Reconstructing Keynesian Economics with Imperfect Competition

Reconstructing Keynesian Economics with Imperfect Competition

A Desk-top Simulation

Robin Marris
Emeritus Professor of Economics
Birkbeck College, London University

Edward Elgar in association with
the United Nations University World Institute for Development
Economics Research, Helsinki, Finland

Published by
Edward Elgar Publishing Company Limited
Gower House
Croft Road
Aldershot
Hants GU11 3HR
England

Edward Elgar Publishing Company
Old Post Road
Brookfield
Vermont 05036
USA

British Library Cataloguing Publication Data
Marris, Robin *1924-*
Reconstructing Keynesian economics with imperfect competition: a desk-top simulation
1. Economics, Theories, Simulation. Keynes, John Maynard 1883-1946
I. Title II. WIDER
330.156

Library of Congress Cataloguing in Publication Data
Marris, Robin Lapthorn, *1924-*
Reconstructing Keynesian economics with imperfect competition: a desk-top simulation
327 p. cm.
1. Keyensian economics – Computer simulation. 2. Competition.
Imperfect – Computer simulation. I. Title
HB99.7.M355 1991
330.15'6'0113536 – dc20 91-16255
CIP

ISBN 1 85278 541 1

Printed in Great Britain by
Billing & Sons Ltd, Worcester

Contents

List of Figures

Note: figures are numbered approximately according to the chapters and sections in which they lie. To locate a figure, please refer to the table of contents.

Preface

This book is unusual. It will stand out in the crowd of contemporary books and monographs written on macroeconomics for at least three reasons. First, although it is primarily a theoretical monograph seeking the microfoundations of Keynesian macroeconomics, the book is written mainly in prose with a minimum of algebra. It is to the credit of the author that despite its almost deceptive simplicity on the surface, the book has a quite tight underlying theoretical structure.

Second, this book makes a contribution to macroeconomic modelling techniques. The use of "desk-top" simulation to demonstrate the theory and the invitation to the reader to carry out his own simulations is not merely an intrusion of modern technology into model building. It performs the important task of coping with non-linearities in a sequential period analysis as well as permitting examination of the sensitivity of the simulated paths to changes in the parameter values. Since analytical solutions to non-linear systems are often difficult, the use of simulation is a valuable venture. True, it does not have the rigour of an analytical solution, but it is equally true that it may do less violence to reality where a conventional model builder ends up over-simplifying for mathematical convenience.

Finally, this is an exceptionally readable book. Only part of this readability is explained by the author's style. This book is also so readable because it mixes Cambridge (England) "gossip" and personal anecdotes of the author with developments of ideas that shaped the *General Theory* of Keynes and the professional views of a subsequent generation of economists.

The essential thrust of the monograph is to find an appropriate theory of the firm which fits the broader idea of demand-driven output enunciated in the *General Theory*. The author rejects, in my view rightly, the Marshallian notion of the firm as a price taker with rising marginal cost. Instead, he puts forward a theory in which the "mark-up" on (constant) marginal cost is determined by profit maximization and, therefore, depends solely on price elasticity of demand. So long as firms do not anticipate drastic changes in the price elasticity, the mark-up remains constant. Any increase in aggregate demand can then be seen to be transmitted directly to output and employment without going through the rigmarole of price adjustment which, in the "traditional" interpretation of Keynes, is supposed to induce price-taking Marshallian firms to expand output. A twist in Professor Marris's argument comes at this stage. The higher output and employment caused by higher demand for goods may raise nominal wages in the next round and thereby lead to upward revision of profit-maximizing prices. In this sequential model, the price rise is a consequence of the macro-demand rise, not the cause for or "signal" to firms to produce more. This is a difference from much contemporary "mainstream" theory which must be pondered over.

The book has also other delights and innovations, for example a plausible theory of investment (a flexible accelerator based on an endogenous, profit-maximizing, capacity-stock adjustment rate) for modern corporate firms and generally throughout a serious attempt to give the firm a corporate identity.

This is not a book which develops along mainstream trajectories of utility maximizing households and docile, price-taking firms. This book implies rather convincingly that getting away from some current fashions may be necessary if Keynesian economics is to serve as a powerful aid to our understanding of the changing world we live in.

Lal Jayawardena
Director, WIDER
Helsinki, March, 1991

Dedications and Acknowledgements

This book is professionally dedicated to two people, without whose support and encouragement it would never have appeared.

The first person is Dr. Lal Jayawardena, graduate and Honorary Fellow of King's College Cambridge (Keynes's alma mater), sometime Ambassador to the EC, Secretary to the Treasury and to the Ministry of Finance and Planning, of Sri Lanka, and currently Director of the UN University World Institute for Development Economics Research (WIDER). It is a fact that his Institute, in employing me as a part-time research associate for the specific purpose of this project, made it materially possible. But Dr. Jayawardena has also personally given me constant moral and intellectual support, which has been a joy and inspiration to receive. In addition, the remarkable nucleus of permanent and visiting economists gathered in his institute, from whose comments and criticism the project has strongly benefited, is in no small part due to his leadership.

The second person is my brother, Stephen Marris, sometime Economic Advisor to the Secretary General of the OECD, Senior Fellow of the Institute for International Economics in Washington DC, and author of *Deficits and the Dollar: the World Economy at Risk*, who has given me the benefit of his extensive knowledge of world macroeconomic history since 1960. The discussion in the second part of the Author's Introduction is much influenced by him, but the two of us disagree on a number of points, and he can in no way be held responsible for any of its content. He was also one of the first people to see the advantage of a sequential simulation modelling in the study of imperfectly competitive microfoundations and to encourage me to continue to pursue the idea.

I must also mention Michael Posner who, before WIDER came on the scene, in his then capacity as Economic Director of the UK

National Economic Development Office, provided a seed grant at a critical juncture.

In addition to the professional dedications, there is also a crucial professional acknowledgement. Professor Hiro Odagiri, of Tsukuba University, Japan, kindly supported by WIDER, spent a summer working with me to design the whole of that part of the model where the theory of economic growth interacts with the theory of imperfectly-competitive price formation. He contributed the major part of the economic design and programme structure and a substantial proportion of the ideas. Explicitly he contributed the idea of the capital-stock adjustment process and the simultaneous optimization of this with price. So great has been his contribution to the project that I would have liked to have included his name on the title page, but he prefers the present form of acknowledgement.

A considerable number of people have also written with comments on the first draft of the manuscript and they are to be collectively thanked. All have been at minimum helpful. I single out the names of Roger Backhouse, Geoffrey Harcourt, Edith Penrose, Richard Startz and Ferdinando Targetti, in alphabetical order, on account of the exceptional length and detail of their commentaries. Hiro Odagiri also gave detailed comments plus one major piece of advice (namely that the whole of the first part of the manuscript needed to be rewritten!), which was accepted.

There must also be an unusual, some might say backhanded, but neverthless warmly-intended acknowledgement to my friend and Birkbeck colleague, Dennis Snower. In the early 1980s we embarked on a project to co-author a world-shaking new textbook of macroeconomics with explicit microfoundations. After we had each written many thousands of words, the project collapsed, essentially because we had not realised how far apart we were on what we were actually trying to say — Dennis being a complete and elegant modern neo-classic. On me, the traumatic effect of this episode was the reaction that provoked the present project and book!

Finally, my Constant Companion, Rachel Austin, suffered in the usual way of constant companions to people trying to write books. I personally dedicate this book to her.

Robin Marris
March 1991

Author's Introduction

This book has four main aims. The first is a piece of intellectual surgery: to replace an Achilles heel in the Keynesian theory of aggregate demand, and in so doing help to reduce confusion concerning the relation in Keynesian economics between employment and the real wage. The second is to support the revised theory with an economic model based on computer simulation. The third is to apply the model to the macroeconomic problems of the industrialized market economies in the 1970s, 1980s and after. The fourth is to embellish the narrative with a personal view of the relevant history of thought.

There is also an incidental aim, namely to strengthen the connection between macroeconomics and what is known as "the theory of the firm", which is in turn a major part of the professional field known as industrial economics. This stems from the author's previous interest in the theory of the modern corporation.[1] Consequently the computer model has been provided with a feature of a type which, to the author's knowledge, except in the work of Hiro Odagiri,[2] is found nowhere else in theoretical macroeconomics, namely an ability to consider the macroeconomic consequences of the hypothesis that high management has power and motivation to pursue objectives other than pure profit.

A bouillabaisse?

One kindly critic[3] has likened the book to a bouillabaisse. According to this person, professional economists tend to be like Anglo-Saxon eaters. They desire their foods apart. Meat, potatoes, carrots, greens. Macroeconomics, microeconomics, theoretical economics, industrial economics. For better or worse the present author is not of that ilk.

1 Marris, R., (1964b, 1972).

2 Odagiri (1981, 1991).

3 Professor Ron Smith, of Birkbeck College, London University.

Being a lover of Provence, he is happy to be called a Mediterranean economist/cook. The role, however, does present some problems.

One arises from the fact that the author also happens to be one of those people who fell in love with the microcomputer from the first day, little more than a decade ago, the creature came to market, and is therefore also proud of what he believes to be a flexible, teachable and user-friendly simulation programme, written largely by himself, given away free on the disc at the back of the book.[1] He is convinced that computer simulation is an essential method for the task in hand. The jacket cover of the book shows the programme in operation.

But other potentially sympathetic readers may be less enthusiastic about this aspect of the work and many professional economists seem secretly wary of computer simulation as a tool of theory. The pros and cons of the debate are further discussed in Chapter 2.

Another problem has been difficulty in maintaining a consistent level of exposition. The argument combines ideas drawn from different branches of economics which have become increasingly specialized. But we want to communicate with the general reader, including, at a certain level, the general student of current affairs who has never taken a course in economic theory. Inevitably, in so attempting, one may irritate the specialist. Of the reader, specialist or generalist, who encounters a passage where the compromise seems to be failing, we ask only a little patience: if you can hold on or hang in, you may learn something to your advantage.

The style of the resulting text varies and is often more chatty than is customary in solemn monographs. Readers should therefore know that the author is extremely serious about economic science and for that very reason feels strongly that economists should avoid the mistake of presuming that because a person makes massive contribu-

---

1 The programme is believed to be bug-free, but any bugs are entirely the responsibility of the author. No legal or moral responsibility for any deficiency in the programme lies with the publisher. The discs were provided by the author and the price of the book would have been the same without them. Written queries may be addressed to the author, care of the publisher. Instructions for installing the software and running the programme are found in the Appendix.

tions to our discipline, he or she is thereby immune to error or nonsense. Never forget that Isaac Newton spent much of his later career writing papers on alchemy.

Economics and sex

In addition, some readers may need warning that the book could be dangerous to their psychic health. Robert Skidelsky, introducing his brilliant account of Keynes's life up to 1920,[1] describes a double standard separating the biographical conventions for public persons, such as statesmen or economists, from those applying to bohemian persons such as writers and artists.[2] In particular, Skidelsky points out, public figures are not supposed to have sex lives. Skidelsky vividly documents a previous conspiracy of silence concerning the Keynesian sex life. As a direct result of it (the conspiracy, not the sex life), the present author, first an undergraduate and then a teacher at Keynes's own alma mater (King's College, Cambridge, England), had had the impression that Keynes had been a typical English public (i.e. private) schoolboy who, like many of his kind, had entered the adult world undersexed, misogynistic and faintly bisexual, but who had eventually settled into a plausibly normal married life with a great ballerina. Not until reading Skidelsky did your author learn that, on the contrary, before marriage Keynes was highly sexed, passionately homosexual, somewhat foul mouthed[3] and not averse to venturing

---

1 Skidelsky (1983). Skidelsky's period ends before the publication of both the *General Theory of Employment, Interest and Money* in 1936, and *A Treatise on Money* in 1930 (see References). By contrast, contemporary professional economists are more familiar with the post-Skidelsky Keynes. This fact makes his book especially valuable in setting the character of the man who did all that and should therefore be read in tandem with the lucid and comprehensive account of Keynes' total intellectual development as an economist by Donald Moggridge (1976), who is also, of course, the substantive editor of Keynes' collected writings.

2 Skidelsky op cit, pp xvi-xvii. In the text above, the words from this footnote to the end of the current paragraph represent embellishment by the present author, not paraphrase of Skidelsky, who cannot therefore be held in any way responsible for the way his original point is developed here.

3 "Maynard's lack of delicacy, which offended even Lytton [Strachey], excited the bawdy Vanessa [Bell], who wanted to be one of the boys." Skidelsky, op cit, p 294-95.

the street. Skidelsky, however, then cautiously added, "...no one would want to argue that knowledge of Keynes's sexual and emotional leanings gives one a better understanding of his economic theory... .".[1] But in the present book, in Chapter 4, we will attempt to show how sexual, or shall we say more delicately, "personal" jealousy may have significantly contributed to the genesis of the Achilles heel we see in the Keynesian theory. Thirty years of professional literature has been devoted to attempting to live with the theoretical problem which resulted.

Structure of the book

In this present Introduction we summarize our view of the problem with the Keynesian theory and the outlines of the method of reconstructing it. This is followed by a personal testament describing how the author came to the problem and his view of the relevant aspects of world economic history since 1970.

In Chapter 1 we first summarise the main features of the economic model and the simulation programme and then look at some of the assumptions in more detail, with special reference to our views on the theory of the firm.

The next four chapters in one way or another continue the latter process. In Chapter 2 we digress to discuss the implications for economics of recent developments in computer related theory building and theory about the human brain. Surprisingly, the reader will find, this discussion also supports discussion of the author's current views on expectations formation and the economic role of money, and the treatment of both in his model. Chapter 3 expands on the nature of "imperfect competition". Chapter 4 expands on Keynes. Chapter 5 discusses the recent history of other contributions to macroeconomics based on imperfect competition.

Chapter 6 gives the specification of the economic model and simulation programme in detail.

Chapter 7 describes results, conclusions and policy implications from various experiments on the model itself, complete with graphs of the relevant programme runs.

---

1 Op cit, p. xvii.

The Keynesian theory

In order to proceed, it is necessary, for the benefit of the general reader, to give the author's version of the essence of the Keynesian theory as such. Professional readers will sigh, but if they choose not to skip the next paragraphs they will notice a certain twist.

The Keynesian thesis is not an attack on the virtues of the market economy. Under full employment conditions, a general network of self-adjusting markets is an excellent system for following consumer tastes, for encouraging innovation and productive efficiency, and for allocating scarce resources between ends. It is not a criticism, but rather A statement of the obvious, however, that such a system, using money as the means of exchange, must almost inevitably be to some extent macroeconomically unstable. If it were catastrophically unstable, it would no longer exist. The Keynesian theory is a theory of finite instability. One day in 1933 most banks in the US were closed and the unemployment rate was 33%. Half a century later total unemployment in the OECD countries[1] went from 10 million to 30 million and back to 15 million inside five years. But in neither of these two historically extreme cases did production fall to zero, or capitalism disappear. The problem is a manageable one. But the management has to be public and purposive, and also, as Keynes's earliest interpreters quickly saw,[2] should best be based on a battery of instruments of which fiscal policy is one but only one.

Instability in a system of linked processes is caused by "positive feedback".[3] The process of amplifying the input signal of a Hi-fi system may distort it. The distortion may be reduced by feeding the errors back into the circuit as correction factors. If an error is *X*, to

---

1 Organization for Economic Cooperation and Development, headquarters in Paris; members, most W. European countries, N America, Australasia, Japan.

2 See especially Nobel Laureat Jan Tinbergen's classic essay on macroeconomic policy (Tinbergen, 1952), where the author extended the Keynesian theory to show that it is logically impossible to manage an economy with fewer instruments than objectives. The quotation from an article written in 1990 by the economics editor of the London *Times*, given at the end of the present Introduction, represents a direct application of the theorem.

3 The first person to suggest this terminology was Arnold Tustin, a Professor of control engineering who wrote a much under-recognized book (Tustin, 1953) applying cybernetic theory to Keynes.

correct it we feed back some fraction of -*X*: because of the minus sign the feedback is called "negative" and, by design, is effectively stabilizing. But if a live microphone is moved near live speakers, so the sound goes around and around, distortions are cumulatively reinforced to produce the familiar rising scream: the feedback is positive and, accidentally, destabilizing.

The economy is seen as a circuit with goods and services flowing in one direction, money in payment in the other. Positive feedback occurs when a disturbance in consumer expenditure disturbs, in the same direction, the demand for labour and workers' earnings, thus feeding back further to disturb consumer expenditure itself. For various reasons however (one of which is that in the short run households may be expected to vary their expenditure less than their income), as the initial shock is successively recycled, rather than amplified, it is attenuated. Consequently, unlike the case of the screaming Hi-fi, the Keynesian economic system eventually steadies, and remains at the new level unless reshocked.

Despite the rather obvious plausibility of this implicit explanation of the ever recurring phenomenon of macroeconomic fluctuations, no corresponding theoretical model was developed until the best part of two centuries after the science of economics had been founded. The historic paper in question, published in 1931, was the work of Keynes's close associate and the present author's subsequent tutor, the late Richard Kahn.[1] The crucial political significance of the theorem is that, between shocks, the stable position is by no means necessarily one of full employment; in the absence of public policy, "under employment" may be stable.

As most readers will know, the past quarter-century has seen the appearance of a substantial literature arguing the precisely opposite; arguing, that is, that a market economy is inherently stable at full employment. If the present author believed that he would not be writing this book. And surely the truth is that few governments or political groups, anywhere in the world, genuinely believe it either.

---

1 See Kahn (1931). It is generally accepted that the first significant work of theoretical macroeconomics was the book of Richard Cantillon published twenty years after the author's murder in 1734 (Cantillon, 1755).

The Achilles heel

Kahn's "multiplier" theorem formed the core of Keynes's *General Theory* published five years later. But although the multiplier is an inevitable element in our model, it is not our primary point of concern. The Achilles heel is located further back in the process, implying that it might never start.

The multiplier theorem implies that the main weight of the initial shock to demand must fall on the physical quantities of goods that employers desire to produce, thus affecting the demand for labour and initiating the feedback cycle. However, contrary to the way the story is often told, it is impossible to escape the fact that the initial change in aggregate demand is not a physical or "real" event, rather it is intrinsically a monetary or "nominal" event; consumers are spending more or less money on goods; an effect which can be translated into real terms only if we know the prices of goods. If prices were fixed, producers would have no alternative but to change output exactly in proportion to nominal demand; the nominal disturbance would be synonymous with a real disturbance. But in a market economy prices are not fixed. So why should not the effect of a change in nominal demand fall on prices, rather than on quantities? For example if monetary demand falls by ten per cent, why should prices not fall by ten per cent, leaving physical volume unchanged? As S.C. Tsiang, in an apposite passage of a profound paper originally written in the early 1960s and recently propitiously republished,[1] has implied, this was the assumption of the classical economists, and is therefore the essential point of departure of Keynes from the classics. Yet Keynes and most of his followers "fudged" it.

A simple solution: imperfect competition

We believe the simplest answer is the one pursued in this book, namely the market process which in their zany way economists insist

---

1 The general argument of pages 144-145 of Tsiang (1989), using original words as much as possible, may be paraphrased as follows, "The classical economists believed that money is not wanted for its own sake but in order to buy other goods with it. It is true that the aggregate demand for goods in physical units determined by the available quantity of money might be smaller than the aggregate supply of goods at the current price level. This possibility, however, did not seriously worry the classical economists because they believed that the price level was highly flexible."

on calling "imperfect" competition.[1] Picture each producer as having a reasonable idea of the demand curve for his product, that is the graph of points showing how much could be sold at various different prices, given competitors' prices and consumer demand. Now assume that at the moment before the macro demand disturbance occurred, the typical producer had gradually adjusted price until it had seemed to him that, given his production costs, he was earning maximum gross profit: the economy was stable with producers believing that, given the prices of other producers, it would be unprofitable to change their own price. Clearly this state of affairs also requires that the production of the resulting outputs demands a total amount of labour such that the total earnings of workers (plus other incomes such as distributed profits and other expenditures such as on capital goods) will create a total nominal demand just sufficient to purchase all the goods currently produced at the prices currently actually asked for them: "ex ante" and "ex post" nominal demand must be equal. But after the shock, they will not be.

Consequently producers will perceive that their demand curves have moved. What, then, should they do? Clearly the answer is that they must recalculate optimum price. But now comes a surprise. It is possible to show that unless productive capacity is already fully utilized, the new optimal price may well be little different from the old optimal price, while the new physical quantity of sales will differ from the old quantity virtually in proportion to the change in nominal demand. In short, free-market behaviour yields much the same result as if prices had in fact been frozen; prices will remain constant because it is not profitable to change them. In consequence the feedback process essential to the Keynesian theory works unambiguously. The conclusion is just the same whether the shock that moved the demand curves was monetary or fiscal: if the monetary authorities do something that tends to increase the money supply, firms will perceive the effect, in one way or another (interest rates, credit availability) as leading to an increase in nominal demand, with the consequences described.

---

1 The classic works on this subject are Kahn (1929), Chamberlin (1933) and Joan Robinson (1933).

The foregoing theorem, although (as will be seen Chapter 3, subsection 3.1.2, below) easily proved in a couple of lines of maths, is not completely easy to explain in words, but an intuitive explanation runs as follows. The gross profit earned from selling a given quantity of product at a given price can be expressed as the quantity multiplied by unit prime cost, plus the percentage, known to business as "the mark-up", by which unit price exceeds unit cost. Turning this around one can say that if one knows the unit cost, and knows the mark-up, one knows the price. So selecting a profit-maximizing price means selecting a profit-maximizing mark-up. If one sets a low mark-up, one sells more product, but gains less profit per unit. If one sets a high mark-up, one sells less product but earns more per unit. Clearly, the less "elastic" the demand curve (elasticity of demand is a measure, based on the demand curve, representing the sensitivity of demand to price; it is the percentage change in quantity demanded, with aggregate consumer demand and competitors' prices constant, for a one per cent change in own price), the smaller the penalty factor in choosing a high mark-up, and vice versa. Consequently the profit-maximizing mark-up is mathematically determined by the elasticity of demand: in fact, if we substitute for mark-up the concept of "profit margin", meaning the percentage share of profit in price (it is smaller than mark-up, because price, the base of the percentage, is greater than cost), it turns out that the profit-maximizing profit margin is exactly equal to the reciprocal (inverse) of the elasticity of demand, divided by 100: e.g if the elasticity of demand is 3, the profit-maximizing profit margin will be 33 and a third, per cent.

When, as a result of a macroeconomic shock, the demand curve of the typical producer moves, it is perfectly possible that the elasticity of the curve may also change. But since demand elasticity is a quality deriving from the general substitutability of products, and since economists have developed no theory about or data on the subject, we have no presumption as to either the extent, nor, more importantly, the direction, of such an effect.[1] Consequently, when thinking

1 A few economists have speculated from time to time on the point, but there has been no consensus and no econometric study. Barely 2000 words on the topic can be found in the whole of economic literature. Just before World War II, Keynes gave it a few, somewhat scratchy, paragraphs (Keynes, 1939), and referred to earlier writings by Pigou and by Harrod which are not cited in our

through the effect of shocks, as a first approximation, we may assume that every firm perceives that, although the location of its demand curve has changed, the elasticity has not. (The book jacket shows the macroeconomic effects of spontaneous changes in elasticity of demand, inserted from outside by the model user, with results which are discussed in Chapter 1 below, in the sub-section describing demonstrations of the programme.) Consequently, the profit-maximizing mark-up may be assumed approximately the same before and after the shock. In turn this means that unless unit costs change (as a depression or boom develops, they may well change, but there is no well established direction of effect on labour productivity of varying capacity utilization[1]), profit-maximizing price does not change. And if the price set by the typical producer does not change, the quantity demanded for the typical product must change strictly in proportion to the change in nominal aggregate demand.

In due course, the resulting change in the demand for labour may influence nominal wages and hence, with given mark-up, prices. But this price change has a totally different implication from the kind of initial price change, discussed above, that could inhibit the start of the multiplier process. We now have new stable levels of macro production and employment, and a new nominal wage and price level or alternatively a new steady inflation rate. There, in principle, the economy remains until shocked again.

---

references. The subject then went virtually dead for 45 years, at which point the celebrated Joe Stiglitz (Stiglitz, 1984) gave it a few hundred more words in a rather similar vein to Keynes. In the present book, more precisely in the simulation model, without any specific theoretical basis, we provide the user with the option to make the elasticity of demand move anti-cyclically, in the sense that, with a sensitivity selected by the user, the micro elasticity of demand facing firms tends to decline as the macroeconomy expands. Since, for the reasons given above, a fall in elasticity implies an increases in the profit-maximizing profit margin, if this option is used, the expanding economy will see firms attempting to raise prices relative to wages. If the user has also selected the option for indexing nominal wages (workers fight back), the familiar inflationary spiral will begin even though the user may have disabled the normal direct effect of rising labour demand on wages.

1 For further discussion see Chapter 1 below.

So we have a highly convincing competitive process that gives a strong microfoundation for the multiplier and Keynesian theory generally, i.e. replaces the Achilles heel. But, apparently supported by Keynes himself, professional students of the problem have until recently mainly preferred another story, called "perfect" competition, which the present author believes to be inherently unsatisfactory.

The "perfect" competition story

In this story economists suppose that the typical producer, rather than perceiving a distinct demand curve for his own product, sells in a market that is like a commodity market or the stock market, in other words an organized market containing specialist intermediaries called "brokers", "jobbers" or "market makers". There is a large number of traders on both sides of the market and the commodity is fully graded and standardized, i.e. "homogenous". The market makers periodically "call" prices at which they are for the moment prepared to buy or sell in unlimited quantities. This means they must be prepared to hold buffer stocks. If they find their stocks rising, they call lower prices, so encouraging demand, discouraging supply, dampening or reversing the unwanted movement and generally correcting the market: the law of supply and demand operates in the market as a whole, rather on individual firms: at any instant producers face "given" prices called by the market makers; producers are "price takers" rather than price setters. In order to maximize profits, given the price, they adjust only production. Economists also call these kinds of markets "auction" markets (rather misleading because a key feature is lacking, namely an auctioneer!).

In such a market, evidently, the first effect of a fall in demand is a fall in price (more precisely, a fall in the price called by the market makers). Therefore, as a microfoundation for the Keynesian multiplier process, it seems a non-starter. With some effort, however, it is possible to make up a story where the initial change in price subsequently induces profit-maximizing producers to reduce output and hence employment, so restarting the multiplier. Surprisingly, a rather fuzzy version (see Chapter 4, section 4.3, below) of this uncomfortable scenario actually appears in the *General Theory*. Numerous subsequent economists have produced more rigorous versions: one of the best, in the present author's opinion, is to be found in the lucid survey of microfoundations theory, by Roy Weintraub, published in 1979.[1]

The grave weaknesses the present author sees in the story are detailed in Chapter 4 (op cit). Here we anticipate two of them. The first is simply a matter of realism. In the modern industrial economy only a tiny proportion of GDP is produced for "auction" markets. The producers in question are mainly farmers[2] (whose goods are graded and often sold literally at auctions). Agricultural employment, however, is typically a small proportion of total employment and also, typically, does not fluctuate in boom and depression in the manner of industrial employment. The other point is strictly theoretical. The Keynesian theory is a theory of how changes in aggregate demand affect the quantity of production. The excitement which the theory created among young economists in the late thirties[3] was due to the shift of the traditional emphasis on prices, to emphasis on quantities. It therefore seems quite strange to base such a theory on a story whereby the immediate direct effect of demand fluctuation falls on prices, and subsequently only indirectly, via the presumed incentive effects of the price changes, on quantities. It is a story that no industrialist can recognize, nor is it supported by the typical statistical profile of events occurring in booms and slumps. For these reasons, and for others given in Chapter 4, except as a matter of history, perfect competition plays no role in the present book. Finally, the present author does not believe that either Keynes or Kahn originally saw their theory this way. We believe (in fact we virtually know) they conceived it as a theory of direct quantity effects and later, for reasons discussed in Chapter 4 (which include the "personal" factor

---

1 Weintraub (1979), pp 40-42. Although Weintraub's own account is clear, we cannot agree with him that the same is true of Keynes's. For other good discussions see Sargent (1979, Ch 2) and Casarosa (1981).

2 Intermediate industrial products are often standardized and in the past were sometimes produced in industries containing a largish number of small or medium-sized firms. But owing to the economies of large-scale production, with hardly any exceptions, the competitive process has converted all these industries into oligopolies or monopolies. As we shall see in Chapter 3 and 5, conditions oligopoly or monopoly can also provide strong microfoundations for Keynes.

3 I am grateful to Kenneth Berrill for this point.

mentioned above), decided to patch up a reconciliation with perfect competition.

Alternative repairs

In the intervening years practical macroeconomists have rather sensibly evaded the problem described in the preceding paragraphs by an approach used in the great majority of contemporary statistical computer macro models of actual economies, called "mark-up pricing". Here the mark-up is not assumed to be the profit-maximizing mark-up, but rather a mark-up that yields some reasonable profit, not theoretically predicted, but statistically observed.

For economic theorists, however, such a pragmatic approach would be unprofessional. A significant number of distinguished theorists have therefore made various attempts to reconstruct Keynesian economics, disdaining to use our simple solution, by other means. One of these is the "disequilibrium" approach, where it is assumed that although prices in a market economy are not fixed, they tend in general to change more slowly than quantities. Consequently at a given instant, buyers and sellers of goods and labour seem to perceive a fixed set of prices, to which they must adjust quantities. At such an instant, supply will not equal demand in many markets, and firms, consumers and households must conform to this fact, as if they were "rationed". The result is complex and the field has naturally attracted good mathematicians. The concepts and methodology developed do have important general implications for practical Keynesian modelling.[1]

A personal testament

The foregoing completes the thumbnail overview of our book: the work is a mixed-fish medicinal soup intended to cure an otherwise fatal weakness in the Keynesian theory by providing microfoundations of "imperfect" rather than "perfect" competition. The rest of this

1 The main authors, in alphabetical order, are Barro (with Grossman), Benassy, Clower, Drèze, Leijonhufvud, Malinvaud and Muellbauer (with Portes). See References. Robert Gordon (1990, p 1138) has pointed out that whether or not one regards these scholars' approach as the best general explanation of macroeconomic instability, they contribute a crucial theoretical message, namely, "that the failure of one market to clear imposes constraints on other markets", for example if firms cannot sell their goods, households cannot sell their labour.

introduction consists of a personal account in the first person singular of how the author became interested in the problem, and why it is relevant to the year 2000.

Many years ago, when a teenage schoolboy, I bought a copy of Keynes's pamphlet, "How to Pay for the War", which contains a Keynesian model of inflation. At the time it also carried a political message: if we were serious about World War II, we should be serious about it; Keynes, as well as inspiring my schoolboy patriotism, also provoked my interest in a subject of which I then knew nothing. As a result, after a rather easy war-time entrance test, I was admitted to study economics at King's College Cambridge, the college of Keynes. But he, together with his close associate, Richard Kahn, was away for the duration.

At the end of the year I got a surprising exam result and the College awarded me a prize to buy books. I became an RAF transatlantic ferry pilot and had time for reading. Among the books I had bought with my prize was the first edition of *The General Theory*, which I still possess, with annotations made around latitude 50 north, longitude 30 west. The annotations indicate, however, that I was already having trouble with the passages concerned with what today we would call the microfoundations.

The war ended and I returned to Cambridge at the end of 1945. In my final student year I was allotted two supervisors, R. F. Kahn and A. C. Pigou, for whom I wrote essays in alternative weeks. One day, by nature a trouble maker, I wrote a note to Kahn asking, in so many words, "Please Sir, may I have a lesson on the relation between the level of employment and the degree of monopoly?", the latter being the term the then current for the profit-maximizing mark-up under imperfect competition. With the benefit of hindsight I like to think I had the idea that the degree of monopoly could influence the extent to which changes in aggregate demand went to quantities or to prices. Kahn replied that my enquiry suggested the time was ripe for a personal session with the great Joan Robinson[1]. She received

---

1 Author of the world's first book on imperfect competition (Robinson, 1933). As will be seen in Chapter 4, the present writer is convinced that the theory there presented was essentially a development of a theory created five years earlier by R. F. Kahn, deposited, unpublished, in the library of King's College, Cambridge, there to remain until eventually published first in Italian and later in English

me graciously and said the answer to my question was that an increase in the share of profit in the National Income could cause a fall in aggregate demand because profit receivers tended to save more than wage earners. Reasonable as it was, the point was not, at the time, the one I was after. When I tried to explain further, Joan seemed not to hear, and the session closed. The incident began a concealed distance between us which affected my whole career.

When I later became a "don" the problem continued to bug me. I began to believe that Keynesian macroeconomics must have deep microfoundations that everyone understood but me. The truth finally dawned. The problem lay not in me but in Keynes! What a shocking claim! In Chapter 4 of this book, below, however, as already hinted, I shall attempt to justify it.

In the 1980s people were saying that Keynes had been abandoned.[1] To me that is rather like trying to abandon the theory of relativity. Of course, a country, or more precisely its government, may behave as if they did not believe in either relativity or Keynes. In the first case there will be no immediate consequences until, on the outbreak of Star Wars, everything misses. In the second case there may also be circumstances where nothing much happens. Alternatively, as did occur in the period 1980-85, there may be a collapse of output and a recurrence of mass unemployment on a scale not seen since the 1930s depression which had provoked Kahn to invent the multiplier and Keynes and Kahn to create the *General Theory*.[2]

These remarks will be applauded by some readers, jeered by others. I hold however an additional opinion which is unpopular with almost everyone (according to friends, my favourite posture). The circumstances of 1980 were those of severe inflation: how they came about is a question shortly to be reviewed. In the meantime we note that unlike the depression of 1930-38, the depression of 1980-86 was the medium-term consequence of a cumulation of politico-economic shocks from 1970 onwards and the immediate consequence of the

---

(a few months after the author's death) more than half a century later.

1 See for example the position taken by the Director General of the UK National Economic Development Office, Walter Eltis, in Eltis (1988, 1989).

2 Kahn (1931), Keynes (1936).

1980s OECD governments' desperate responses to a shock (the second oil shock) which they did not at the time fully understand, but were nevertheless determined to defeat. Politically speaking, a traditional modern Keynesian is not well suited to such battle (Maynard Keynes himself was another kettle of fish; there is a case for arguing that his work in the two World Wars represented as great a contribution to the theory and practice of war finance as his more famous work to the theory of economic fluctuations.) I personally believe that given the balance between fear of inflation and dislike of depression and other political realities, it was probably literally true that at that time "there was no other way". In such circumstances, the fundamentally as-always Keynesian economy may be better managed by political anti-Keynesians than by even reconstructed Keynesians. That does not (cannot) imply abandoning the fundamental theory. It is my personal view that it was a tragedy that as the events of the decade unfolded, economists, instead of speaking with one voice, split into groups with different weird and elusive interpretations of what was happening.

Be all that as it may, it is common ground that after 1970 stagflation has predominated, and that after 1973 economic growth in the West dramatically decelerated and has not fully recovered. We have still not recovered the path on which the OECD economy seemed set before 1973, a path of low inflation, moderate but steady growth by the US, with sharp catching-up by the continental OECD countries, explosive growth by Japan, and persistent falling back by the UK.

Economists and politicians hold strongly differing views of the world's economic history since 1950. The differences are patently correlated with open or hidden political premises. To be honest I must set out my own view, although I hope this will not deter those who disagree with it from taking the technical aspects of this book on what I hope they would see as its own merits. My personal view is that the first cause of the great slow-down in economic growth was the series of politico-economic shocks arising from the super-power confrontation combined with a decline, following the death of President Kennedy, of responsible economic management in the world's largest economy. A sound response based on sound economic theory (i.e. a Keynesian theory of stagflation) was, in most countries, and especially in large countries, politically difficult if not impossible to manage. Hence, superficially, "Keynes" did have to be "abandoned". The result in the real economy was exactly what the theory predicts, a major depression and loss of growth.

This thumbnail sketch, though irritating to many economists with Left-centrist opinions, will not seem to them totally outrageous. Conservative and "hyper-liberal" economists, however, may be outraged. The difference between their view and the policy outlook of this book is closely connected with differing interpretations of world economic history since the year 1970. I tag the opposing interpretations "revisionist" and "neo-Keynesian": but there are probably numerous economists who would describe themselves as "neo-" or "new" Keynesians, who will not agree with my historical dichotomy. The same would apply to some "post" Keynesians. The root of the problem is that one group, including some neo-Keynesians, believe that the cause of the era of troubles was a previous indulgence in an exaggerated or "degenerate" Keynesianism, paying too little attention to the needs and benefits of the free market and to society's aversion to inflation. By contrast, some radical economists who rather monopolize the "post-Keynesian" label, believe at heart (or at least, they used to; it is difficult to know what any of one's old friends think about such questions after the extraordinary events in the "Second World" since 1988) that market capitalism cannot be made to work under traditional Keynesian policies without much more extensive government micro intervention than is believed necessary by your typical old-fashioned Keynesian, such as myself. So what I am about to say may raise hackles at both ends of the hidden political spectrum, but, by the same token, I appeal to passionate moderates.

In its strongest form, the "revisionist" school hold that the causes of the collapse of Keynesianism were inherent in the Keynesian theory itself: so long as Keynesian policies were pursued it was only a matter of time before creeping disaster occurred. In contrast, the "neo-Keynesian" interpretation, as I define it, holds that all would largely have been well with the world, if the evolving consensus, gradually improved by experience in international Keynesian-oriented macroeconomic co-operation, as mediated by the OECD in Paris, had not been disrupted by the series of politically-originating economic shocks to which the world economy was subjected from a time around 1967 onwards. Even some of those most sympathetic to this view do not always appreciate the full strength of the political element in the story.

Now follows a satire against the revisionist story. Readers likely to be upset by it had best jump to the subsequent account of the "neo-Keynesian" story: they may disagree with that, but are less likely to be upset, and will have heard my case.

The "Revisioner's Tale" begins from the proposition that the wage explosion which began with the student uprising in France in 1968 was the end-product of an accelerating inflation that had been creeping up since the Keynesian era began. Maybe the creep could not be seen statistically, but he was around the corner. When the first incident of stagflation occurred in 1971[1], governments, especially including the Conservative government of Edward Heath in Britain, in a misguided paroxysm of "degenerate" Keynesianism, simultaneously expanded their national economies, not only by means of fiscal policy but also by major increases in money supply; the total OECD money supply in consequence increased sharply.

All this produced a commodity price boom in 1972, followed by the oil-price shock of 1973. Ever since that year, in virtually every OECD country, the long-term rate of growth of productivity, measured in one way or another, has failed the standards achieved in the previous two decades, a phenomenon which has been much investigated but not so far conclusively explained. The most likely explanation has been the least investigated,[2] namely that the next two decades were a period of unreliable growth of demand.

After the oil shock, in foolish countries, such as the UK, Italy and Japan, governments "rode with the punch", while in sensible countries such as Germany and the US of President Ford, fiscal and monetary policies were kept tight. In consequence, inflation in 1974 was less in the "good" countries, and also came down faster, against a fall in aggregate output which, though sharp, was short. As President Carter

---

1 For the first time since appropriate records began, between calendar year 1970 and calendar year 1971, in the United States, and only in the United States, the unemployment rate and the inflation rate moved in the same direction, namely upwards.

2 A major exception is found in the opinions of Christopher Dow, see especially Dow (1990).

walked through the streets of Washington DC to his "Peoples' Inaugural" in January 1977, US inflation was down to 5%.

Then came the second oil shock. Within months, the US, now in the last throes of the failed Carter presidency, had inflation up to 10% again. But the presidential election of November 1980 brought in the good and supposedly monetarist Ronald Reagan only a short time after Mrs Thatcher's first victory in England. With change also occurring in Japan, the "goodies" club, including its permanent German member, although still numbering only four, now represented a massive proportion of total OECD GNP. By the heroic efforts of monetary and fiscal restraint among them, inflation was brought down (e.g. by 1982, in the US, to as low as 5%), and thereafter held reasonably in place. There was of course a rather large increase in so-called "involuntary" unemployment, but in the US this was fairly quickly reduced to a reasonable 5-6%. It lingered on at much higher levels in Europe, mainly the result of a sudden affliction called "Eurosclerosis" (mysterious increase in restrictive practices, rigidities, immobilities and the like among European industrialists and their employees[1]) and also because the European workers, flying in the face of the productivity slow-down, doltishly vetoed the necessary reduction in real wages.

The story which I call neo-Keynesian, begins with a point of agreement. There was certainly a decline in the profitability of industry. In the US the cyclically adjusted real internal rate of return in manufacturing appears to have fallen from a little under 25% in the middle sixties to about 15% in the mid-seventies, fallen another couple of points in the mid-eighties and has since barely regained the mid-seventies position. In Europe the time pattern was similar to the US, although OECD Europe, in the mid-60s showing a figure nearly ten points lower than in the US, over the twenty years thereafter, on average suffered a smaller decline, so at the time of writing the average rates for the US and Europe are not significantly different. In Japan, the story is spectacular. She began the period with a rate of return in manufacturing recorded as no less than 40%, which has now fallen to about 20%![2]

---

1 For a classic account of the Eurosclerosis thesis, see Lindbeck (1983).

2 Figures derived from various issues of OECD *Economic Outlook*.

To say that the fall in profitability was "caused" by excessive real wages is to state a tautology. Real wages are the statistical result of two numbers, one of which is prices. It is just as likely, as Christopher Dow[1] has pointed out, that the first cause lay in various difficulties and uncertainties faced by firms in raising prices quickly enough in face of the unprecedented shocks.

But if I do not doubt the broad story of those numbers, I suggest that if the "revisionist" story implies that the world slow-down in growth and increase in unemployment was caused by a fall in the profitability of business, these numbers do almost the opposite of support that view. The conventional wisdom is that the US came through the long depression better than Europe, and it is certainly true that the US managed to find work, outside manufacturing, for a large number of people, while in Europe high unemployment has persisted. But that historical relationship is hardly consistent with numbers which show that, comparatively speaking, profitability in Europe, over the two decades, rose relatively to the US. And what about Japan, the world's most successful economy, whose profitability figure, comparatively speaking, fell the most drastically of all?

But the more crucial difference between neo-Keynesians (or my brand of neo-Keynesian) on the one hand and revisionists on the other concerns the question of whether, as a matter of fact, there was a creeping acceleration of inflation from the beginning of the sixties. The answer is that if we examine statistical series for retail prices and nominal unit labour costs, in each of the main OECD countries, 1960-1973, and apply various tests of acceleration (e.g. simple correlation of inflation rate with time, averages of first and second half of the series, and etc.), in only one series, namely one of two alternative calculations of labour costs in the US, is there any confirmation. Despite the events of the late seventies, one cannot, therefore detect any objective sign of "in-built" inflation carried over from the sixties.

So what was really going on after 1965? There was undoubtedly some international Keynesian macroeconomic overshooting. The problem of Keynesian-oriented international macroeconomic co-operation can be likened to trying to sail a yacht close to the wind, steered not by a person, but a committee. Considering the difficulties,

---

1 Dow (1990).

over the course of history since 1950, international manifestations of this imaginary committee have performed rather well, and have shown they can learn from experience. So, had it not been for other events, it is unlikely that such mistakes as did occur would have been repeated.

The "other events" were fundamentally political. They begin with the assassination of President Kennedy. I have read a number of books on this subject, both cranky and serious. Many friends have begged me that the topic is irrelevant, but it is not. As a person with some experience with telescopic sights, I am quite satisfied that the wounds which killed the President could not have been inflicted by even an expert marksman (which Oswald was not) positioned in the Texas Book Depository. If I say in more detail what I think did happen, my friends (at least those over the age of 60) get upset. But until very recently I had no idea that Jack Ruby, the man who purposefully found his way into the police station and killed Oswald, and later met his own death in prison, had had a long career and a number of convictions as a minor mobster. Furthermore I have found that most of my friends to this day do not know this. The economic significance of the event was that Kennedy was known to have been reconsidering not only his whole policy in Cuba, but also in South East Asia and the economics of the super-power confrontation generally. His murder, combined with the later murder of Robert Kennedy, initiated a profound change in the quality of government of the world's largest economy, a change which persisted until the middle of 1990. The point at issue is that this was an absolutely exogenous political-historical event which can literally be seen as the first cause of the chain of economic events which produced the subsequent shocks.

In the United States, the inadequate conservative-liberal Lyndon Johnson was elected on an internal programme that was to create for the first time in the US a Welfare State. Over the Viet-Nam War he was out of his depth and devious. His successor, supported by H. Kissinger, may have been less out of his depth but was certainly even more devious. Neither president had the power to induce the Congress to authorise the taxation for simultaneously fighting a substantial war and sustaining social expenditures. The resulting public deficit was not, in fact, so large a proportion of GNP as has been the Reagan deficit (which occurred through analogous motivation in different world circumstances), but the global inflationary force of war deficit-financing under peacetime economic regimes is normally greater than that of the same deficit, even for re-armament, incurred when there is no actual fighting. A hidden message of Keynes's *How to Pay for the War* is that on the one hand it is possible, with the aid of strong measures, to fight a major war without a major inflation (the UK and the US ended World War II with a record of about 5-10% annual inflation and low nominal interest rates), but on the other hand, nothing is more inflationary than fighting a major war under normal economic freedoms. In the first part of World War I the UK tried to do that, with consequently high inflation.

In the case of the Viet-Nam War, as the US military involvement became increasingly heavy from 1965 onwards, the world economy became increasingly like the economy of World War I. The combination of these forces with the more modest contribution from "international Keynesian overshooting" was quite sufficient to cause both the wage "explosions" and the commodity price boom of the period up to the first oil shock of 1973.[1]

Where did the wage explosion really begin? Answer, (as William Nordhaus's careful contemporary research showed[2]) not in fact in France, but in the country from where the underlying inflationary pressure was coming, i.e. the US. And which component led the rocketing world commodity-price index? Answer, "wheat". And where lay the cause of that? Answer, "in Washington DC". Weak management of farm price support not only found the Federal Government holding large grain stocks but also desirous of ending the embarrassment. Despite the generally poor state of international relations, large

---

1 Alogoskoufis and Smith (1989) present elegant econometric evidence for an upward creep in the statistical persistence of inflation from the late 1960's. They attribute this to international monetary laxness permitted by the break-down of the Bretton Woods fixed exchange rate system. I attribute both the increased persistence of inflation and the breakdown of Bretton Woods to war. The authors find a similar, and statistically stronger, story after World War I, which they attribute to the break-down of the old gold standard. I make the same reply.

2 Nordhaus (1972).

quantities of wheat were sold to the Soviets and so kept off world markets. But the story only begins.

The US was involved not only in the superpower confrontation, but also in a chronic military confrontation, via Israel, with the whole Arab world, a state of affairs made complex by the US connection of ARAMCO. But, and this is the crucial point, before around 1968 the US was not a net oil importer. She might import some oil, but she was also an oil exporter. She had never up to that time been dependent on Arab oil in the way her allies were.

The dramatic change which then occurred was not the simple result of renewed Arab-Israeli fighting. That event certainly strengthened the political bonds among the OPEC countries and hence also strengthened the potential economic power of the cartel. But the power could not have become effective without the economic power which had previously been lacking. Coincidentally, something happened within the US to halt the previous upward trend of domestic crude production. The reasons have never been explained. They may have been connected with struggle between the well-owners and the Federal government over a question of taxation. (Whatever the cause, it wasn't Keynesianism!) In direct consequence, as the US real GDP continued to expand, the whole weight of increased demand for oil was thrown onto imports. And because the US not only held a large proportion of total OECD GDP, and because her oil consumption per dollar of GDP was much higher than that of the other countries, the leverage of this force in comparison with the then existing level of world trade in oil was very great indeed. Even without the political consolidation of the OPEC, the effect on the international price of oil would have been strong. The political crisis produced the immediate shock, the price rising fourfold, but in the longer term a major rise would have been inevitable.

From there, most subsequent events, bar one, follow naturally. The exception, however, is the most important, namely the second oil shock. How did that come about? For the last time we must answer "cherchez à l'ouest". After 1973, US domestic energy policy, rather than helping abate the international oil situation, exacerbated it. The Executive was unable to resist the populist insistence of the Congress that the internal price of energy be held down much below the world level. Americans passionately believed it would be morally wrong to allow the wicked Arabs to dictate the people's energy price. The price of car fuel was especially taboo. The political reasons were completely reasonable: a rise in the price of car fuel in the US shifts purchasing power against families in the next two quintiles from the bottom. These are important voters. In addition there was the obvious fear of the heavy adjustment costs for a nation which had, over a century past, been adapted to extremely cheap energy by virtue of domestic natural resources. Only a strong Executive could have quickly overcome such difficulties. In the meantime, lacking that type of government, the share of imports in total US oil consumption continued to rise for some years after 1973, with again powerful effects on the world balance of oil supply and demand, and the final result was the second shock. The biggest sufferer was Europe. Japan ought to have suffered worse, but, being Japan, she didn't (maybe she did but not visibly).

After that, given the political constraints, the 1980s were inevitable. With some exceptions in a group of small countries said to have "corporatist" economies,[1] and, in the case of France, a certain delay, the OECD countries pursued tight monetary policies, supported in some countries, such as the UK, by tight fiscal policies. Shortly after Paul Volcker succeeded Arthur Burns as chairperson of the Federal Reserve Board, he attended an economists' dinner at which were present a clutch of past, current and future chairpersons of the Council of Economic Advisers plus at least a score of America's leading applied policy economists, mostly, but by no means all, Keynesian or neo-Keynesian. They asked him what he planned to do.

---

1 See Matti et al (1991). The usual definition of this group is Austria, Denmark, Finland, Norway and Sweden. In that group, as compared with average performance in the OECD "Big-Six" (France, Germany, Italy, Japan, UK, US) average peak inflation rates after 1979 were about the same, but the unemployment performance was greatly superior, average peak rates being little over 5% compared with 10%. If Belgium and the Netherlands are included, as is sometimes done, the comparison is less favourable. Both Japan and Switzerland performed at least as well as the first group, but unfortunately, owing to counter-cyclical government regulation of immigrant labour permits, Swiss unemployment figures cannot be used to evaluate macroeconomic performance in the usual way.

In a few words he replied, "restrict the money supply". "What else?", they cried. "Nothing else", he replied, and meant what he said. That is virtually sufficient to explain the 1980s; those present saw an economic experiment in the making; we saw the valves being closed, and the results followed.

The measures taken did not prevent severe inflation ranging from 10% to 20% in the OECD world (worse elsewhere) for the best part of two years, but did destroy a large quantity of real demand and real balances, producing the depression we know. The justification is, or has to be, that otherwise there would have been hyperinflation. For political reasons it then became necessary to say that Keynes had been abandoned (if not discredited). Governments could not say openly that they were "squeezing out" inflation by means of unemployment. It was therefore necessary to make up other explanations of what was happening, a game in which, as I have already complained, the economics profession joined only too easily.

It is also quite easy to explain how the depression in the growth rate of output lasted longer and was more severe in Europe than in the US. While Paul Volcker remained unflinching at his post, President Reagan, the "degenerate" Keynesian of all time, was at his. The combination of a huge public deficit with tight money (although possibly better for the US, overall, than if Reagan had had control of the Fed as well) was like flying a plane with the rudder turned one way, the ailerons the other. High real interest rates were obviously inevitable, an effect which, as graphically described by my brother,[1] destabilized the US dollar and, exported around the world, seemed to have a more dampening effect on European business expectations than the positive effect of the US overseas deficit, a large part of which latter, in any event, was with Japan. (This does not say that Europe, or the US, had sclerosis, but rather that Japan, as we all know, enjoyed whatever is the opposite condition.)

Statistically measured unemployment in Europe has also had a markedly "worse" history than in the US. In 1973, in the whole OECD world, about 11 million souls were officially recorded as unemployed, of whom about 4 million were in the US; so the non-US share, mostly in Europe, was under two-thirds. At the peak of the

1 See Marris, S. (1984) and *Deficits and the Dollar* (1985).

bad times in the middle eighties, the figures were 8 million US, 23 million non-US, total 31 million. In 1992 there will still be at least 25 million recorded as statistically unemployed (we keep using this term because in the US and the UK under President Reagan and Mrs Thatcher respectively, rightly or wrongly, but not in the other countries, the definition of unemployment has been narrowed and the adminstration tightened), in the OECD world, of whom the huge figure of 20 million, or nearly three-quarters, will be non-US. The formal reason for the difference is that although the general slow-down caused a general decline (since 1973) in growth rates of GDP per person employed, this was very much more marked in the US than in other countries. But in US manufacturing industry the differential productivity slow-down cannot be observed. Consequently it is clear that in the face of the macro slow-down, the US has sustained and indeed enhanced employment possibilities by a heavy movement of working population into labour-intensive non-manufacturing industries, with resulting effect on the GDP-related average output per head.

The foregoing events have been beautifully analysed in a public lecture by Jim Tobin[1] in the course of which he said, "The striking differences in macroeconomic performance between Europe and America are no accident. They are related to striking differences in demand management; in practice, not in rhetoric."

History since 1965 does not even begin to make a case that a Keynesian world economy, managed as e.g. in the period 1950-65, or ideally somewhat better, is any more prone to creeping inflation than is indicated by the average actual OECD inflation rate of that period. Of course, during that time (1950-65), in many countries, especially my own, the average inflation rate was not considered satisfactory.

---

1 Lecture entitled "Is Keynesian theory relevant to the world economy today?", given at the Banco di Napoli, in Naples, 21 November, 1988. This lecture was translated into Italian, re-translated into English and published in Baldassarri (1989). The quotation above is from the original English text which can be obtained by writing to Professor Tobin at the Cowles Commission, Yale University. Either version is the best few thousand words on the Keynesian theory and its contemporary relevance as is ever likely to be published. Apart from the question of microfoundations, and a more judicious style, it agrees entirely with our own account, above, but says much more and better.

There were indeed problems and improvements to be made. But the apocalyptic story is absolute nonsense.

Since I wrote the first draft of this Introduction in November 1989, world events have moved at an incredible and dangerous pace. The trend of opinion on macroeconomics is also in the process of an Atlantic sea-change. In September 1989, on the op ed page of the London *Times* I read the following words of wisdom from the pen of that august paper's house political writer,

> The majority [of British public opinion] sees no inherent contradiction between a free market and properly financed and run public services...[But] few want to return to the *defunct post-Keynesian assumptions* which dominated all politics between 1945-1979.[1]

Tiptoeing past the delicate question of what the writer, in contrast to your average professional economist, means by "post-Keynesian", we come to a passage written in the *Sunday Times*, not strictly a dependency of *The Times* but under the same ownership, barely two months later,

> The political landscape is littered with signs that a new order reigneth. I find it hard to detect any route back. The 1980s are clearly at an end...Here is Mr Major coaxing old John Maynard Keynes out into the limelight. "Come on, no hard feelings, Maynard", he says, "Give us one of the old ones, *like counter-cyclical public spending*!"

Four months later, the author of those[2] lines had become editor (in chief), no less, of *The Times* itself. (Mr Major was the Chancellor of the Exchequer who replaced Nigel Lawson, forced out of office in late 1989 by Mrs Thatcher, many think, because he was too successful and also, despite public pronouncements, a Keynesian![3]) Soon after becoming editor-in-chief, Mr Jenkins appointed a new economics editor, Anatole Kaletsky, a descendant relative of the great Polish economist Michal Kalecki who, as will be seen in Chapter 5, basically anticipated the main theme of this book (that the Keynesian theory

1 Ronald Butt, *The Times*, London, 22 Sept 1989.

2 Simon Jenkins.

3 See for example the position he took in Lawson (1988).

requires imperfectly competitive microfoundations) more than half a century earlier. On October 22 1990, in the business and financial section of *The Times*, Anatole Kaletsky wrote,

> It is not just in Britain but even more importantly in the US that single-target monetarism has been gradually abandoned in favour of a pragmatic type of interest rate and exchange rate management. This has affinity to traditional Keynesian demand management... . There is, however, a crucial element missing from the new type of economic fine tuning... . While the intellectual content of monetarism has been effectively abandoned, the political commitment to using monetary policies alone has remained. The tax and credit policies that were a vital part of the economic toolbox of Keynesian demand management have been deliberately thrown away. As a result policy makers...have had only two instruments...to try to influence a multiplicity of objectives. [Tenses changed from past to present.]

Finally, in November 1990, Mrs Thatcher, perhaps the only genuinely anti-Keynesian political leader the Western World has ever seen, was deposed by her own party, and Mr Major became British Prime Minister! The Keynesian revival is rolling. The research for this book began in the middle 1980s when it had hardly begun. Naturally I knew it would come! In the coming decade the European Community hopes to form a new and stronger economic union based on a common currency maintained by a virtually Federal Central Bank. I passionately support these ambitions. But there is a school of thought, stemming especially from Germany, that would impose constitutional conditions virtually blocking intelligent neo-Keynesian macroeconomic management of the new federation. That would be not only ridiculous but tragic.

1 Setting the Stage

In the first part of this chapter we summarize the background and main assumptions of the economic model on which our thesis is based and the procedures of the computer simulation programme. We also demonstrate the latter in operation. In the second part we further discuss our picture of the firm, which is central to the model and in our opinion essential to the Keynesian theory. As in the Introduction, there is a difference of style between the two parts of the chapter. In the first part we are trying to describe the model as concisely as possible, in the second we are more inclined to let our hair down.

The model, being that of a macroeconomy based on imperfectly competitive microfoundations, is called the **Imp-Mac model**. The software is called the **Imp-Mac programme**.

The programme is intended to be a user-friendly tool of analysis of the model. Therefore it is essential that the user can change, or "shock", important parameters while the programme is running, in order to see the results. Unfortunately, for practical reasons the number of shockable parameters has to be restricted, and the ones we have selected relate to fiscal policy, nominal wages, the competitiveness of the goods market (as indicated by the elasticity of demand) and the motives of management as indicated by their bias, if any, in favour of efficient employment creation at the expense of some profit. There is, however, a significant difference of interpretation for the first two of these as compared with the last two. The former can genuinely be characterized by the name "shock": fiscal policy can change within the space of a year, economies have been known to experience sharp one-time increases in the general level of nominal wages. By contrast, the two last named "shocks" relate to long-term structural or behaviourial factors which in real life are unlikely to change suddenly. The purpose of making them nevertheless "shockable" in the Imp-Mac programme is to enable the user to see how they affect the macroeconomy. In the case of the first two shocks the transition dynamics are economically significant (what happens after a positive wage shock if wages are also indexed?), in the case of the last two less so. The dynamics of the last two shocks are not uninteresting nevertheless. What happens if the elasticity of demand falls, initially pushing up prices relatively to wages, but wages are indexed? (See the jacket cover, which shows the results of shocking demand elasticity when wages are not indexed, but neither is government expenditure, with results discussed in subsection 1.3.11. below.) Or if firms wake up one morning with a sudden onset of employment-creation bias (for answer see also subsection 1.3.11)?

For the user to assess the effects of shocks, a base of comparison is needed. Therefore it is arranged that however the programme's editable constants (see below) have been set, it always runs in a steady state (see box) until it is shocked.

> ECONOMIC STATES
>
> In this book the term **stable state** is used loosely to refer to any condition of the system which should be self-sustaining. A **steady state** is a stable state where some variables are constant and others growing at a constant proportional rate. A **stationary state** is a stable state where all variables are constant, in effect a steady state with growth rate zero. Because some economists prefer to reserve it for a steady state where all markets clear, we are cautious with the term **"equilibrium"** and limit its use in this book to an imperfectly competitive goods market where no firm wishes to change its mark-up.

The response of the model to shocks is much influenced by the fact that it is a model which, from the outset, was designed for computer implementation. Consequently it is inevitably sequential. As operations occur in successive moments of computer time, so the model emulates events in imaginary real time. It follows that shocks create an extensive amount of small scale short-term disequilibrium in the model (some prices not yet optimized, some imbalances between production rates and corresponding quantities of demand) which in our view has less economic significance, however, than in the "disequilibrium" interpretation of Keynes discussed in the Introduction. In the Imp-Mac model the disturbing effects of demand shocks, for example, are immediately reflected in changes in unsold stocks of, or unfilled orders for, finished goods. Individual firms' production rates are influenced not only by current and expected future demand, but also by their stock levels and the states of their order books. The economic implications are further discussed following the summary of the actual programme sequence, below.

1.1 Keynesian background

In the Introduction we pointed out that the Kahn-Keynes multiplier leads to stability not necessarily at full employment. In a closed economy, the GDP ("gross domestic product" or national production) will be stable only if it is precisely matched by the total domestic demand for consumer goods and capital goods (private investment) plus government expenditure net of taxes; otherwise there will be aggregate excess demand or supply. Keynes argued that in a monetary economy there was no direct link between consumer demand and investment demand, so investment demand, as well as government net expenditure, could be taken at any point in time as given or, in later terminology, "exogenous". Consumer demand, by contrast, clearly depends on consumer income, which is related in turn to GDP. If this relationship is known, then only one value of GDP is consistent with any pair of values of private investment and government expenditure. The theorem is proved in three equations that lie behind thousands of elementary macroeconomics exam questions set around the world every year,

$$\begin{aligned} Y &= C + I + G \\ C &= cY \\ Y^* &= (I + G) / (1-c). \end{aligned}$$

Y is GDP, C is consumption, I is private investment, G, net government expenditure, and c is the proportion of consumer expenditure to GDP divided by 100, for example a number like 0.75. The third equation is the simultaneous solution of the first two. Y^*, the solution value, is the stable GDP. As discussed in the Introduction, except for c, all these numbers are monetary aggregates, but somehow prices must be assumed given, so, in an elementary presentation the aggregates are implicitly physical, or "real", concepts. The final equation is typically employed to show that if, for example, the government increases G, after the system has settled, Y^* will be found to have increased by the amount of the increase in G divided by $(1-c)$. The latter, being the proportion of consumer income which

THE THEORY OF LIQUIDITY PREFERENCE

Keynes supported the dichotomy between investment and consumption decisions by a theory he named liquidity preference, the essence of which was that interest was the reward for sacrificing liquidity by not holding money, and that, in consequence, the money market and its price, the interest rate, could not function as an automatic coordinator of savings and investment. This theory is now somewhat discredited and some writers now argue that it was literally invented for the purpose of making the *General Theory* work. (See for example Meier Kohn's provocative introduction to Tsiang, 1989.) As a student, the present author found the liquidity preference theory attractive; it had a feel of freshness and realism as coming from the mind of a man who speculated on the markets with his own and his institution's money daily, a feel which was enhanced when the theory was taught to the author by Kahn who had succeeded to Keynes's bursarial duty of managing King's College's money (if one accidentally arrived early for a lesson one might find Kahn still in the bath, with a white telephone beside it, talking to the College brokers in London, revealing the strength of his liquidity preference). Unfortunately the theory, as also the subsequent Hicksian "IS-LM" interpretation, implies that in a modern economy the function of money as a store of value is important. For reasons given in Chapter 2, we support the school of thought that denies this. The concept of money as a store of value is both unnecessary for and (by possibly licensing real balance effects) potentially damaging to the Keynesian theory. From the very first time that the human race invented money as a medium of exchange there has been a permanent tendency for its use as a means of payment by consumers to get out of balance with its use as a means of payment to producers. Why? Because, in the absence of a coordinating mechanism (such as an actual Walrasian "auctioneer", see Chapter 2) no automatic balancer exists.

is not spent, can be considered the proportion saved, or "propensity to save", often denoted as s; so we say that the "multiplier", meaning the ratio of the increase in Y^* to the increase in G is $1/s$. Because s is less than 1 we expect the multiplier, in simple cases, to be greater than 1.

1.1.1 Neo-Keynesian superstructure

On this platform economists and econometricians over the past half century have built extensive structures; rather than only a handful of equations a typical econometric macro model will contain literally hundreds. Such models (as further discussed in Chapter 4) are widely used by public and private institutions around the world.

The main developments cover foreign trade, monetary forces, the wage-price relationship, productivity, labour supply and economic growth. Since many of the main relationships are included with time lags, the models are markedly dynamical in their behaviour. Typically, when observing one of these models in actual operation one is rarely, if ever, observing a steady state. Even if all exogenous variables are constant for several years, the time required for the model to settle down may be even longer.

Typically the wage-price relationship is represented by some form of "Phillips-type" equation[1] in the labour market combined with mark-up pricing by firms in the goods market. By the former is meant any connection between macro demand pressure in the labour market and the level or rate of change of nominal wages. By the latter, as explained in the Introduction, is meant assuming that the mark-up of price over cost is determined pragmatically rather than by explicit profit maximization.

The econometrician building a typical neo-Keynesian model observes the average mark-up in the economy over a period of years and projects this into the future. When combined with the Phillips-type equation for predicting the average nominal wages for given real GDP, and another equation predicting labour productivity for given real GDP, the projected mark-up completely determines the nominal price level of goods for given real GDP. Consequently any level of real GDP is now associated with a unique corresponding nominal value.

Clearly this is a plausible and practical method of dealing with the difficulty in the Keynesian theory of moving between real and nominal aggregates as is required to validate the multiplier. The essential difference between it and the method pursued in the present book is that in the former, the mark-up, although statistically observed, is unexplained, while in the latter it is explained but not "observed".

---

1 The term stems from Phillips (1958). For the historic role of this paper in the history of applied economics, and subsequent theoretical and applied developments in the field created by Phillips see the corresponding entries in Eatwell et al (1987) op cit.

1.1.2 Absent microfoundations

Generally speaking, with a major exception in Sweden, (the Swedish micro-to-macro model, discussed in Chapter 2, section 2.3, and also below, subsection 1.4.6), despite the complexity of their equations, all the macro models of the kind discussed above are to be described as "aggregated" rather than "disaggregated". Typically they identify block entities, such as "all households", "all firms", "government" and so on, although by now it is not uncommon to see partial disaggregation, for example into some different classes of households. This means, that with exception of the Swedish case, the microfoundations of contemporary neo-Keynesian models are implicit rather than explicit. The assumptions, especially concerning households, may be quite complex but are applied to households in the mass; individual households are not identified. Given the number of households that exist, this is hardly surprising. In the case of firms, however, where typically less than a thousand firms contribute a large part of the industrial output of a national economy, the case is less obvious.

Macroeconomic theory has also tended to fudge the implications of the fact that in a modern economy a large part of private investment is financed by retained profits. Since this money does not reach households, the link between GDP and consumer expenditure is disrupted. How should it be remodelled?

1.2 The Imp-Mac model

Because the main objective of the present project is to resolve a problem in the micro/macro theory of the goods market, the Imp-Mac model has unusually detailed assumptions about firms. But an economic model cannot be made only of firms. Assumptions about other entities such as households, government and money are also essential. Here our priorities are reversed. We desire minimal assumptions for the task, and we especially desire to avoid assumptions that would enforce important conclusions however the goods market were modelled. We make no apology for thus evading some major concerns of contemporary macroeconomics. We do not imply that the omitted topics are unimportant. We simply clear the decks for battle in our own sea. Consequently, outside the theory of the firm, some of the assumptions are extremely simplistic.

We assume a closed economy (it could be a large country such as the US, the European Community or the whole advanced industrial world) containing households, firms and government. There are only two macro markets, the goods market and the labour market. There is no money market.

The goods market trades distinct products made by specific individual firms, one product per firm, so the number of firms in the economy equals the number of products. Each firm is a separate price setter and investment-decision taker. Investment is entirely internally financed. Firms retain just enough profit to finance already-decided investment; distributed profit is the residue.

Household income consists of wages and distributed profits. In effect, given the level of output per household, the distribution of income between wages and profits is uniquely related to the real wage. A higher real wage raises the marginal reward for work and reduces household profit income from non work and should therefore increase the supply of labour. There could also be a change in the propensity to save. In the Imp-Mac model, however, both these implications, widely recognized in other models, are ignored.[1]

Households are the main customers of firm, but goods are also bought by the government and by firms from other firms for the purpose of investment. Government and investors buy goods in exactly the pattern of households (following the same price elasticities), to be subsequently transformed by costless magic into public goods or investment goods. These specially outrageous assumptions are also made for good reason: there is little evidence on the question of whether in real life the elasticities of demand for investment goods or government goods are particularly high or low,

---

1 It must be conceded that these assumptions may be contradictory. With share ownership unequally distributed, an increase in distributed profits at the expense of wages will twist income distribution in favour of the rich who (subject to theoretical and empirical controversy) may be heavier savers. Alternatively, if, unrealistically, share ownership is assumed to be equally distributed, a rise in distributed profits at the expense of wages presents the average citizen with a situation where not only does he need to do less work to achieve a given consumption, but also, the prospective wage-rate being lower, his incentive to sacrifice leisure for goods is decreased; hence there should be a reduction in the macro labour supply, or, in the case of the opposite change in the balance of profit to wages, an increase.

so it is essential to avoid non neutral assumptions whose macro effects could be significant.[1]

Products are physically commensurable, measured in a common quantity unit, but qualitatively different, serving different needs and purposes. Buyers obey the traditional laws of consumer demand; if the price of one product rises, with others constant, they buy less of that product and more of other products, and vice versa, but the adjustments are constrained to leave the total nominal value of consumer expenditure unchanged. We further assume that the demand elasticity is the same for all products and the same through the entire length of each product's demand curve and also remains constant when buyers' total expenditure changes: if demand curves' locations change, their elasticity does not.[2]

The actual numerical value of the common elasticity is an important constant selected by the user before the model runs. Given that it represents consumers' general perception of the substitutability of products, one will expect the normal figure to be relatively high (it cannot be less than 1 or every firm would be trying to raise prices to infinity) and the simulation programme begins to run uncomfortably if it is set below 2. The initial "suggested" ("default") value is 3. As already told, this can subsequently be altered ("shocked") while the model is running, either by the user making the change directly, or by the user selecting a procedure to make it anti-cyclically endogenous,

---

1 For an example of these dangers see the discussion of Robert Solow's model (Solow, 1986b) in Chapter 5 below.

2 These assumptions have an important practical implication which is especially valuable in designing a computer simulation. Because a single point, combined with the numerical value of the elasticity, completely defines the demand curve, a firm can in principle discover the whole graph of its own demand curve, at a point in time, by simply by setting a price and observing the resulting flow of orders, i.e. quantity demanded. This means in the programme writing we can fully define any demand curve by the elasticity and by a reference point - three numbers only - and do not need to specify a more complex mathematical equation. The computer can store the entire information concerning the present state of the whole demand system by means of two numbers specific to each product, price and quantity, plus the common elasticity of demand.

that is systematically to fall when aggregate demand is relatively high and vice versa.

Households do not spend all their incomes, they save a fixed proportion, the propensity to save. Where they place their savings is discussed shortly. As already indicated, the socio-economic structure is such that the propensity to save is not affected if there is a change in the make-up of consumer income as between wages and profits. It follows that aggregate nominal demand for goods consists of wages and distributed profits, reduced by the propensity to save, plus investment expenditure and net government expenditure. If aggregate demand increases, when all prices happen to remain constant, the quantity demanded of every product changes in the same proportion ("expenditure elasticity" constant and equal to 1).

The only employers of labour are firms. Each firm is initially endowed with a stock of productive capacity and a partly specialized pool of labour. The utilization of capacity and the employment of labour are subsequently variable. Variations in utilization of capacity and labour by firms are therefore the micro causes of macroeconomic instability in the economy.

There is no technical progress and no substitutability between capital and labour.[1] Before the model begins to run the computer fixes values for **opph** (output per person-hour) and for capital per person-hour of labour (and hence capital per operating hour of output[2]) that subsequently apply throughout the run whenever any

---

1 The substitution is capital for labour or vice versa is a "classical" and not a Keynesian phenomenon and therefore outside the scope of this book. The assumption of no technical progress was necessitated, to the disappointment of the author by programming exigencies. The author is associated with the view (see Marris, R. 1964, 1980 and Odagiri, 1981) that the macroeconomic rate of technical progress in a modern economy is heavily influenced by the microeconomic growth motivation of the typical firm. The creation of technical progress is an internal activity of firms. It would be extremely interesting to simulate this micro-to-macro process, but not easy to write the programme.

2 This coefficient has also been called the instantaneous capital-output ratio (see e.g. Marris, R., 1964a). It is the true measure of the capital intensity of an economic activity. The more familiar measure is the ratio of the stock of capital to the annual flow of output. The latter, however, is the product of the instantaneous capital output ratio and the number of operating hours per annum. Hence the conventional measure depends partly on the rate of capital

firm is operating at a standard or "normal" utilization rate. If the utilization rate varies from normal, opph may be systematically affected in a manner over which the model user has some control and which is further substantially discussed later in the present chapter.

The pool of labour the firm initially inherits is just, and only just, sufficient to operate the initial capacity endowment at the normal utilization rate, in turn determining the "normal" output. Thus firms can subsequently increase their capacity (which never depreciates) by investment, but investment does not affect labour productivity or the normal-utilization capital-labour ratio.

The macro supply of labour is determined by demographic or social factors and, as already indicated, is completely unaffected by the real wage and associated distribution of household income between wages and distributed profits. The long run proportional growth rate of this labour supply is a constant selected by the model user and is called the **initial growth rate**. This is also the steady state macro growth rate of capacity and output.

If macro demand for labour falls short of the demographic supply, employment equals demand, and it may be assumed there is unemployment of one kind or another and also (see next sub-section) that nominal wages may fall. The programme however displays no number representing unemployment as such. What it computes and displays is the employment level of each firm and the aggregate of these, the macro labour demand.

If macro labour demand exceeds the long-term labour supply, the model implicitly assumes that firms somehow succeed in filling all their posts by sucking in more labour than the society would naturally supply, at the cost (see next sub-section) of higher nominal, but not real, wages. Why this labour was not previously classified as involuntarily unemployed is not explained. (This is probably the most unsatisfactory feature of the model. The sole justification lies in programming constraints. In any macro model without some

---

utilization which not only varies cyclically but is also under full employment conditions affected by the economic and social factors determining normal utilization such as the average length of the working day and social and legal forces resisting shift-work. Hence the conventional measure is a bad indicator of capital intensity.

assumption that clears the labour market automatically, for conditions of excess demand it is necessary to programme a scheme for rationing labour among employers, with consequentially complex effects on output. In effect, we have run away from the disequilibrium problem on the "short" side of the labour market by means of inconsistent assumptions.)

At the micro level, as previously mentioned, each firm faces a local labour pool whose size grows with the macro supply. If therefore a firm increases its capacity at the same rate as the macroeconomic initial growth rate, the firm's local labour pool will remain constant in relation to the firm's capacity. What happens when a firm varies its local demand for labour is now to be discussed.

1.2.1 The nominal wage

The model contains a not necessarily constant macroeconomic nominal wage norm which forms the base for variations in the actual wages paid by firms. Firms pay the nominal wage necessary to obtain the labour they require. If this happens to be the amount required for normal capacity utilization, the required nominal wage is the macro norm. If they require less labour, they pay the same. If they require more, they must offer overtime premiums or organize additional shifts (somehow inducing the new shift workers to come forward) and pay the corresponding shift premiums. The sensitivity of micro wages to micro capacity utilization is controlled by a coefficient selected by the user.

The model user also has the choice of including explicit macro effects in the labour market. One is price indexing: the macro wage norm can be indexed with a flexible lag or alternatively not indexed at all. Another is macro supply and demand: the programme periodically calculates the relation between the current total labour demand and the current demographic supply. If the former rises in relation to the latter, the macro wage norm is increased with a user selected sensitivity; if vice versa, the wage norm (a nominal number, remember) literally falls. This is the Imp-Mac model's version of Phillips, and is in fact basically similar to the wage equations used in most contemporary econometric macro models world-wide.[1]

1 The main difference will be that in the typical modern economy, when total supply and demand for labour are (in some sense) balance, average nominal

The case where the model user chooses not to include the macro effects described in the previous paragraph is **called wage model 1**; the case where both macro and micro effects are included (i.e. effects described in both of the last two paragraphs) is called **wage model 2**.

1.2.2 The real wage

The real wage is essentially a statistical entity, the national wage bill (payroll), divided by national aggregate person-hours employed, deflated by the price index ("deflator") and displayed as an index number. As most readers will know there is major controversy over whether the macroeconomic real wage can be interpreted as a "price" that equalizes macro labour supply and demand thus creating negative feedback circuit to stabilize the macroeconomy at full employment. The idea may be logically viable in models which permit not only Keynesian but also "classical" unemployment (caused by substitution of capital for labour in conditions of weak economic growth) but for reasons we shall now discuss is otherwise impossible. In the Imp-Mac model, as described so far, it would in principle be possible for unemployment to occur through lack of capacity, but, on account of the assumption already mentioned (that when capacity utilization is normal, the coefficient representing the ratio of capital to labour is fixed), the real wage could do nothing to alleviate the problem.

The real wage is not a price in the ordinarily understood sense. It consists of one number, which is the nominal price of labour, divided by another, the deflator, which represents the price of goods. If all firms produced an identical product, shall we say corn flakes, then it is apparent that the real wage is the quantity of corn flakes a worker can buy with the nominal wage she or he is paid for an hour of work. In turn, this must be the quantity of corn flakes produced by the average worker per hour (opph), less profit. Thus changes in the real wage can be fully decomposed into changes in average opph on the one hand or changes in the average profit margin on the other.

Suppose the profit margin is the profit-maximizing margin under imperfect competition as described in the Introduction. There we saw

---

wages are normally increasing. In some economies this "core" growth of nominal wages exceeds the trend of opph, implying a positive core rate of inflation of unit labour costs.

THE WISDOM OF DOW

Not long before the present book went to press, and well after the adjoining paragraphs had been drafted, the distinguished British macroeconomist Christopher Dow, sometime Senior Economic Advisor in the Treasury, sometime Deputy Director of the National Institute for Economic Research, Assistant Secretary General for economics and statistics in the OECD, sometime Director of the Bank of England, author of two classic books on the history of macroeconomic policy, gave the annual Keynes Lecture to the British Academy (Dow, 1990) on precisely the question of whether, in a Keynesian context, it is possible to make any sense of the statement that real wages are "too high". The following telescoped quotations have a telepathic relationship to the present author's thinking and the theoretical philosophy of the Imp-Mac model.

> **It is widely taken as self-evident that, since it is labour that gets unemployed, unemployment must represent a malfunctioning of *the labour market* - a malfunctioning attributed to the stickiness of wages. If wages declined when there was unemployment, full employment (it is implied) would then be restored. Since they fail to do so wages are "excessive". Such reasoning has an intuitive appeal, but rests I think on a confusion. For capital as well as labour gets unemployed. Should we say that unemployment of capital is due to capitalists demanding excessive profits? Can wages and profit both be excessive at the same time? These lines of thought suggest that unemployment must be due to some general blockage of the economic system, not confined to a single market. ... Real wages are nominal wages divided by product prices. ... The high-wage theorists say something about how nominal wages are set but nothing about how prices are set.**

This is precisely the reason why the Imp-Mac model places such strong emphasis on the goods market, and the price-setting process therein.

that the profit-maximizing profit margin depends on the goods-market elasticity of demand (as we shall see in Chapter 3, it may alternatively depend on more complex goods-market processes, for example oligopolistic processes). Opph, as already indicated, is given when the rate of capacity utilization is given. Consequently it appears imposs-ible to see a circuit for the supposed feedback.

The conclusion does not depend ignoring the fact that the real wage may affect the supply of labour. Suppose the supply of labour is, in reality, uniquely determined by the real wage. Only by coincidence will the real wage, itself determined as in the preceding paragraph, happen to be the one to generate a supply of labour equal to the demand created by the multiplier equations. This is the heart of the Keynesian explanation of the non clearing labour market, but unfortunately neither Keynes nor his followers were ever able to describe it so clearly.

The profit-maximizing profit margin is, we know, the inverse of elasticity of demand, so, given opph, it is demand elasticity in the goods market that sets the real wage, rather than supply and demand in the labour market. The book jacket shows the effects of changing demand elasticity in conditions when the incidental change in the nominal price level also affects aggregate demand, but the effect on the real wage is clear. When elasticity rises, profit-maximizing profit margin falls and real wage rises; and vice versa.

1.2.3 The firm

The firm is a financially autonomous organization responsible for the pricing, production, stock-holding, finance and capacity development of a single distinctive product; the conflict between the single-product assumption and the reality of the modern diversified corporation discussed later in the chapter. The firm's decision-taking criteria are based on the motive of maximum long-term profit (discounted cash flow) and also, if the model user so desires, by the size of the firm as measured by employment. The management accordingly sets prices and investment strategies to maximize a concept of expected benefit which is a weighted combination of discounted future cash flow and discounted future employment. The weighting factor is selected by the programme user, who may select conventional profit maximization by setting the weight for employment to zero. This in fact is the default setting.[1]

The number of firms is selected by the user before the start of each programme run and is thereafter fixed until the end of the run: the problem of reconciling this absence of entry with the case of a growing economy is discussed at the end of Chapter 3.

---

1 For background on the motives of management and the growth of firms see Baumol (1959), Galbraith (1967), Marris, R. (1963, 1964b, 1970, 1979, 1980), Mueller (1972, 1980), Odagiri (1981, 1991), Penrose (1959), Solow (1970), Yarrow (1976).

Except for the fact that their products are distinctive from the point of view of consumers, firms are homogenous. We have already stated that their products are measured in common physical units and that the demand curves defined in these units are iso-elastic. We now add the assumption that firms' physical production capabilities have a similar symmetry. When working under comparable conditions (in effect at given capacity utilization rates; see box) each firm has the same physical opph and the same amount of capacity per hourly unit of labour. Variations in the capacity utilization rate affect the efficiency of labour (as measured by opph) and the relationship between the two is closely related to the economist's concept of the short run marginal productivity curve of labour. The shape of that important curve is also discussed at some length later in the present chapter. Here we merely note that before the programme is run the user has considerable flexibility in choosing the shape of the curve, but thereafter it is frozen throughout the run and is the same for all firms.

THE UTILIZATION RATE

The stock of capacity with which each firm is endowed at the beginning of each run may be thought of as a bundle of plant, equipment, high management and some upper-middle management. The output per week obtained from the bundle depends on the operating hours per week, a number which ranges from zero to 168 (= 7 x 24), and may in real life vary in different parts of the plant or organization. We assume that when the capacity was originally planned, it was intended to produce a given output at an economically efficient operating rate, for example (out of many possibilities) 80 operating hours per week, representing five working days with two eight-hour shifts. We call this efficient rate the standard or normal rate and then define the actual utilization rate as the ratio, multiplied by 100, of actual weekly operating hours to the weekly operating hours of the normal rate. So the normal utilization rate is defined as 100, but, owing to the possibilities of overtime working and shift work, it is not the maximum possible rate. For background theory and empirical findings see Marris, R. (1964a) and Winston (1982).

Capacity may be expanded by investment. But capacity expansion is subject to a key constraint called the **Penrose effect**, also substantially discussed later in the chapter. The effect puts a premium on the real cost of capacity expansion related to the rate of expansion. The faster the rate of expansion, the greater the premium, the greater, that is, the required real investment expenditure. Again, the Penrose effect takes the form of a curve (relating rate of expansion to cost of expansion) the shape of which is initially determined by the user.

Thus the firm must make its key economic decisions on price and long-term capacity adjustment against four fundamental constraints, the demand curve, the nominal-wage curve, the opph curve and the Penrose curve, the shapes of each of which are completely under the control of the programme user. In the case of the last three, the programme permits the user to display the curve he has selected, and if necessary change it, before the programme is run, but not thereafter. In the case of the first, the demand curve, the "shape" is well known; it is a falling curve with the property that if both its dimensions are transformed into logarithms it becomes a straight line; unlike the other constraints, the elasticity of demand can be changed ("shocked", as illustrated on the book jacket) during a run; alternatively, as already indicated, it can be made endogenous.

Firms periodically estimate future long run growth rate of demand, hereafter called the **expected growth rate.** In the early stages of a run a firm's expected growth rate is effectively the same as the macroeconomic initial growth rate already selected by the user. Later it may be adapted, to an extent determined by a user selected coefficient, by the firm's past experience of the outward movement of its demand curve.

In association with the expected growth rate the model identifies a key variable, entirely the creation of Hiro Odagiri,[1] called the capital stock adjustment period, hereinafter called simply the **adjustment period** or AP. It is defined in the box. Briefly it is the length of time over which the firm decides to bring actual capacity into line with the capacity required to meet long-term demand with the normal capacity utilization rate. But long-term demand is affected by price, so the maximization of expected benefit requires a simultaneous selection of price and adjustment period.

Given the AP, current capacity and required capacity, it is possible to calculate the desired growth rate of capacity and hence, by the

---

1 See author's dedication and acknowledgements at the beginning of the book.

THE ADJUSTMENT PERIOD

From current price and quantity, together with expected growth rate, the firm can perceive its entire present and future demand curve. Any price set now therefore defines a future path of capacity required to produce future quantity demanded at the normal rate of utilization. It is not necessary to make actual capacity hit this path overnight. It is possible to reconcile actual and normally required capacity by non-normal utilization rates: there is trade-off between Penrose costs of fast expansion, on the one hand, and the effects on labour costs of non-normal utilization rates on the other. Subject to the simplifying assumption that whatever growth rate of actual capacity is decided upon, it is a constant proportional rate, the AP is defined as the number of units of model time from the current time to the time when the actual path of capacity cuts the normal-utilization path. There is therefore a planned discontinuity in capacity growth rate at the end of the AP, after which the firm hypothesizes that growth will be steady and that discounted cash flow may be calculated by the standard mathematical formula applying to a series that grows to infinity at a constant rate. During the adjustment period, however, when capacity utilization rates may be planned to be non-normal (with predictable effects on labour costs), and the absolute values of important variables are growing non-linearly (although the Penrose effect is constant, its financial consequences on cash flow, which latter, it will be remembered, is defined as profit net of investment, are not), the programme must make a separate calculation of each element in the series of future cash flows. These are aggregated and total discounted cash flow is then computed as the sum of the dcf during and after the AP.

application of the Penrose effect, the needed current rate of real investment. Converted into current nominal values, this gives current nominal investment expenditure. As already indicated, we then assume that although firms never issue new shares, they retain just sufficient profit to finance this predetermined investment expenditure, distributing the residual as dividends.

Given the criterion of expected benefit, the implicit choice of investment rate (in combination with price) is the best choice possible for the circumstances. The combined result will yield an expected rate of return. But because investment is entirely internally financed, and because there exists no money market rate of interest, there is no provision in the model for intervention by outside bodies, such as banks, to restrain investment in the event that the actual expected return resulting from the management decision criteria falls below some minimum. We thus capture the internal managerial flavour of the investment decision in a modern economy but simplify away the clearly important external financial forces.

To the extent that firms determine investment according to their perception of the expected growth rate of required capacity, the foregoing has some similarity to "accelerator" theories of investment already familiar to economists.[1] In those theories, however, the rate of capital stock adjustment, defined in our model by the AP, is often exogenous, and certainly never, to the author's knowledge, endogenous and simultaneously optimized with price with imperfect competition. Since, as indicated, the AP concept, and the idea of the simultaneous optimization was entirely the creation of Odagiri, the present author has no hesitation in claiming that this element in the Imp-Mac model represents an original contribution to economic theory in its own right.

In addition to the price and adjustment period decisions, firms make operational decisions concerning actual current production, actual current investment, stock holding and finance. A key feature of these operational decisions is found in the handling of orders and deliveries. Firms regularly accept, at their current posted price, all orders received resulting from consumers' response to the price as indicated by the demand curve. The orders are placed in a queue. Consumers pay in advance of delivery and firms place the payments in monetarily sterile holding accounts, to be transferred to revenue accounts only when the goods are actually delivered. In parallel with the queue of orders, each firm also holds finished stocks and maintains a target minimum level for these, which latter may, however, be violated in face of shocks. Consequently, both stocks and unfilled orders may fluctuate. Orders are delivered in historical order. Current revenue (transfers from the holding accounts), therefore, represents an aggregate of revenues from past orders at past prices and only in stationary state will necessarily equal the expenditure indicated on the demand curve at the current price.

---

1 The literature is large. For bibliographies see the two most relevant articles, namely the one entitled "Accelerator Principle" and the one entitled "Investment" in Eatwell et al (1987) op cit.

The production decision (which determines the employment decision) is not a simple equalization of production with current demand. It is based on the current levels of unsold stocks and unfilled orders on the principle that the normal state of affairs should be one where the two are equal to each other and jointly equal to a target minimum. Whenever firms find this target condition unsatisfied they adjust the current production rate on the plan of smoothly re-establishing normality within a given length of time, on the expectation that during that time new orders will run at the current level, growing at the expected growth rate.

1.2.4 Expectations

If any general readers are still with us, they need to know that by "expectations" economists mean something rather different from the contents of grandma's will. They mean the general way in which the actors in an economic model perceive the future for the purpose of taking current decisions. Keynes placed great emphasis on the evident fact that the production, employment and investment decisions of firms will be based on expected demand which is not necessarily the same thing as actual demand. His general view of the subject was based on his early work on probability theory[1] with special reference to the capacity of humans to make decisions relating to possibly unprecedented future events. Since then the subject has seen major controversy which the present work will largely evade. The author's own current views, for what they are worth, strongly influenced by recent developments in the theory of the human brain, are briefly set out in Chapter 2. Here, for the Imp-Mac model, we simply summarise what has been assumed.

The main expectational assumptions of the model are in fact implicit in the foregoing description of the assumed behaviour of firms: households have only short run behaviour, responding instantly as consumers to current prices, and as labour suppliers to labour demand; the government, as will be seen, is an abstraction.

The expectational behaviour of firms is essential "local"; it is based on past and current data relating to events affecting this firm and this firm only (albeit in reality often also affecting other firms as well).

---

1 See Keynes (1921) and further discussion of the history of this work in Chapter 2 below.

The managers of firms may read the newspapers or watch TV or even in extreme cases conceive that they know what is going on in the wider world from reading the published Minutes of the US Federal Reserve Board. But they do not regard information received from such sources as hard news until they have felt its actual impact on their own operations. In the words of another, namely Robert J. Gordon, "Individual firms maximize profit by setting *their own* marginal cost equal to *their own* marginal revenue."[1] More precisely, we should say that in the Imp-Mac model this local maximization relates to both current and future time. It has two aspects, each of which is affected in its own way by the future path of demand implied in the firm's estimation, described above, of the expected growth rate. The first aspect is represented in the assumptions governing the price and adjustment period decisions, the second in those governing the current production decision.

However the user sets the degree of adaptivity to recent experience in the formula for calculating the expected growth rate (see

---

1 Gordon (1990) p 1161. The empirical case for this approach is in our view overwhelming. It is supported by any industrialist whom any economist is likely to know or interview. Alternatively, consider the counter case. Let any firm which experiences a change in the location of its nominal demand curve take this as a signal that the national price level is about to rise in the same proportion. So, rather than calculating their new optimum price on the assumption used in this book, that competitors' prices are given, they assume that competitors' prices are about to be raised in proportion to the increase in nominal demand; this raises their own optimum price, and the prophecy is self-fulfilling. Clearly this is a possibility if for example an increase in aggregate demand occurs when the economy is already at the height of a boom. In strict logic it could occur to some degree during an earlier phase of the upswing, a possibility recognised in the Imp-Mac Model by the facility to endogenize the demand elasticity. But in a story of this kind, the predicted nominal price change is essentially relative to nominal wages, hence the story also predicts systematic counter-cyclical movement of the real wage, i.e. precisely the systematic movement that is denied by the evidence. We are satisfied that the empirical evidence reviewed at the end of this Chapter (subsection 1.4.6) once and for all finally demolishes all support the counter-cyclical real wages over any period, in any country. (A simultaneous increase in the nominal wages demanded wage-setting workers will not do; the demand for goods is an experience of firms not workers. If firms kill off the goods-demand increase by raising prices, no increase in the demand for labour, by contrast, will occur.)

above), the future path of demand is assumed to be a path of constant proportional growth (with a zero growth rate one possible case). If the forecast were actually correct, it would be impossible for the firm to earn greater expected benefit by a different choice of price and AP. In practice the forecast may be wrong in two ways; the path of future demand may not be a constant proportional path, but rather for example a path of depression and recovery; or, because a relatively high degree of adaptivity has been chosen by the model user, a shock or shocks has created a false impression of what is going to be the actual proportional growth rate. In the former case the firm plans a constant proportional path of capacity whereas a more complex path would yield slightly higher expected benefit. In the latter case, as events unfold, the error will be progressively corrected, but the firm must earn less benefit than it would have done if the error had not been made.

In the case of the production decision, as described above, the adjustment procedure takes account of current stocks and unfilled orders plus current demand projected forward according to the expected growth rate, for a relatively short period. Consequently, if the actual path of demand for goods follows an up-down curve of one shape or another, the path of actual production is adjusted relatively quickly and in practice deviates from the path of demand only modestly. Loss of profit or benefit, therefore, is on this account relatively trivial.

To the extent however that the constrained forms of the expectational assumptions create the possibility of some loss of profit, the Imp-Mac expectations are not perfectly "consistent", meaning that a person, such as the user, who understands the model (for example knows that in certain circumstances the initial effects of certain types of demand shock will in due course inevitably be reversed) could make better decisions for the imaginary firms in the model than the model itself permits them to make (for further discussion see Chapter 2, section 2.2.4). Where a high degree of adaptivity (in the expected growth rate calculation) has been introduced by the user, expectational "inconsistency" is the inevitable and, in fact, deliberate result of the user's choice. But it can be seen from the foregoing discussion that a small amount of loss of profit is also possible when no adaptivity has been introduced at all. The author cannot don sackcloth and ashes on account of this. It is the price of evading unfeasible programming complexity and cannot, as far as the author can see, affect any prime conclusion of our project.

1.2.5 The micro-macro interface

In the Imp-Mac model the multiplier process works in a sequence in which firms successively choose benefit-maximizing points on their demand curves. These decisions lead indirectly to production and employment decisions which, in conjunction with the nominal wage and government expenditure, create an aggregate demand which re-locates the micro demand curves. If the model is in stationary state, the demand curves will be re-located exactly where they were before, and firms will repeat their original decisions. If it is not in stationary state, the demand curves will have moved, and firms will make new decisions, and, after repetition, further new decisions until every firm has no desire to move to a different point on its demand curve. Such a situation (see Chapter 3) can also be called a "conjectural equilibrium" because, on the conjecture that other firms' prices will be constant, every firm wishes to hold its own price constant. The process of steady economic growth, described below, is a moving conjectural equilibrium.

1.2.6 The government and money

The role of money in the Imp-Mac model, and the associated treatment of government, is untypical of contemporary fashions in economic theory and model building. From one point of view the role of money is crucial, from another, de-emphasized. The difference hangs on the distinction between the role of money as the means of payment and, in our view, its elusive role as a store of value.

Because the means of payment for all transactions is money, Imp-Mac model variables, such as prices and wages, which in real life appear to the ordinary citizen as nominal values, appear in just the same form in the model and in that form play their causal roles: consumers make choices on nominal prices, workers see earnings as nominal wages. Macroeconomic aggregates such as those appearing in the equations above, and others, such as aggregate wages, are primarily computed in nominal terms. Finally, because we are indeed interested in the problem of inflation, the programme in which the model is embodied calculates and displays at frequent intervals a general price index ("the deflator"[1]) and also the rate of inflation. The deflator is also fed back into the model itself for various purposes such as indexing wages or government expenditure.

Apart from these features resulting naturally from the fact that transactions are made in money, the model is also endowed with a potentially powerful mechanism to emulate macroeconomic monetary effects on the real economy, namely the option for the model user to index (with a variable lag) or not to index, as the case may be, government expenditure. If the general price level changes and government expenditure is not indexed, or is indexed with a long lag only, in the absence of any other counter-effect there will be a multiplier effect in the opposite direction to the price change, due to the altered purchasing power over goods represented by a given nominal government expenditure. This process, which we call the "real fiscal effect", if selected by the user, has a similar macroeconomic effect as the "Pigou" or "real balance" effects further discussed in Chapter 2.

Where the Imp-Mac model parts company with most other contemporary macro models is in the treatment, or rather non treatment, of the stock of money as such. There is no macro variable representing the "money supply" and no micro variable representing the cash holdings of firms. There are no bonds, no money market, no interest rate. The money supply that finances transactions is implicit rather than explicit. It is implicitly assumed to have come into existence at some time in the past by some unspecified means and is now flexible. When the macro real GDP varies, or the price level varies, or both, firms and households may need more or less money to finance transactions, and either the government or the monetary system, by one institutional means or another, always precisely responds. The effect of this totally passive behaviour is that other than through the real fiscal effect, in the Imp-Mac model, the much studied monetary forces of the modern economy have no impact on

---

1 It is a current-weighted index expressed on a base of model time = 1. That is to say, it is the aggregate of current demand-curve indicated expenditure divided by the sum of the same quantities multiplied by the corresponding time 1 prices. As, however, all time 1 prices are always = 1, the deflator in the Imp-Mac Model is in fact simply the indicated current expenditure divided by physical aggregate of time 1 quantities measured in the common quantity unit.

the imaginary simulated economy whatsoever. The primary reason for what will seem to many contemporary readers an unusual or unfashionable step is quite simply that the inclusion of more familiar monetary elements in the model would have no effect on the distinctive implications of introducing imperfectly competitive microfoundations into Keynesian macroeconomics. If one introduces a strong real balance effect into any macro model, the model will have strong negative feed back and tend to stabilize at full employment, whatever its goods-market microfoundations.

1.2.7 The financial balance

Given the monetary non assumptions, how does the government conduct its business? What happens to household savings and to financial transfers between firms and households?

The answers to these questions are as follows. In the Imp-Mac model "the government" is in truth no more than an abstraction; it can also be seen as a proxy for any institutional influence on macro demand. Although the Imp-Mac model contains no interest rate, one might imagine an alternative version with a well-modelled money market, in which the government, in place of fiscal policy, preferred to attempt to manage the economy exclusively by interest rates. This could reduce the propensity to save and act as a negative fiscal shock. It is our contention that the basic implications of our thesis, concerning Keynesian microfoundations in the goods market, would remain inviolate.

The government levies no taxes and finances all its expenditure by printing money or borrowing from the banks. We assume it has sufficient power over the banking system that it is able to avoid all monetary side effects of this procedure, preventing the banks, in one way or another, from using government debt as a base for expanding the money supply, sterilizing other money in the system or somehow evading the long-term consequences of increasing national debt. In real life, of course, such tricks cannot be permanently sustained, but in real life there are taxes.

Households devote their savings to purchasing shares in firms. But as firms (see above) issue no new shares, there should be an upward trend in share prices relative to the price level. The very real possibility that the resulting chronic capital gains will in the long term induce households to reduce savings (i.e. reduce net share purchases) and increase consumption is ignored; as in the case of the money market, no representation of the stock market is included in the model.[1] As already mentioned, firms finance all their investment from profits, distributing only what is left to households. Consequently, quite unlike Keynes's assumptions, savings and investment among firms are directly equalized: since household disposable income is GDP less retained profits, household income is GDP less private investment. Consequently, household savings represent a total loss to aggregate demand. This loss, however, is counteracted by government expenditure. It follows that the condition for stability in the economy is that government expenditure equal household savings. It follows in turn that the government (in effect the model user) in setting expenditure, fully determines the stable value of GDP,

$$\begin{aligned} Y &= C + I + G \\ C &= (1 - s)(Y - I) \\ Y^* &= (G / s) + I \end{aligned}$$

The explanation of the second equation is that part of GDP never reaches households because it is retained by firms to finance investment. In the Imp-Mac model, as more fully discussed below, firms decide their investment according to their forecast of the long-term growth of the economy. In the event that the expected growth rate is zero (e.g because the model user has set the underlying growth rate at zero and there have been no shocks), I is zero. Then we can read the third equation is telling us Y^* for given G, or required G for a target Y^* (namely $G = sY^*$).

1.2.8 Economic growth

Alternatively, in place of the case of constant G and Y^* there is provision for positive economic growth at the speed of the initial growth rate. The purpose, however, is not to make a significant contribution to the general theory of growth (a topic which clearly involves the supply side at least as much as the demand side of the

---

1 This assumption, acceptable in a model, departs from the tradition of placing major emphasis on the relationship between the firm and the stock market found in previous work by the present author and in other associated writings in the field such as those of Kaldor and Odagiri. See Marris, R. (1964a, 1972), Kaldor (1966) and Odagiri (1981).

economy[1]) but rather to provide a basis for the investment decision of the firm. The Imp-Mac growth model, largely designed by Hiro Odagiri, demonstrates the possibility of a steady growth path of demand and capacity, and the effects of shocks therefrom. The government, all foreseeing, knows that the economy has the capacity to grow at say 3% per annum, and therefore benevolently validates the corresponding growth of demand. Therefore it increases expenditure in real terms at this rate, e.g. if inflation, pushed along by wages, were running at 2%, *G* would be increased in every period by the equivalent of 5% per annum. Then it will be found that firms, following the procedure of constantly re-assessing their price and output decisions, would each time conclude that their demand curves and nominal wage levels had changed since the model equivalent of one year back, so as to indicate a new profit-maximizing price up by 2% and a new rate of flow of quantity demanded up by 3%, leading, in due course to corresponding growth in production and employment. We label both pictures "steady state", but the case where the steady growth rate is zero is also, as already indicated, called "stationary state".

1.2.9 Model recap

This completes our canter over the general picture of the Imp-Mac model and its assumptions. In the next section we shall try to give the horse more life by summarizing the actual programme. In the meantime, let us recap. The model is founded on a concept of a firm as an undiversified producer organization which earns profits, finances investment and distributes dividends. Firms face distinct demand curves whose locations are determined by household income and government expenditure. They choose expected-benefit-maximizing locations on these curves while simultaneously choosing their capacity adjustment period for investment planning. These choices lead to effects on stocks, orders, production, employment, current

---

1 The present author and Hiro Odagiri, particularly the latter, are both associated with efforts to incorporate into macroeconomics the idea that in modern economies a major factor on the supply side of the growth rate factor, namely the rate of technical progress, is partly endogenous to the growth efforts of firms. (See Marris, R. 1964b, last chapter and Odagiri, 1981, whole book.) We wanted to incorporate this idea into the Imp-Mac model but were deterred by programming constraints.

investment costs and distributed profits. Passing through the micro-macro interface, the firms' decisions lead to the macro multiplier, which re-locates demand curves and sets in train the Keynesian process. For example, if government expenditure is down-shocked, there will be a smooth decline in output and employment to a new stationary state as predicted by the multiplier theorem.

In the course of these developments, nominal wages may be affected by pressures in the labour market, leading to changes in the price level (deflator) and possibly leading to changes in nominal wages and or government expenditure if these are indexed. A permanent inflation is possible. If wages are indexed and government expenditure is not, the real effect of government expenditure will be progressively reduced with a corresponding macro effect.

The real wage is mainly determined by the elasticity of demand. If, with government expenditure indexed and wages not, the elasticity of demand is changed, the result will fall entirely on income distribution. With both wages and government expenditure indexed, there will be chronic disequilibrium, symptomized by chronic inflation or deflation.

Of course, many other plausible combinations of assumptions are possible with correspondingly diverse results.

1.3 The programme

As already mentioned, the complete description of the Imp-Mac programme, including definitions of the considerable number of constants, micro variables and macro aggregates, together with precise descriptions of programme steps, functions and procedures, is found in Chapter 6. After reading only the following summary, however, it is possible to use the disk. The technical instructions for installing the software and starting the programme are found in the Appendix.

When the programme is running, macro variables are displayed graphically, in colour, in the upper part of the screen; micro data (prices, quantities demanded, production rates, capital stock, capital utilization rates, opph, nominal wages, investment, orders, stocks and others, 20 in all, for each firm) on the lower part, where necessary by scrolling. As well as current values, it is also possible to view the value of any macro aggregate or, for any firm, any micro variable, at any past point in model time since the run began. Alternatively, the user can call other numerical displays on the lower screen, e.g. the states of firms' order books or a review of the settings of constants. The lower screen is also employed for inputting shocks.

Although current variables can be viewed, or shocks introduced, while the programme is running, it is often more convenient to view the lower screen displays while the programme is temporarily stopped (paused). This is done by pressing the space bar on the keyboard, pressing again to restart. The facility completely freezes the programme, and has no effect on the model's behaviour. The upper screen graphs stop moving and the lower screen data remain constant. If it is desired to view retrospective data, use of the facility is essential.

1.3.1 Initialization

Before the programme is actually run the user must select values for various constants such as the number of firms[1], propensity to save, elasticity of demand, initial growth rate, wage or government expenditure indexing lags and coefficients controlling the strength of the Penrose effect or the shape of short run opph curve, and others (18 in all). Full definitions are given in Chapter 6, where user selectable constants are called **editable constants**; they may also be thought of as external constants, in contrast to **internal constants**, which are calculated by the programme itself. If the user elects not to edit any external constants the programme runs either with a set of default values inserted by the author or with the values of the last run whose data is still in the computer's core memory.[2]

---

1 We said above that a realistic micro to macro model of a modern economy need not contain more than a thousand firms. But in the Imp-Mac Model, designed for a micro rather than main-frame computer, the number is constrained by the amount of core memory and the size of the screen. With 640k of core memory the maximum number of firms is likely to be nearer ten, and the default setting is five! It has been established that for most perhaps the main significant results can be obtained with this setting. It is undesirable, however, to use less than five firms, and the user will find the programme will frustrate attempts to do so: it contains a simple instruction "If number of firms less than five, then number of firms equals five".

2 Constants, micro data and macro data of a run are stored in separate memory arrays (for example the micro data array stores variable i, of firm j and time t, and has thus the dimensions, number of micro variables, number of firms, run length) and there remain unless replaced or memory is cleared due to quitting the programe.

Among the editable constants one is called **smooth length** which is used for smoothing or averaging certain variables such as the expected growth rate or (see below) shocks. On the editing screen, smooth length is displayed in **imaginary real years** but when the programme runs it is converted to **model time** as defined in subsection 1.3.5 below.

After the editable constants have been set, as already explained, the programme must adjust itself to start the model in steady state. This has both macro and micro implications. There is first defined an internal constant called "**Keynes**", an arbitrary number representing the initial full employment aggregate output of the economy[1]. From this is calculated "**Keynes per firm**", derived from the value of "Keynes" and the user selected number of firms, representing the initial output and quantity demanded for each firm at full employment. Initial government expenditure is then set to create initial full employment aggregate demand and will thereafter be programmed to grow at the initial growth rate unless shocked, so that, in the absence of shocks, full employment and steady growth will be sustained. An exception occurs in the case where the user initially sets the weighting for the editable constant called **employment-creation bias** to a non zero value. In that case the programme initiates itself as if the employment creation weight were zero, then as it begins to run immediately absorbs the user created value. The effect is an immediate disturbance which eventually settles into a steady state consistent with the user selection.

At the micro level firms must invest at a rate consistent with the growth rate of capacity equal to the selected initial growth rate. In addition firms must be setting prices that not only imply quantities demanded equal to "Keynes per firm", but also, on testing these prices, firms must be satisfied that they are profit-maximizing prices, confirming a conjectural equilibrium. In practice this is done by initializing each firm's nominal price and opph at the arbitrary value 1; the programme then computes and sets the nominal hourly wage to produce a profit margin equal to the profit-maximizing margin implied in the user's already-made choice of elasticity of

---

1 It is actually 10,000. Consequently, if the number of firms is, say, 10, the initial value of Keynes per firm consistent with the initial steady state is 1000.

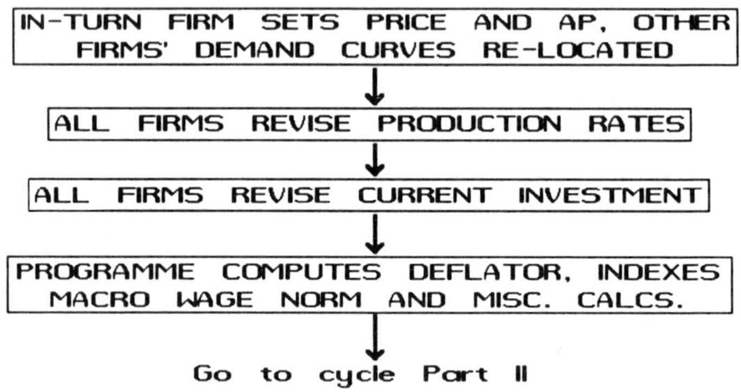

PROGRAMME CYCLE PART I FIGURE 1.1A

demand.

Finally the programme needs to compute the **discount rate.** Temporarily employing an old terminology used by Keynes, we may define a "marginal efficiency of capital", or *mec*, as the rate of discount to set discounted cash flow just equal to the initial value of capital. Then the initial *mec* is based on initial discounted cash flow, being the expected stream of cash flow, discounted to infinity, implied by the initial profit-maximizing profit margin applied to initial prices and quantities, resulting from the user's choice of elasticity of demand. The editable constants include an **initial return,** to be selected by the user as a positive rate of economic return at a reasonable level for the model's initial steady state. After the user has selected the editable constants, but before the run starts, the programme calculates and fixes the actual discount rate for the run at a level to equal the initial *mec* less the initial return. The effect is to create initial conditions where the return to investment exceeds the initial *mec* by the amount of the initial return. Subsequently, when running, the programme calculates and displays a current **expected return,** that is the current *mec* (based on the expected future cash flow implied in current run conditions) less the run discount rate. (Hence initially, expected return equals initial return and will so remain until the run is shocked.) This display is for the user's information only: it will be remembered that there is no provision in the model for external intervention to reduce investment if expected return falls below a minimum.

1.3.2 The programme cycle and programme time

In the programme, micro decisions are taken sequentially. A run is divided into cycles, during which one firm, designated the **in-turn firm**, takes optimizing decisions; and all firms (including the in-turn firm itself) take various practical operational decisions.

The programme cycle represents a unit of model time which can also be interpreted as a small unit of imaginary real time. It corresponds to the amount of real time required for all the firms in the imaginary economy to make all the adjustments prescribed by the programme. The model user determines this by selecting a value of an initial constant called **optimizing frequency**. If, for example, the optimizing frequency is set equal to 4, then it is implied that every firm in the economy can take the optimizing decision four times a year.

Precise details of the programme cycle sequence are given in Chapter 6. A visual summary, slightly re-arranged for presentation, is shown here in *Figure 1.1A* and *Figure 1.1B*. The economics of the main procedures have already been discussed. We now describe, summarily, how the programme implements them and the frequency and the sequence (frequency and order) in which they are carried out. In the final sub-section of the section we review the economic significance of the sequence.

1.3.3 In-turn firm sets price and AP

The economics of this first step in the sequence were discussed in sub-section 1.2.3. The in-turn firm enters the procedure knowing its current price, quantity demanded and actual capacity. It also implicitly knows the capacity it would require to produce current quantity demanded at the normal utilization rate. It then proceeds to find the optimum pair of values for price and adjustment period by iteration, that is by calculating the effects of small variations in one or the other variable until it appears that discounted benefit cannot be improved. The assumptions of the model, as described above, facilitate this process by ensuring that if it is found that moving either price or AP in a certain direction would decrease expected benefit, it is sure that this direction should be no further pursued; there are no local optima.

The programme iterates by first setting AP at an arbitrary low value, namely 2, then calculating discounted expected benefit assuming this AP and current price. Then small variations of price in either direction are tried, and a possible direction of improvement ascertained; if one exists, it is then pursued until price is optimized for this AP and the resulting discounted expected benefit recorded in memory. The trial value of AP is then increased by 2, and the process continued until the double optimum found.

The key calculation is that of discounted expected benefit for given price and AP. Its outline has already been introduced in the box above where we first defined the AP concept. Hypothetical future time is divided into two parts, before and after adjustment period, the latter being regarded as infinite in length. For example, if the trial AP were 20, then the first segment is from current model time to time 20, the second from time 20 to infinity. The programme needs to calculate discounted future cash flow in the two segments and add them together, and do the same for discounted future employment.

The post-AP calculation is simpler than the during-AP calculation and is done first. It begins by projecting forward the hypothetical quantity demanded indicated by the trial price, to the point in time at the end of the AP, by means of the expected growth rate (see above). This quantity is multiplied by the trial price to obtain projected (end of AP) revenue, production costs are deducted assuming the level of opph based on normal capital utilization combined with the current nominal wage norm (no future inflation is built into the calculation; if it were, the effects would cancel out). Investment expenditure at the current price level is calculated and deducted by applying the Penrose effect to the expected growth rate. The net result is projected hypothetical cash flow at the end of the AP. This is then assumed to grow from that time to infinity at the expected growth rate, discounted at the discount rate and aggregated by the standard formula (in effect divided by the discount rate less the growth rate, see Chapter 6). If discounted employment is required, a corresponding calculation is made based on projected quantity demanded produced at normal utilization opph.

The during-AP calculation is more complex because discounted values for each hypothetical model time period during the AP must be separately computed and aggregated. The computation for a single future period takes account of the fact that length of the trial AP

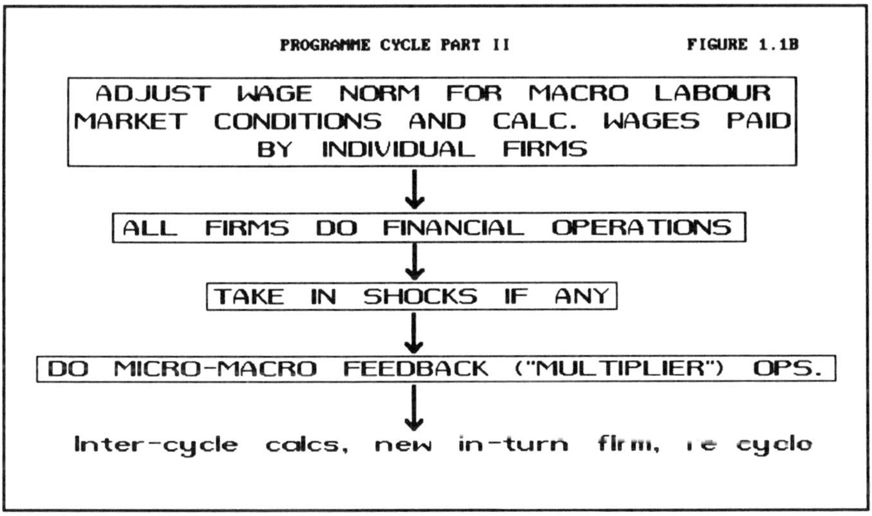

implies a path for planned capacity during the AP different from the path of normal utilization required capacity, and hence implies for each time during that AP an explicit, non normal rate of capacity utilization. The latter, in turn, implies specific levels of opph and local labour costs. Planned capacity and its rate of growth, at that time point, is also known, so real investment expenditure can also be calculated after applying the Penrose effect. In combination with the trial price these computations are sufficient to yield cash flow for the time period, which is then discounted before inclusion in the during-AP aggregate. Again, a similar calculation yields discounted employment. After repeating all this for every hypothetical time period during the trial AP, we now have aggregate during-AP discounted cash flow and employment.

Finally, if the user has not selected conventional, pure cash flow motivation, that is has assumed that the management give a positive weight to employment per se, it is necessary to transform discounted employment, both during and after AP, as more precisely described in Chapter 6, so that it is commensurable with cash flow. This done, all the data are then available for obtaining a numerical value for discounted future expected benefit, for given price and AP.

1.3.4 All firms revise production rates
All firms revise investment rates

Firms arrive at the current production decisions knowing the current levels of unsold stocks and unfilled orders (see next sub-section) resulting from previous programme cycles. They then revise production rates on the principle that, by the time they again become in-turn, unfilled orders should equal unsold stocks and both should equal target stock, this combined objective to be achieved smoothly over the intervening time.

In the case of investment, the fundamental decision is that of AP, already taken, but must now be translated into actual current orders for goods to become investment goods. The first step is to calculate the one-period physical proportional increase in capacity. If the firm has completed its capital stock adjustment, i.e. is outside its AP, the required proportional increase in capacity is simply the expected growth rate. Otherwise it must be calculated from the known current capacity, the known target capacity at the end of AP, the amount of the AP remaining, and the requirement for smooth growth. In either case, to obtain actual current investment expenditure, it is necessary first to apply the Penrose effect and then to convert the numbers into nominal values by means of the deflator.

1.3.5 Programme computes deflator, misc calcs, etc.
Adjust wage norm, etc.

These procedures have already been introduced in 1.2.1 and 1.2.6 above. The implementation is largely mechanical. "Miscellaneous" includes, inter alia, the steps required to derive the macro wage bill from micro production rates: given current actual capacity, a firm's current production rate implies a capacity utilization rate, which, as described in the general overview of the model given in the opening paragraphs of section 1.2 above, implies a level of opph, thus determining employment. The utilization rate, combined with the macro wage norm, determines the hourly nominal wage in the manner described in sub-section 1.2.1 above, thus implicitly determining the wage payroll. In Figure 1.1A these are called "misc calcs".

1.3.6 All firms do financial ops

The economics of this key procedure was given in sub-section 1.2.3. Firms accept and queue all current orders as represented by the quantity demanded currently residing in programme memory, which for the in-turn firm is the quantity demanded at the price emerging from the optimizing procedure, and for other firms is the quantity demanded resulting from their last optimizing turn, successively modified by the expenditure effects of any price changes made by firms who have optimized in the interim, including, of course the expenditure effect of the price change, if any, made by this programme cycle's in-turn firm.

Each firm delivers all orders that are more than one programme cycle old subject to availability of stocks. From the resulting revenue (transfers from holding account) is deducted current nominal investment expenditure as determined in sub-section 1.3.4 above. The residue is recorded in memory as the firm's current distributed profit.

1.3.7 Shocks

The user shocks the programme by calling a display which lists the four types of shock discussed at the beginning of the present chapter under the names **fiscal shock, wage norm, base demand elasticity** and **employment-creation bias.** The first two default to zero, the last two to the initial values of the corresponding constants.

After the user inputs a shock the new value of the variable or constant in question is not fed into the programme instantly but is built up in an S-shaped curve, to reach full effect at the end of a period of model time equal to the constant called smooth length (see 1.3.2). The shocks display shows two values, **raw shock** and **smoothed shock** for each shock, the first being the value set by the user (before shocking, these will be the default values), the second the actual value progressively developing on the S-curve. When the top of the curve has been reached, the raw and smoothed values become equal and the smoothed value remains constant unless and until the shock in question is again changed.

Adding one point to the **fiscal shock** has the effect of implicitly administering a one-time increase to nominal government expenditure sufficient to expand the economy so that at the end of the multiplier process, nominal aggregate demand would have increased by one per cent. In practice the shock is administered directly to the nominal value of the internal constant "Keynes" (see 1.3.1), the computer then calculating the required change in government expenditure.

"Complications" in the labour market would mean, for example that the user had initially selected a strong Phillips-type effect whereby the change in the macro demand for labour had a strong effect on nominal wages, leading, in the model, to corresponding effect on profit-maximizing (more precisely, expected-benefit-maximizing) prices. If the user had also elected not to index government expenditure, the resulting inflation will in due course devalue the fiscal shock and the economy will in due course relapse to its previous state. Alternatively, if government expenditure is indexed, the real expansion will be sustained at a higher but stable price level. If wages are also indexed, there will be permanent inflation.

Adding one point to the **wage norm** increases by one per cent the base from which all nominal wages in the economy are calculated. There will be a corresponding one-time increase in wages and (profit-maximizing) prices which will then deflate macro real demand and output unless government expenditure is indexed. If wages are also indexed, so that the real value of the nominal wage shock is sustained, there will be permanent inflation but in simple cases no permanent increase in the real wage.

The **base demand elasticity** is the normal value of elasticity of demand set by the user when initiating the run. If the user has not selected the option for making demand elasticity vary systematically counter cyclically, base demand elasticity is the same thing as actual demand elasticity. If the user initially selected the constant value 3.0, the shock screen will display this value unless and until the user changes it. (Examples of results of this shock are shown on the jacket cover of the book.)

Alternatively, if the user initially "endogenized" demand elasticity (by setting a non zero value for the coefficient to make it move counter cyclically), then base demand elasticity is the base from which the cyclical effects take place. Shocking it will have quite complex results.

Changing **employment-creation bias** is straightforward. An example of the effects will shortly be presented.

1.3.8 Micro-macro feedback

The micro-macro interface is implemented by deriving an aggregate called "ex post" nominal demand from current employment, wages, investment and government expenditure (household incomes are wages plus distributed profits, distributed profits are firms' revenues less investment, household expenditure is household income reduced by the propensity to save, aggregate demand is household expenditure plus investment expenditure and government expenditure). This is compared another aggregate called "ex ante" nominal demand, defined as the sum of household expenditure generated by firms' price decisions on their currently-located demand curves, that is to say, the quantities demanded emerging from the first step of the programme cycle multiplied by the corresponding prices. In the case of the in-turn firm the price will be the price emerging from the optimizing procedure in the present programme cycle; in the cases of other firms it will be the prices they set after the optimizing procedure when each respectively was last in-turn.

In stationary state, the ex post and ex ante aggregates will be equal. If they are not, the programme resolves the discrepancy by adjusting the quantity demanded of each product proportionately. Since prices are not changed, this amounts to a proportional "expenditure effect" and, given the iso-elasticity of demand curves, amounts to a general proportional "re-location" of them. (Notice that the question of whether the multiplier effect might go to prices does not arise here; all we are doing is re-locating demand curves. The effect on prices, if any, and on quantities will be first felt in the consequences of the optimizing adjustments made by the next in-turn firm at the beginning of the next programme cycle.)

1.3.9 Intercycle calcs and recycling

The foregoing completes the main story of one programme cycle. Between programme cycles model time is advanced one unit and all current data carried forward into the initial data of the new period; firms update their expected growth rates; the macro and micro data displays are updated; the user is given an opportunity to pause or quit the programme; and finally the next firm in line is designated to be in-turn.

After the intercycle calcs a new programme cycle commences and the programme continues cycling until either the user orders **quit** or the model time is reached already designated by the user as (maximum) **run length** (an initial editable constant).

1.3.10 Economic significance of the cycle sequence

Now that the sequence has been described, it is reasonable to ask why it, rather than some other sequence has been programmed. Why are the steps within the programme cycle placed in this particular order? Why is only the in-turn firm permitted to optimize price and AP, but all firms are permitted production and investment adjustments? Have we introduced the basic assumption of the "disequilibrium" school (that quantities adjust faster than prices; see Introduction) by the back door? Why is the micro-macro interface activated at the end of the programme cycle, and why, for that matter in every programme cycle, rather than less frequently?

The first answer to make is that the actual reasons for the choice of sequence were largely practical, and largely the result, in fact, of experiment. Given a decision that certain adjustments should occur within a programme cycle, it follows that certain things cannot be done before others are done: for example the micro-macro feedback procedure requires the data of the micro "financial ops" procedure. In the case of adjustment frequency, especially in respect of production and investment-expenditure adjustments, the physical limitations of the microcomputer are the key factor. We are supposed to be modelling a state of affairs where each firm's output represents a small fraction (a hundredth or a thousandth) of the output of the economy. In practice most users are going to run the model in a condition where each firm represents a much as a fifth of the economy. Most of the time this does not matter, but in the case of both production and investment, when the number of firms becomes small, there are certain circumstances where, if the adjustments are reduced to the same frequency as price adjustments (i.e. are permitted only to the in-turn firm), small systematic perturbations appear in an otherwise steady state, or alternatively the programme runs too slowly for most users to be likely to tolerate, after being shocked.

The practical answer, however, will not satisfy the economist; her questions remain. Nor is it sufficient for the author to assert, with his hand on his heart, that an alternative version of the model, in which production and investment-expenditure decisions were made only by the in-turn firm, has been tested and except for the problems mentioned at the end of the previous paragraph, behaves in all essential economic respects in the same way as the current versions (i.e. version on the disk).

The economic answers to these questions are to be found not so much in the structure of the Imp-Mac programme but in the basic character of the Imp-Mac model. The behaviour of the model will be largely independent of the relative adjustment rates of prices and quantities, because it is founded on a deeper principle, profoundly respected in economic science, namely profit maximization! More specifically profit (more precisely expected benefit) maximization by price-setting "imperfect" competitors. Price is set in the expectation of inducing consumers to demand the corresponding profit-maximizing quantity. That this revision occurs, in the current version of the model, less frequently than the indirectly affected stock adjusting production rates, however arguable, cannot affect the general thrust of the result.

The micro-macro feedback procedure is deliberately implemented in every programme cycle in order to capture the idea that it is in fact a frequent process whereby small, i.e microeconomic, events feed back into the macro circuit. Is it significant that we have put it at the end of the programme cycle? The answer is negative. Basically (see above) the procedure represents a periodic testing for discrepancy between ex post and ex ante aggregate demand. If we put it at the beginning of the programme cycle, or in the middle even, it would need to be based on data from a slightly different time phase, but it would still do the same job.

In short, the answer to the question, "what is the economic significance of the Imp-Mac programme sequence, as compared with other possible sequences that would validly implement the Imp-Mac model?", is, "little or none".

1.3.11 Demonstrating the programme

The reader who is already in a position to install the disk can try it now. Other readers, no doubt the majority at this stage, can follow in spirit. The book jacket gives an idea of what the user will see. (It is the effect of "shocking" elasticity of demand. It is discussed at the end of this sub-section.)

For installation instructions see Appendix. Start the programme and select "Do/display new run" from the main menu; it is the default, so pressing "Enter" will do.

The **constants editing** display will appear (for definitions, see Chapter 6). We will experiment with a fiscal shock.

Set govt indexing lag to 10. Government expenditure will be updated to the nominal price level indicated by the value of the deflator (see above) ten model time periods before the current period.

Set wage indexing lag to 10. The programme will compute a projected inflation rate (expected proportionate increase in deflator per model time period) representing that average inflation rate over a period of length equal to the constant named smooth length, ending ten model time periods before the current period. In each programme cycle the macro nominal wage norm will be increased proportionately by the projected inflation rate thus calculated.

Set demand elasticity endogeneity to 0.5. The effect will be that if, for example, the economy is booming by 10%, as measured by the percentage excess of the macro demand for labour over the demographic labour supply, the elasticity of demand is reduced by 0.5, from the base value, 3, to 2.5. (If the coefficient was set to 1, the reduction would be by 1, from 3 to 2; with coefficient = 0, no effect.)

> NOTES ON THE DISPLAY
>
> **Smthd** = moving average of length = "smoothlength"
>
> **Amplfd** = original data with amplified fluctuations
>
> **Rl** = "real" = nominal data adjusted by deflator
>
> **Goods Demand** = physical aggregate of quantities demanded
>
> **Log Scale** = vertical axis labels are natural numbers; the plotted numbers are as follows,
>
> $NORM \times (1 + \log y_1 - \log y_o)$
>
> where *NORM* = display base for variable in question [e.g. for **Labour Demand**, *NORM* = 110] and y_1 and y_o represent current and model time 1 values of original data of variable in question, respectively.

Leave all other constants at their default values. This will mean, inter alia, initial return 10% (per imaginary real year), wage model = 1 and wage coefficient = 0.5. Wage model 1 creates only micro (see sub-section 1.2.1 on the nominal wage, above) effects, in firms' local labour pools; with the wage coefficient = 0.5, the effect is that a firm which desired to increase capacity utilization to 1% above norm would have to pay 0.5% more in nominal wages on account of overtime payments or shift work premiums. With further increase in capacity utilization, the effect strengthens. (To inspect the full shape of the wage curve, return to main menu, select "display curves", from the resulting submenu select "wage".)

From submenu beneath the constants editing display, select "run" (as this is the default, pressing "enter" will do). Do nothing until the display reaches time 30. Pause the programme by pressing space bar, call up lower screen shocks display (by pressing "enter" until it

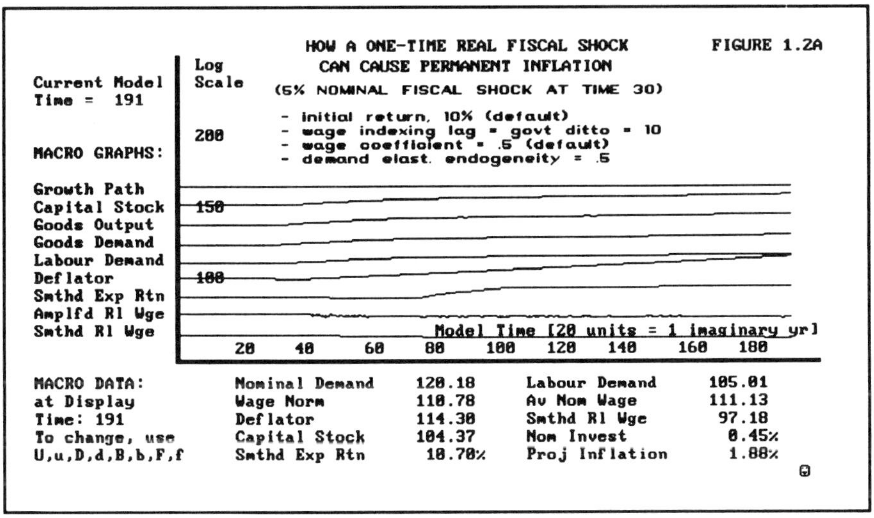

appears) and follow the displayed instructions to insert a 0.05 (5%) fiscal shock. Unpause (by pressing space bar again). Let the model run almost to the end of the screen and pause to inspect. The result, in colour, should appear as *Figure 1.2A*, the latter sadly transformed (owing to the fact that the wonders of technology will not yet allow economical disk transfer from colour monitor display to colour printer) into shades of grey. After time 30, there is a general expansion, which leads, via the selected coefficients, to a rise in average nominal wages (due only to local micro effects under wage model 1) and a fall in elasticity of demand, causing a rise in profit-maximizing profit margin, so there is both wage and profit inflation. At each programme cycle wages are indexed by the lag-calculated projected inflation rate, government expenditure is indexed, sustaining the real value of the shock, and the in-turn firm is free to raise prices in response to wages and profit-maximizing mark-up. There is permanent inflation with a fight over distributive shares. At the end of the day, the real wage (with inflation still continuing) is permanently reduced (by 3%) and the expected return permanently increased. With these dynamics, wages always win. In Chapter 7 we demonstrate another dynamic pattern, simulating the events of the late 1970s, where the opposite occurred.

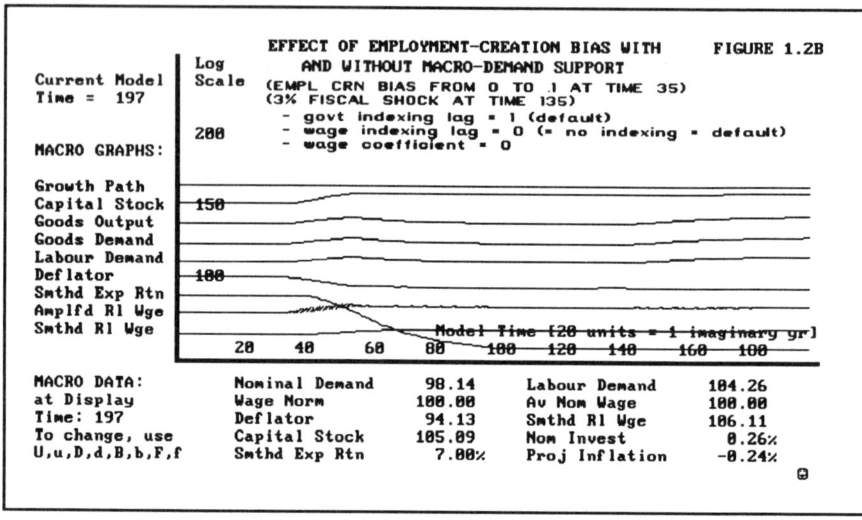

Figure 1.2B demonstrates an experiment with employment-creation bias. The coefficient was changed from 0 to 0.1 at time thirty, implying a corresponding change in the weight given to discounted future employment in calculating expected benefit, in other words a modest change towards an element of "managerial" motivation in the optimizing decisions (see end of sub-section 1.3.3 above, and Chapter 6). To simplify interpretation, wages were not indexed and all effects of labour demand on the nominal wage in both micro and macro labour markets were suppressed (wage indexing lag set to the disabling value, namely 0; wage coefficient set to 0). Government expenditure, however, was tightly indexed (indexing lag = 0) in order to ensure that government expenditure and fiscal shocks are held into real terms.

What must a firm do to implement the new motivation? It must increase its demand for labour by increasing its demand for goods; consequently, it must reduce price. As Figure 1.1B shows, as the "shock" takes effect, firms indeed reduce prices and temporarily succeed in raising the demands for their products. But, after initially rising by 3%, macro demand, including labour demand, falls back. Why? Because, in the absence, of any change in real government expenditure, the new micro data, when aggregated and fed back, generate insufficient aggregate demand to be self sustaining (why? because, given the constant propensity to save, there is an increase in the absolute leakage of household income into savings). So we see the situation shown in Figure 1.2B around time 100.

But it is by no means the case that nothing has changed. Prices have fallen, nominal wages are unchanged (there is no reason for them to have changed), so the real wage has increased. The effect of the burst of desire, on the part of firms, to create more employment has been to create none, but to raise the real wage of the already employed. The change in the distribution of income is marked by a fall in the expected return (from approximately 10% to approximately 7%), which, on account of the new motivation, is accepted by firms.

The period after time 135 shows what has to be done to rectify the situation. By means of a 3% fiscal shock, government expenditure is increased by a sufficient amount to ensure that the demand will be there to make the new motivation effective (it is the amount necessary to offset the increased leakage into savings; see above).

But notice an interesting and probably for most people (certainly for the author) unexpected additional result. In the stationary state achieved at the end of the run, with the demand for labour now permanently increased by 3%, the distribution of income does not return to the initial state; the real wage is permanently increased and the rate of return permanently reduced. Since it would have been possible, by means of a fiscal shock alone, to create the same permanent increase in the demand for labour, with no addition of employment-creation bias, it is impossible to escape the logical conclusion that under the assumptions of the Imp-Mac model, the true effect of employment-creation bias is to create, not employment, but higher (real) wages and lower profits.

This is an excellent example of the fundamental laws of the Keynesian universe determining the results of an otherwise unfamiliar experiment. In the work of Hiro Odagiri,[1] at first sight it appears that a different result is obtained because, in his work, management motivation favouring the growth of the firm does have macroeconomic effects. In his work, unlike in the Imp-Mac model (see the opening paragraphs of section 1.2 above) technical productivity is not fixed, but rather varies with the intensity of management growth effort as expressed in R&D expenditure. Consequently the

1 Odagiri (1981).

supply-side macroeconomic growth potential of the economy is affected. But the demand side is not. The original Odagiri model was also a full employment model, in other words carried the implication that by one means or another aggregate demand is made to grow at the same rate as potential supply. In his subsequent collaboration in the design of the growth aspects of the Imp-Mac model, Hiro has shown how to give effect to that implication.

Finally, the time is ripe for another look at the book jacket. At first sight the story is simple; demand elasticity is varied up, then down and then back to the initial 3.0; the macro real wage moves up, down and up accordingly. But, in addition, there are disturbances to macro output and employment. Why? Because, in the book jacket example, government expenditure was not indexed. The response of firms to their (correct) perception of a change in elasticity is, as we know, a change in (profit-maximizing) mark-up. Therefore, since they cannot change nominal wages, they must change prices. Consequently, as the reader can see, the curve of the deflator moves counter to the changes in elasticity. Consequently, with government expenditure unindexed, its real value moves in the same direction as demand elasticity, and real aggregate demand likewise. It is another example of the operation of Keynesian laws in unfamiliar circumstances. We change something (demand elasticity) that is generally regarded as a microeconomic parameter and we produce unexpected macroeconomic results.

1.4 The concept of the firm

In sub-section 1.2.3 above we were mainly concerned to describe, rather than to justify, the assumptions of the Imp-Mac model in relation to firms. In this second part of the present chapter we go about the task of amplification and justification. It is an expositional task fraught with the handicaps of an unfriendly terminology arising from what we see as a paradigm. We suffer in a situation where terminology that is most familiar to economists seems almost designed to prevent us describing that which we wish to describe, but if we create more appropriate, but unfamiliar, terminology we are liable to fail to communicate. It is a situation the author has elsewhere called "paradigmatic crucifixion".[1]

1 See Marris, R. (1990) and, of course, Thomas Kuhn (1962).

1.4.1 Alfred Marshall

The trouble starts with the great Alfred Marshall, one of the founding fathers of neo-classical economics, in whose work the concept of the firm was intended to be realistic, but, certainly as far as the 20th Century was concerned, most definitely was not (the first edition of Marshall came out around 1890, the last around 1910). He confused two conceptual roles of the firm, the one that of producer and seller of a product, the other that of an administrative organization. Both roles are essential to market capitalism, the legal framework of which has never suggested that they must be separated. In the early years, it was sometimes argued that a limited company which diversified beyond a list of products specified in its founding charter, was "ultra vires" (acting beyond its powers). In every state where this was tried, either the doctrine failed in court, or the law was briskly changed.

By contrast, the Marshallian neo-classical concept of the firm is that of an entity, implicitly owned and managed by one man (women were quite out, see box on Marshall and sociology) producing, by assumption, only one product. This concept certainly had more reality in the 19th century than today. But, writing at the turn of the century, Marshall still claimed that his argument stood for all time. In response to the total failure of that prediction, modern neo-classical economics has substituted a theoretical abstraction. The firm becomes an algorithm; a constrained routine for taking what are, to the modern corporation, the relatively low level decisions of price and output.

This modern neo-classical approach may in turn be severely criticised because important economic questions implicit in the assumptions expressed in the constraints are all too frequently either not discussed or only superficially discussed. The reality, which is inevitable, is that products are produced and marketed by administrative organizations (which may range from the one-person business to a multinational megacorp), and that one organization may produce any number of them.

WHY ECONOMISTS SHOULD AVOID AMATEUR SOCIOLOGY AND BOTANY

Quotations from Alfred Marshall

> Here we may take a lesson from the young trees of the forest as they struggle up through the benumbing shade of their rivals. Many succumb on the way, and only a few survive; those few becoming stronger with every year. They get a larger share of light and air with every increase in their height, and at last in turn they tower above their neighbours, and seem as though they would grow on for ever, and for ever become stronger as they grow. But they do not.
> – first edition (circa 1890) of *The Principles of Economics.*

> There are few exceptions to the rule that large firms....are, in proportion to their size, inferior to businesses of more moderate size, in energy, resources...and inventive power. – address to British Association for the Advancement of Science, 1902.

Why did the successful firms not grow on for ever? In the first edition Marshall explained that eventually the founder would grow old, and assumed that he could only be succeeded by a son. But the son, by virtue of the father's very success, would have been brought up indulgently. In particular, rather than the paternal rod, his back would have felt the soft hand of the nursemaid. So, ipso facto, he will tend to be inferior in business energy to his father, and the firm will go downhill. The author has mixed feelings about this story, because his family had a Birmingham manufacturing business that was founded well before Marshall wrote his *Principles* and survived, rather feebly, through the generations until the holocaust of 1982.

The point is that in the above quotations Marshall completely ignores the shareholder corporation, although in the US, Britain and Europe the institution and its legislation had been established for some time. It was true however that before 1900, most manufacturing businesses were private companies or partnerships. But after 1900 things changed rapidly on both sides of the Atlantic and when Marshall revised the book after the end of the century he struck out the nursemaids, and qualified the phrase "but they do not" with the words "at least until the recent great growth of joint stock companies which, although they rarely die, often stagnate". He was recognizing reality with reluctance. Setting a neo-classical fashion?

1.4.2 The firm and the quasi firm

Two economists, Heflebower in 1960 and Oliver Williamson ten years later,[1] attempted to popularize "quasi firm" for the neo-classical entity, reserving "firm" for the administrative organization. The idea did not catch on, and in his more recent work, Oliver Williamson has not encouraged it, but because the distinction is so fundamental to our present project, in this book we not only revive the term but shall make persistent use of it. In our terminology, a **quasi firm** means a lump of management, other overhead labour and physical capacity specific to a product, the utilization rate and weekly output of which can be varied by varying inputs of labour and materials. The **firm** is an organization, typically a shareholder corporation, probably made up of a number of quasi firms.

1.4.3 The cost curve and economies of scale

The place in economics, especially in classroom economics, where failure to distinguish between the firm and the quasi firm creates the most pernicious confusion lies in the standard discussion of the relationships between output, capacity and unit cost. So, as preliminary, let us clear the air.

When we speak of the expansion of *the firm* we have to be referring to a time period (not necessarily very long in real time) sufficient to permit the addition of whole new quasi firms, their production labour, their overhead labour and their physical plant. Therefore any "economies" or "diseconomies" associated with the expansion of firms are what are called economies of scale, i.e. the result of all quantifiable inputs being expanded in appropriate proportions.

When we speak of expanding a *quasi firm*, we may be speaking of the long run, as just mentioned, or of a shorter-run cyclical period, during which for some reason the entity varies the utilization of its "fixed factors" in association with varying inputs of labour and materials. The concept of returns to scale relates only to the fomer case. The long run average unit cost curve of the quasi firm represents the effects of adding capacity. Major questions then arise as to what costs associated with capacity (such as interest, depreciation or

1 Heflebower, 1960 and Williamson, 1970.

"normal" profit) should be included. These questions are discussed in Chapter 3 at the point where we discuss problems of interpreting the so called "excess capacity theorem" of imperfect competition theory. Since it is always possible to replicate a plant, the points on this curve which pass through a given utilization rate must lie on a flat curve. Intermediate points, with non-normal utilization rates, may show a "saw tooth" appearance, although, except at low levels of output, managers are usually able to some extent to smoothe these by using various combinations of shifts and hours worked per person per shift. So, **it is logically impossible for a quasi firm to have anything but constant returns or increasing to scale.**

As regards the firm, if nothing else happened when it expanded than the addition of quasi firms, then the firm, too, must have constant returns to scale. However, as the firm is in fact an administrative organization, we must consider the question of administrative economies or diseconomies of scale. Administrative economies, due for example to resource pooling, are obvious. On the other side, the majority of economists fervently believe that after a firm passes a certain size, administrative diseconomies set in, due to problems of coordination. Your author is in a customary minority position on this matter. He is confident that the case for the inevitability of eventual administrative diseconomies of scale in large commercial organizations is not supported in fact or theory.[1] For reasons that will become clear in the next two sub-sections, the controversy is not too important for this book, although, to the extent that in the Imp-Mac model, as the economy grows, so firms grow, and we assume that in a static sense this has no effect on costs. Instead, as already briefly indicated, we assume a dynamic effect, i.e. that the speed, in contrast to the scale of expansion has a most important influence.

The effect on "internal" costs, mainly the effect on the marginal productivity of labour, as we vary the utilization of capacity, is a

---

1 For a review of the arguments, see Marris, R. and Mueller (1980). The relevant passages are the work of the first author. The second author does not entirely agree with them. More specifically Dennis Mueller believes that large organizations suffer from general bureaucratic inertia, whose potential adverse effects on profitability are often offset by monopoly power and other benefits of non-price competition, described in the passages on this topic, mainly contributed by him, in the paper cited.

question of great importance in price-taking competitive economics (because it affects short-term stability), and is also of importance when discussing the viability of the apparent perfectly competitive microfoundations of the *General Theory*, is not so crucial in the field of imp-comp microfoundations, but is certainly important in this field. The central question is whether, as the utilization of capacity increases, the marginal productivity of labour, after an initial phase (on which all agree) of increase, then smoothly declines with increasing steepness; or whether, alternatively, after the increasing phase, the curve is approximately flat until capacity is utilized 24 hours a day, whereupon the curve disappears down its own verticalis.

In engineering logic, as we reduce the utilization of our plant below the level for which it was designed, we must experience the effects of technological indivisibilities inherent in the equipment itself and in its use of inputs such as labour. Therefore, as we reduce utilization, we expect output per machine-hour and output per-person hour to decline. This confirmed by conversation with any industrial engineer, production engineer or plant manager. As soon, however, as we reverse the statement into the proposition that over a major part of its range, the curve of marginal productivity of labour is flat, many economists, even to this day, turn green. They are conditioned to the analogy of the ancient case of the peasant working a potato patch.

1.4.4 Equipment hierarchies

Many economists who accept the foregoing arguments nevertheless "believe" that an assumption of a smoothly declining marginal productivity curve of labour is justified by another assumption, namely that in the typical quasi firm in the typical modern economy, production of the single product is supported by separable equipments which, having been acquired over historical time during which there has been technical progress, represent a historical hierarchy of "vintages" of efficiency. Consequently, the argument runs, if business declines, the older equipment is stood down first; when business recovers, it is reactivated, and therefore, on the upswing, the marginal productivity of labour is less than its average productivity. The "approximate smoothness" of this assumed relationship implies that in a plant producing a given product, there are not two or three, but maybe five or six vintages of equipment standing ready and fit for work at a given time.

There are a number of problems with this story.

(i) It is not supported by direct evidence from industrial establishments; the author has met economists who have sampled vintages of wine, but he has never met a single one who has visited a factory to sample vintages of plant.

(ii) Different equipment requires different skills; so the story also requires the existence of a pool of unemployed workers who remember the old skills and are available to be called back.

(iii) The story is technologically dated. Consider a modern business making sails for yachts. Despite a considerable turnover each order is one-off. The sails are designed on a computer which then untouched by human hand draws a full sized template on the working floor. The cloth is cut to these lines and stitched by workers using power tools. Out the back lies a "vintage" of traditional electric sewing machines kept there "in case they come in useful". But they never do. Why? Because they could not be used with the computer.

These points do not completely destroy the vintage hypothesis, but they surely cast a bucket of rather cold water on it.

1.4.5 Cost curve terminology

For the rest of this book we shall refer to any short run smoothly rising marginal cost curve, in principle derived from a presumed smoothly falling marginal productivity of labour, as the **neo-classical cost curve**. The "alternative" curve is based on the presumption that as utilization is increased, the marginal productivity of labour either increases or remains constant until the situation finally reaches an absolute constraint on any further increase in output. This is often called the "L shaped" curve, although of course the "L" is presumed turned left onto its side. In our view that is not an entirely happy name, and we prefer, for reasons which are fairly obvious, the term the **empirical curve**. But because that is not yet in general use, we shall sometimes employ the two terms together. And because so many economists still use the neo-classical curve, we have made it, albeit disapprovingly, a user option in the Imp-Mac model.

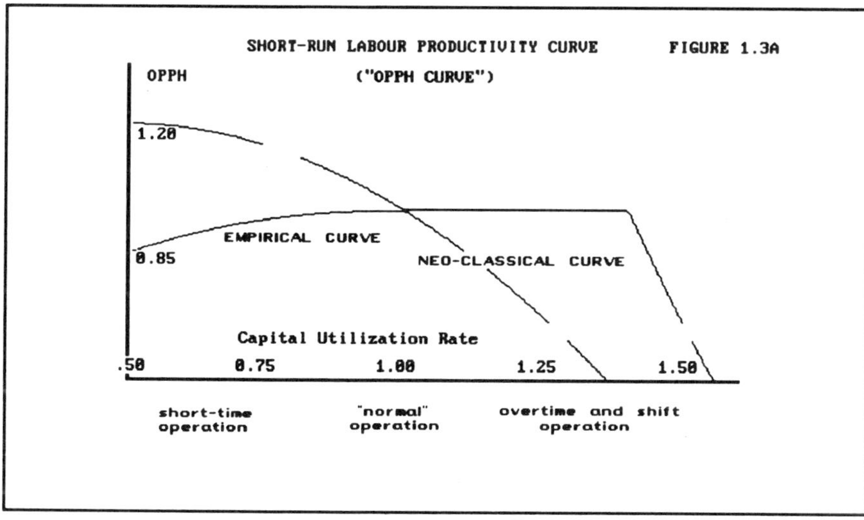

The user can choose among a family of empirical curves or among a family of neo-classical curves. See *Figure 1.3B*.

1.4.6 Empirical evidence

The foregoing deductive propositions are confirmed by various empirical studies, for example the case studies of British industries undertaken by none other than R. F. Kahn in the research already mentioned, the work of John Dunlop and Laurie Tarshis in the immediate wake of the *General Theory*, the industrial case studies undertaken by the present author 30 years later, the study by Wynne Godley and Robert Neild in the same era, the numerous econometric studies of the United States and elsewhere surveyed by Robert Lucas around 20 years after that.[1] The Kahn and Marris studies represented direct observations of the empirical curve. Dunlop and Tarshis for the 1930s and Godley/Neild for the UK 1955-65 either found either no cyclical movements or found *pro*-cyclical movements of average real wages, implying that the neo-classical curve could not exist unless the mark-up of profits on wage costs moved counter cyclically, a pattern for which no theoretical argument or empirical evidence could be found. The US studies surveyed by Robert Lucas

1 Kahn (1929), Dunlop (1938), Tarshis (1939), Godley and Neild (1962), Marris, R. (1964a), Lucas (1970).

were varied in definition but all tended to the same conclusion, namely that no direct or indirect evidence for the neo-classical curve could be found.

More recently, a most important result has been published by the operators of the Swedish micro-to-macro model in Stockholm.[1] It is based on actual data obtained directly from nearly 150 Swedish firms in the period 1976-88. The conclusions represent the strongest statistically significant confirmation of the empirical curve (except that the phase of rising opph with increasing utilization appears to run the whole length of the curve) in the history of the topic to date. The

There are only two apparent exceptions known to the author, one a recent study by Dr Bils of MIT[2] and the second by Alberto Heimler and Carlo Milana in a recent issue of the Italian *Review of Political Economy*.[3] Both are careful studies using sophisticated contemporary econometric modelling techniques. Both, however, have the neo-classical picture as prior assumptions. In the case of Dr. Bils, it is not clear that the phenomena he is observing represent declining marginal physical productivity of labour, rather than increasing supply price (imperfectly-elastic supply) of labour of a given quality: if this complaint is valid, Dr Bills, as we shall shortly see, is in extremely distinguished company. Heimler and Milana are free from this potential criticism, because they hold unit labour costs constant. In a study of two Italian industrial sectors (metal working and textiles) over the period 1956-83, they found that although the short run marginal cost curve was fairly flat, it did appear to be slightly rising. This could be a significant counter result for the "empirical" curve subject to the qualification that, in contrast to the Swedish case, the data are industry wide and the analysis strictly of a time series character. In the circumstances it is not possible to calculate the odds against the result being inconsistent with the hypothesis that a firm by firm analysis of the same Italian industries over the same period, if the data existed, would produce a "Swedish" result. Different as the two countries may be, it is not easy to see how their differences

1 See Chapter 2 subsection 2.3.1, below.

2 Bils (1987).

3 Heimler and Milana (1989).

should produce a major difference in comparable industries in the cyclical behaviour of labour productivity!

The last word is given in a masterwork of empirical and theoretical scholarship by Robert J. Gordon,[1] further discussed at the end of Chapter 5 below, which, published in September 1990, came to the attention of the author only a few weeks before the final date for revising this manuscript. One of the definite conclusions of his new comprehensive macroeconometric study covering the US over more than a century and other countries over half a century is that, taking the economy as a whole, there is no significant or robust cyclical movement of the real wage at all. In industry alone, in the US, a significant relationship exists, but it is pro not anti cyclical! So perhaps at last this debate can be regarded as closed.

1.4.7 The "U-shaped" cost curve

The foregoing discussion is associated with a more or less running controversy in economics concerning the so-called "U-shaped" cost curve. It is a U-shaped envelope of mini-U's, the latter being the short run cost curve (assuming the neo-classical curve), and the former the long run cost curve, of an entity which is not properly distinguished as to whether it is a firm or a quasi firm. The confusion is particularly common in graduate texts. Typically the author explains the short-term curve on the potato-patch analogy (when a variable input, such as labour, is applied to a "constant" factor, such as land) and then either does not explain the long-term curve at all (just leaving it as a pretty drawing) or resorts to the argument concerning coordination. So suddenly we are in a firm, not a quasi firm. The envelope is the surround of a group of quasi firms. Are they then all producing different products? Usually the answer is "no" (for as the authors above point out, the context may well be perfect competition). So we are back to the idea that the long-term "U" is the long-term expansion path of a quasi firm. In which case, for the reason given above, not only under perfect competition, but from in our view deeper reasons concerning adminstration, the "U" cannot exist. More precisely, its right arm is bent flat.

Here are some selected quotations, the first embodying the confusion between the productivity of labour and its supply price; the

---

1 Gordon (1990).

second assuming the neo-classical marginal productivity curve without empirical discussion or justification, the third (from the context) assuming, in effect, the U-shaped long run cost curve of the quasi firm in conditions of imperfect competition:

> (1) The distinction between diminishing returns and constant returns partly depends on whether workers are remunerated in strict proportion to their efficiency. *If so*, we shall have constant real labour costs (in terms of the wage unit) when employment increases. *But if* the wage of a given grade of labourers is uniform irrespective of the efficiency of individuals, we shall have rising labour-costs, irrespective of the efficiency of the equipment....Hence, in general, supply price will increase as output from a given equipment increases. *Thus* increasing output will be associated with rising prices... .[italics added]

> (2) If there is [sic] diminishing returns and the economy is competitive, the real product wage should rise as the economy goes into recession. The same is true in an economy dominated by...monopolistically competitive firms... .

> (3) Equation (12) [of our model]....gives the price-wage ratio...as a function of output. If firms operate under strictly decreasing returns...the real wage consistent with firms' behaviour is a decreasing function of output. We shall refer [to this] as the aggregate price rule.

The author of (1) is Keynes, J. M. The author of (2) is Stiglitz, J. The authors of (3) are Blanchard, O. and Kiyotaki, N.[1] A mock exam, intended affectionately to tease these authors (or in the case of Keynes, his shade), is given in the box below.

The cases of Maynard Keynes and Joe Stiglitz will come up again, because both also toyed with the idea (Keynes in 1939 and Joe 45 years later) that there could be interacting cyclical movements of the elasticity of demand in a theory with imp-comp microfoundations. In the meantime it is essential also to remark that the third quotation comes from an article the present author admires very much

---

1 *General Theory* (1936) pp 299-300. [The phrases qualified by "if" lie on the first page, those preceded by "therefore" lie on the second; the reader who would that feel this fateful pagination must be the pure result of coincidence should be reminded that Keynes was notorious for almost literally writing his books in galley proof and re-writing them in page proof.] Stiglitz (1984), Blanchard and Kiyotaki (1987b).

MICRO-ECONOMICS I: THIRD WEEK

Question 1

"Diminishing Returns" means,

As production increases, and more labour is applied to given equipment,

(1) it is necessary to employ less efficient workers,
(2) it is necessary to pay a higher wage to workers of given efficiency,
(3) the additional output from a worker of given efficiency declines.

Question 2

Diminishing Returns to Scale means,

(1) as an industrial plant expands beyond a certain size, it becomes technologically inefficient,
(2) as increasing amounts of labour and capital are applied to a constant amount of management, the management becomes overstretched,
(3) as an organization expands it is impossible to recruit new effective managers quickly enough,
(4) as the size of an organization expands and more managers of given quality are recruited, they suffer increasing coordination problems.

Note to TAs
The right answer to Question 1 is (3). Please report if you get a lot of (2)s and I will take it up again in my next lecture. Of course you all know the right answer to Question 2 - Prof.
Note to Prof from a TA
I've got a student come to see me who in Question 1 checked both (1) and (2); I gave him 0 but he is giving me a hard time, arguing. His name is Keynes. What shall I do?

(apparently more than the first-listed author of the paper from which it is taken, who has written to the present author to say he does not think it is a good paper!) and which will be substantially further discussed in Chapter 5.

1.4.8 The firm in the Imp-Mac model

Despite the foregoing diatribe the reader may already have noticed, from the description earlier in the chapter, that the firm in the Imp-

Mac model is also conceptually a hybrid: the economy consists of a large number of what are effectively quasi firms, engaged, as already mentioned, in imperfect competition on a nationwide scale, yet undertaking important activities, such as finance and investment planning, of organizations.

The reader may ask why the particular set of "bastard" specifications for the firm were chosen. The answer is found in the aims of the book. While the financial and strategic behaviour of large organizations may be of major significance in practical macroeconomics, microfoundations are the province of quasi firms. Whether as profit centres in multi divisional corporations, or, at the other extreme, as small single product businesses, it is the quasi firm, by definition, which takes price and quantity decisions.

Why not then, as in standard neo-classical practice, just model the quasi firms only? The answer is that almost as soon as you embark on a simulation study you begin to face all kinds of simple questions that do not bother the traditional modeller. After programming the taking of decisions, you must programme their consequences:[1] if a firm has set a price, expecting a quantity demanded, is this also automatically a production decision, or is it not also necessary to model the consequential movement of orders, inventories and cash flows? Consequently it is inevitable that we also endow our firm with a degree of administrative structure; at least an order book, an investment-planning unit and a primitive finance department.

1.4.9 The Penrose effect

We now expand on the "Penrose effect", named after Edith Penrose, who invented it, and whose seminal book on the nature and growth of the firm, considered as an administrative organization, first published in 1959,[2] has had a permanent influence on economists' view of the firm. The interpretation, or "theoretical realization" we employ was first suggested, soon after the book was published, by the

---

1 The train of thought set out here was entirely suggested by a similar passage in the opening chapter of the book by Robert Bennet and Barbara Bergmann (1986), of the University of Maryland, describing their extremely interesting transactions model of the US economy.

2 Penrose (1959).

distinguished Japanese economic theorist, Hirofumi Uzawa,[1] and adapted for the purpose of the present project by Hiro Odagiri (how much the science of economics does owe to modern Japan).

To explain the Penrose effect we maintain the assumption, discussed above, of constant returns to scale in the static sense. But because the planning of future growth must be carried out by existing high management, whose knowledge and skills are in the short run firm-specific, there is a manifest constraint on the *rate* at which an organization can expand without experiencing a general decline in current efficiency. Such decline is a "cost of growth", the burden of which increases with the desired or attempted growth rate itself.[2] There are a number of plausible ways of modelling this. Uzawa's was specially aimed at implications for not only the theory of the growth of the firm, but also the economy; in effect implications for the microfoundations of macro growth theory, so especially valuable for the Imp-Mac project. Uzawa represented the additional costs of faster growth as being like a premium on the real cost of investment expenditure required to sustain a corresponding growth rate of effective production capacity. If a firm desires to grow at say the same rate as the initial (underlying) growth rate of the economy, say 3%, then maybe it will need investment expenditure at a rate which, when expressed as a percentage of a measure of its existing capacity (e.g. book value of capital stock), will also be 3%. But if the firm wants to grow at 6%, the second number could rise as high as maybe 9%; the three percentage points (9%-6%) of premium costs representing the additional costs of more rapid growth. In the Imp-Mac model the severity of the effect (from nought to enormous) is a user choice, as illustrated in *Figure 1.3B.* The figure also shows that in the Imp-Mac model we for simplicity assume that if a firm desires a zero or negative growth rate, it cannot sell capacity, therefore the investment expenditure required is zero, while capacity, in the absence of depreciation, stays constant.

The Penrose effect, as incorporated in the Imp-Mac model, has important macroeconomic implications which stretch beyond the

---

1 Uzawa (1969).

2 Penrose op cit (1959), Uzawa op cit (1969), Marris, R., (1964b).

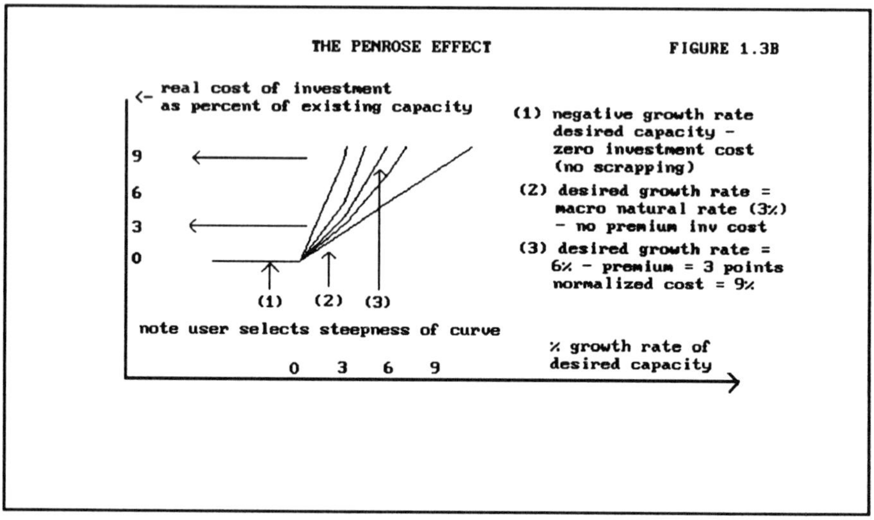

theory of economic growth and which are not easily investigated in traditional analytic models. Macroeconomic models tend to be either "short period", in which case the capital stock and general productive capacity of the economy is assumed fixed, or "long period", in which case, although the capital stock is a variable, the model is usually analyzed only in equilibrium. The process of change between short period and long is not too often discussed in detail. The gap raises a question mark over some traditional conclusions. When macro demand increases, the actual or attempted rate of utilization of existing capacity increases, and various results (e.g. effects on labour productivity) may ensue. But firms can also immediately consider taking decisions to expand capacity, decisions which, in traditional analysis, are thought to require a certain amount of time to carry out. Lacking data, the lag in question has to be treated as arbitrary. The "Penrose" reality, however, shows that the rate at which a firm adjusts general capacity (managerial as well as physical) to a new level is a choice, with a cost. The costs of lacking capacity may be traded against the costs of rapid growth. Consequently, the adjustment period (AP), as explained above, is no longer arbitrary, and becomes a matter for optimization simultaneously with price setting. Thus by a marriage of Penrose and Odagiri we obtain, as already explained above (1.2.3), our endogenous accelerator.

2 Computers, Humans and Economics

This chapter has four purposes. The first, arguably digressive, purpose arises from a desire in the breast of the author to reconcile the very conventional type of software found in the Imp-Mac programme, with recent exciting new ideas about the biological entity that makes economic decisions, namely the human brain. An economic system is a network of brains. But the brain's interior structure is probably inconsistent with the traditional concept of economic man. The consequences are rather pervasive and tend to reinforce, we would argue, some Imp-Mac assumptions, such as our treatment of expectations.

The second purpose, which partly flows from the first, is to justify the mixture of optimizing and "satisficing" (see below) assumptions built into the Imp-Mac model of the firm, in the light of the original ideas of Herbert Simon.

The third purpose is a general discussion of computer simulation as a tool of economic theory.

The fourth purpose is to discuss two topics dear to the hearts of contemporary macro theorists, namely the Walrasian paradigm on the one hand and the role of money on the other, in the light the author's outlook after spending two years writing a large piece of simulation software.

The main subheading relating to the first purpose is called, **"humans and computers"**; to the second, **"the brain and economics"**; to the third, **"the pros and cons of simulation"**; and to the fourth, **"the computer, Walras and money"**.

COMPUTER ANALOGIES

> The mother of a four-year-old boy, observing that he has been unusually cranky and obdurate for several days, decides that he has entered a "phase". A laboratory rat, busily pressing a lever to obtain food, hears a distinctive tone, which is followed by an electric shock. The very next time the animal hears the tone, it hesitates... A nineteenth century scientist observes the behaviour of light under several types of controlled conditions and decides that, like sound, it travels in waves through a medium. These are all examples of induction... In this book we propose a framework for understanding induction that is designed to overcome the limitations of previous philosophical, psychological and computational work on the topic... We have tried to develop a systematic set of principles providing coherence to a diverse set of findings on the nature of inductive processes. These principles will be used throughout the book to develop accounts of specific psychological phenomena, and their computational feasibility will be displayed through descriptions of *running computer programs*.... Since we are concerned with the inductive processes of organisms, notably humans, and those of computers, we will refer to "cognitive systems" to describe the "thought processes" of everything from *man to mouse to microchip*. Whether we are describing organisms or prescribing for machines, it is our intent that all our assertions ultimately be rendered *computational*... [italics added]

– from the opening pages of the recent influential book, *Induction* by John Holland, Keith Holyoak, Richard Nisbett and Paul Thagard (Holland, 1989].

2.1 Humans and computers

Evolution's highest achievement, the animal brain, is an amazing engine. It works without a programme. It can use data that is incomplete or inaccurate. It can make spontaneous generalizations. It can retrieve data without knowing precisely what it is looking for or where it should be looking for it. It records its own activities and records the recording of them. It spontaneously creates internal mental models and at will stores and develops these. It can transfer mental models from one domain to another, and is thus, unlike the

HOW GREAT IDEAS ARE BORN

> The proposition that one human being has more utility than another makes no sense...How could one decide whether prehistoric man was more or less happy than modern civilised man? Or, to push the comparison further, how decide whether the ant is happier than man; the lion than the gazelle?" [trans, present author]

These words from Pareto's *Cours d'Economie Politique* (1897), of which no English translation has ever previously been published, founded the proposition that it is impossible to make interpersonal comparisons of utility, and hence led to the concept of Pareto Efficiency and to a large part of modern neo-classical economics. The great majority of economists have therefore never read the original argument. Non-transferability of utility is treated as an axiom whose acceptability or otherwise is to be judged by subjective or philosophical criteria. While there has been considerable discussion among economists of the desirability of postulating that the individual human mind is a rational optimizing machine, there has been virtually no discussion of the possible biological nature of mental processes in relation to these questions. By contrast, a modern neuro-scientist would be likely to say that although we are a long way from understanding the pleasure-pain decision process, if we could understand it, we would probably find that it is not very different in the human from in the gazelle.

great majority of "artificially intelligent" machines, able to make decisions in unfamiliar situations. At the time of writing, a typical computer can do none of these things, nor can easily be programmed to simulate them.

We speak of the "animal" brain because the difference between our human brain and that of a cow, or even that of an ant, is much less than the difference between animal brains and computers. A century ago when the great Vilfredo Pareto was writing, similarities between man and ant were less apparent. So Pareto was content to base his entire argument against interpersonal comparisons of utility on analogy with presumed differences between ants and humans, gazelles, savages and the like (see box). Today although we know that the ant brain, being smaller, looks physically different from a human brain, we cannot yet be sure how different it is at what we call thinking. We certainly do know that it will be a long time before we can see in detail the relevant physical differences, if any, among the brains of humans with apparently major differences in their performing capacities (e.g. Einstein versus Mozart versus Charlie Parker versus Shakespeare versus Robert Solow).

So why do we need the computer? Why, after the millions of years while evolution has been at work, can the brain benefit from extension? The answer is that the process of natural selection has converged on a machine that thinks in a certain kind of way. In the process it traded calculating power for creativity. So we are weak in mental arithmetic and other logical operations. We take a thousandth of a second for an operation that a computer does in a billionth (the reason may be functional: cybernetic systems with fast learning rates tend to be unstable). There is genetic variation in the extent of the weakness, as there is also, evidently, in creativity. Humans who accidentally inherit unusual strength in both faculties are liable to be geniuses. But it could be that the genetic differences between potential geniuses and ordinary humans are physically quite modest. Maybe geniuses have the capacity to hold a few more items in short-term memory simultaneously: the gain in analytical capacity is likely to follow a power function.

What then is it that makes brain and computer so different? We know exactly how the computer works, but we are only beginning to understand how the brain may work. We know how the computer works because we designed it. In fact the architecture of the typical computer today was suggested by two brains, those of Alan Turing and John Von Neumann, both of whom died young (Von Neumann from cancer, Turing from an overdose of potassium cyanide) over a quarter of a century ago before the invention of the microchip. The design was based on the hypothesis that master wanted his slave to be as fast and accurate as possible. Lateral thinking was not desired. Why? Because it would deny the whole point of the exercise, which was, as already indicated, to compensate for the weakness of the brain by reversing the trade-off between creativity on the one hand and speed and accuracy on the other. To be fast, one exploits electronic pulses near the speed of light. To be accurate, one digitizes (mechanical/logical procedures where all data is ultimately recorded in switches that are either on or off). To avoid confusion, one connects each memory cell directly to the central processor without cross connections. The hardware miracle of the past decade is simply

A MESSAGE FROM BRAIN SCIENCE

Francis Crick, Nobel Laureate, FRS, following his historic contributions to molecular biology and genetics in the early 1950s, has for the past decade and a half devoted himself to the study of the brain, and has published a number of papers in the field, of which the most recent (Crick and Koch, 1990) could represent a major break-through on the subject of the nature of consciousness. In another paper (Crick, 1989) he recently wrote,

> **It comes as a surprise to neuroscientists to discover that many psychologists, linguists in particular, have very little or no interest in the actual brain, or at least what goes on inside it. The brain, they feel, is far too complicated to understand. Far better to produce simple models which do the job in an intelligible manner. That such models have little resemblance to the way the brain actually behaves is not seen as a serious criticism. If it describes, in a succinct way, some of the psychological data, what can be wrong with that? Notice, however, that by using such arguments, one could easily make a good case for alchemy or for the existence of phlogiston. ...I suspect that within most modellers a frustrated mathematician is trying to unfold his wings. It is not enough to make something that works. How much better if it can be shown to embody some powerful general principle for handling information, expressible in deep mathematical form, if only to give an air of respectability to an otherwise rather low-brow enterprise.**

Only the dimmest economist will fail to recognise how few words would need to be substituted to make this appear like a quotation from our own methodological controversies. A telling incident occurred in Keynes's own Cambridge college, King's College, in the middle 1950s when Crick was proposed for a distinguished fellowship. After taking advice, the twelve electors, in their wisdom, rejected him. Their timing was excellent. Soon after the decision, Crick and his DNA partners received their Nobel prize. Half a century earlier the same body rejected the first application from the young Keynes, based on a dissertation which was subsequently published as *A Treatise on Probability* (Keynes, 1921)! On re-applying the following year Keynes succeeded. So it seems that rejection by the King's Fellowship Electors can be a mark of greatness. The present author must therefore ruefully confess that his own entry (which has never been published) succeeded at first attempt!

due to discovering how to put the central processor on a single chip and wire it separately, via a "bus", to hundreds of thousands of addresses.

One of the most important things about conventional computers from the point of view of the economist lies in the essential character of this method of data storage, which is called "local" storage, or **local representation**, meaning that at any instant all the information on a topic is stored in unique physical locations. This is almost certainly the way the human mind does not work. A second, closely associated feature is "serialism". The terminology probably stems from the jargon of electric circuits.[1] A row of electric units is wired "in series" if the first lead goes from the positive terminal of the power source to the positive terminal of the first unit, the next lead goes from the negative terminal of the first unit to the positive terminal of the second, and so on. Alternatively, if the negative lead from the battery goes to the negative terminal of the first unit, and then the positive terminal of the first unit is connected to the positive terminal of the second, and the negative terminal of the first unit to the negative terminal of the second, and so on, they are "in parallel". The alternative wirings produce very different results. By a fairly large leap, a Von Neumann type computer is called a "serial" system, and systems, real or simulated, involving lateral connections of one kind or another are called "parallel". One can say that a serial computer must be inherently "stupid" in the sense that with this type of architecture it is difficult, if not impossible, to make a genuine learning machine. More specifically, it cannot learn things it has not been programmed to learn. It cannot for example make spontaneous generalizations. It may learn or generalize only about problems or concepts the structure of which has already been fully foreseen by the programmer. If the human mind suffered that restriction it would never have been able to achieve what it has achieved, and it would not have been able to invent the computer!

---

1 Some people, including Richard Startz, have written to the author to deny this origin, but the fact remains that the terminology existed in electrical engineering well before the first electronic computer was constructed.

ALAN TURING

English, born in London 1912; attended Cambridge University in 1931-3, becoming a Research Fellow of King's College in 1935. He was early recognised as an independent and original mathematician, and knew Keynes, who had an extremely high opinion of his work. In the late 1930s he began to think about a typically zany fundamental problem in mathematical logic; whether there could exist an algorithm that could correctly answer any question put to it. To approach the hallowed task, he conceived a universal computer, a totally algorithmic machine consisting of a paper tape with instructions such that, at each move forward of the tape, the machine knew precisely what it must do, and punched the result for the next step accordingly. His paper on the result, published in 1937, is a landmark in mathematical logic and also in the history of computing. His type of machine is called a Turing machine.

During World War II Turing worked at the British Government cypher-breaking establishment at Bletchley, and designed machines to break the codes of the famous German cypher machine, Enigma. People in the know believe that he was among the handful of Britishers of whom it could be said that they personally contributed substantially to winning the war (e.g. comparable to Dowding, the under-recognized Fighter Commander in the Battle of Britain). After the war Turing's career was less smooth though by no means a failure. He continued to work on problems of great interest such as biological processes which seem to involve the so-called Fibonacci numbers. He was a deeply committed homosexual with a taste for undesirable young men. At that time his type of activity was a crime in England and he was once prosecuted, humiliated and put on probation. In due course, possibly because he was in trouble again, possibly from side-effects of court-ordered drugs, and no doubt depressed by the effects of constant surveillance, he committed suicide. For a biography see his mother's book (1959), and for a brilliant account of both his life, work, the philosophical moral of same, subsequently made into a successful play, see the book by Andrew Hodges called *The Enigma of Intelligence* (1983).

In the past three years (i.e. since around 1987) some revolutionary developments have been occurring. These are **Parallel Distributed Processing (PDP), Classifier Systems** and **Genetic Algorithms.**

2.1.1 "Parallel distributed processing"

For at least half a century scientists concerned with the animal brain have had the idea that it may be some kind of "parallel" biological machine, meaning by this that the cells would have many cross connections.[1] But if everything is equally connected to everything else we have anarchy. Therefore it has been speculated that the strengths of inter-cell connections would vary in the sense that if cell A, a neuron, is active at a strength of say X (e.g X millivolts), it may pass on a stimulus of bX to cell B, and cX to cell C; b and c being variable parameters, e.g. lying in the range -1 to +1. There is strong biological evidence in support of the hypothesis that an operating mode of this kind is, if not the only way the brain works, at least a major part of it. The operations can be to a limited extent observed directly on living brains, simulated mechanically, or simulated in mathematical models on computers. Either as biological entities or as simulated artifacts, such systems are known generically as "neural nets".

After stops and starts, jumps and pauses, and more recently with an exciting rush, the idea has developed that the long-term information contained in the state of the brain, or in a neural net intended to simulate the brain, is found not in the short-terms states of the cells (neurons), as such, but in the data representing the whole set of connection strengths (synapses) between cells. In contrast to the case of local memory (see above) this type of memory is called "distributed" memory. The data set representing the connection strengths embodies information on many topics. The information on any one topic is embodied in many (in a sense, in all) the connection strengths.

The essence of the situation is that the brain has evolved without a central processing unit. Apart from the fact that, as we shall see, the arrangement has major advantages in performance of tasks such

1 The path of progress has not been smooth. For an excellent account see Vol 1 of Rumelhart et al (1986). The three volumes of that work, on which the present sketch is largely based, constitute, in the author's opinion, one of the most massive advances in man's potential to understand himself of the current half century.

as content-addressable access to memory, it is also, if one thinks about it, the most likely route of evolution, something, that is, that has developed in small steps rather than by comprehensive design. The Von Neumann computer, by contrast, is quite especially the product of comprehensive design and is, as we have seen, based in fact on principles laid down by Von Neumann and others well before the appearance of the hardware features we know today which so much encourage that particular type of architecture.

Suppose for simplicity we simulate a set of N imaginary neurons as an array of binary numbers. The short-term state of the system is simply a list of which imaginary neurons are on and which are off, which are 1 and which are 0. Now postulate another, N x N, array containing a set of connection strengths; numbers (weights) ranging from -1 to +1 telling that us that if a certain imaginary neuron is on, it will send to every other cell a signal equal to 1 multiplied by the weight appropriate for that connection. Also postulate that a cell "fires", switches on, takes value = 1 (and hence begins to send weighted signals outward) if and only if the weighted sum of its own inputs over a certain period passes a threshold.

Now further suppose that some of the cells, as well as being connected to other cells have also external connections. Apply some inputs. Stimulus will spread through the system and recycle. Possibly, after a time, the pattern of firings may settle down. So we have an initial state, some inputs and a final state. What, then, apart from the inputs, has determined the final state? Answer, the connection weights. So we have an information system.[1]

However, notice, so far there is no learning. The really dramatic idea, which has recently begin to find powerful practical applications, is that of making the connection weights dynamically endogenous, that is making them evolve from learning processes. By systematic application of patterns of data, a net can gradually be trained to a succession of associations, without increase in the number of bits of

1 The description is highly simplified. In particular to make practical use of neural nets it is essential to give them structure of various kinds. The "neurons" are usually arranged in a hierarchy of layers, with connections only between adjacent layers. The obvious example has two layers, one for input the other for output. But in order to avoid logical difficulties it is usually necessary to introduce an intermediate or "hidden" layer.

JOHN VON NEUMANN

Born a Hungarian citizen in Budapest in 1903. Was recognised as a mathematical prodigy when very young. By his late teens was studying in Berlin, consorting with leading European mathematicians and by his early twenties was publishing learned papers. In his late twenties he obtained academic positions in Germany and also invented the Theory of Games (1928), a concept which, apart from its profound contribution to economics, has influenced the whole of modern science and philosophy. Before the Nazis' power became obvious, Von Neumann was fortunate enough, and the United States so enlightened, that he was invited, along with Albert Einstein, to become one of the early Fellows of the Princeton Institute for Advanced Study. There he did many things, twice more entering the field of economics with lasting effect – Von Neumann utility, and the Von Neumann expansion path. During and immediately after World War II he became closely involved with the design of the early computers and also with the development of the hydrogen bomb. In the former role he laid down the "architecture" which, forty years on, is still completely dominant. A recent biographer (Aspray, 1990) described him as the most influential computer pioneer of all time.

On the way he found time to be very pleasant to one and all, male and female. One of his daughters, Marina, is a distinguished economist and a Vice-President of the Ford Motor Corporation to boot. Each of his contributions to human thought and science had the quality of supreme originality and richness, usually containing several fundamental ideas each of which could satisfy many academics as a single lifetime achievement. Had he lived to the era of Nobel Prizes in Economics, he would no doubt have caused significant embarrassment, qualifying for more than one prize and, like Herbert Simon, not being academically classified as a professional economist at all.

In his early fifties he contracted cancer and sadly died in 1957. About that time he had agreed to give some public lectures on a subject that is especially topical today, i.e. "The Computer and the Brain". He wrote them, but died before he could deliver them. They were published posthumously (1958) and even today make compulsive reading. First he describes some rather fundamental things about the computer hardware/software interface which are still relevant even though he was speaking of machines which used valves, not microchips. Then he gave an extraordinarily lucid survey of the anatomy and electro-chemical functioning of the brain, with interesting numerical calculations concerning storage capacity. He pointed out that a neuron was like a digital gate, and not a memory address. He was also clearly already intrigued by the implications of synaptic cross-connections.

information, and the resulting memory is distributed in the array of numbers representing the final connection weights. Every weight contains an element of information on each association and consequently the definition of each association requires in principle knowledge of all the weights: this is the essence of "distributed" memory. After training, the trained entity has an uncanny ability to recognise pattern associations for which it has been trained, to respond to a complex input with a correct complex output. Alternatively, if given a partly erroneous input, it has a good chance of coming up with the correct output. By the same token, in certain circumstances, the correct input triggers an erroneous output. Whom does this remind one of?[1]

2.1.2 Classifier systems and genetic algorithms

During the past decade and a half, cognitive scientists have been pursuing, with increasing enthusiasm and intensity since 1980, a group of ideas connected with the mental processes of search and induction that are known as classifier systems and genetic algorithms, the two being separate but often used in combination. Classifier systems represent a procedure for learning, or, better, for evolving, decision-taking rules. Like the genetic algorithm (see below), and considerably invented by John Holland (see quotation at the beginning of the chapter) the deeply original idea of the classifier system is that the decision-maker starts out with a substantial number of potential decision rules which are loosely (or partly) consistent with the observed exogenous conditions, plus a procedure for selecting among them, but, after repeated experiences, has a further procedure for progressively modifying the selection routine in such a way that he or she gradually improves their ability to make decisions in their own best interests.

---

1 In actual simulation models of neural nets there is a major problem in that one is attempting to adjust the connections to the hidden layers (see preceding footnote) by observations on the comparative performance of the "open", i.e. input-output layers, a process known as "back propagation". Various mathematical or algorithmic approaches to this problem are described in Vol 1 of Rumelhart et al (1988). It seems unlikely that the problem presents itself to the actual animal brain in the same light, or that evolution has developed the same kinds of solutions.

Genetic algorithms are a more general type of search procedures where, in searching some problem for good or best results, in place of conventional, usually calculus-based, mathematical procedures, we copy the methods of nature as found in the process of evolution. Survival, and hence reproduction, of the "fittest" can be seen as a process of search for superior variations. It turns out that by simulating the evolutionary process it is possible to create powerful search procedures that are often superior in practical computing applications to calculus-based procedures, the latter depending, as we know, on smoothness, convexity, single-peaks, etc. The mimicking of evolution is then extended to include the effects of "cross-over", similar to assortive mating, and also mutation.

Because the classifier decision procedure is a form of search, the two approaches are often combined, and indeed, conceptually overlap. In some contexts, they can be seen as substitutes. Unlike the case of neural nets and PDP, these two approaches are at the time of writing rapidly attracting the attention of economists, and we discuss below a most interesting recent contribution[1] in the field of the theory of money.

2.2 The brain and economics

From the foregoing discussion, it appears that on the one hand the mind is capable of holding a vast amount of data, on the other that, at any instant, it is "conscious" of only a small fraction. This raises some serious philosophical problems for social sciences, such as economics, based on the idea of choice. We are faced with the question of whether our science can be validly based on preferences which we don't consciously know[2] and can't consciously feel, a situation exacerbated by reflecting that we don't in fact know the

---

1 See Kiyotaki and Wright (1989) and Marimon, McGrattan and Sargent (1989).

2 In a recent interesting paper (Steuer, 1988) which came to hand too late to influence the above text as much as it should have done, Prof Max Steuer of the London School of Economics discusses the economic implications of the proposition that the main differences between human and animal brains are found not in specific inherited characters but rather in a strong inherited disposition, in humans, to acquire culture. "Culture", Steuer significantly defines as "that part of behaviour which is acquired by *unconsciously* imitating the...example of surrounding society." [Italics added.]

meaning of consciousness.[1] Added to that is the proposition that the memories we call economic preferences are learned experiences, undergoing continuous change. The connection weights representing our preferences (or more likely the reasons for our preferences) are undergoing continuous training, simply in consequence of the daily experience of life. Faced with this general situation, choice-based social science has adopted two approaches, the first of which was initiated by Jeremy Bentham circa 200 years ago, the second by Herbert Simon in a series of publications, as listed in the References for this book, beginning in the middle 1950s. The first is axiomatic and deductive, the second is heuristic and inductive. The first is called "rationalist", the second "behavioral". The first tends to be "normative" the second "positive".

2.2.1 Rationality

The rationalistic philosopher of choice takes as given that the mind is an inscrutable mystery and that, in consequence, it is necessary to adopt an axiomatic approach. One states one's axioms, one deduces ones conclusions, and no empirical observation can challenge the proposition that the conclusions follow from the axioms. In economics this implies the potential existence of "rational" states of society, with the associated quality of "rationality". Kenneth Arrow[2] has described this as a quality of society as whole. But if the society is to be rational so must be its members. The concept of the rational individual is particularly apt for computer analogy. The individual is, it seems, a Von Neumann machine, whose memory contains a preference system

---

1 The Crick and Koch (1990) paper on the nature of consciousness already mentioned in the box on brain science surmises that if the brain were a single neural net it would be impossibly large. They suggest that consciousness is an operating mode of the brain in which more restricted quantities of information are selected for attention and bound together by phased pulsing of the electrical communications between neurons. Waves, at an appropriate frequency, have in fact been detected. If this idea eventually proves to be even approximately correct, the implication for social and cognitive science would seem to be that the distinction between conscious and unconscious information is essentially practical rather than philosophical: the distinction between conscious and unconscious motivation would be considerably weakened. Here might lie the elements of answers to the rhetorical questions posed in the text above.

2 Arrow (1986).

acquired from past experience of pains and pleasures. If the rewards from choices extend into the future, the preference system must be time indexed. If the rewards are uncertain, it must be an ordering of lottery tickets. We then present the machine with a set of inputs, representing the current feasible choice set, and let it choose. If it chooses according to its preference system, it is rational. How it chooses we do not care; it could use random search, efficient search or, after having found some way of representing the system as a smooth utility function, mathematics. So long as it succeeds in finding the decision that is highest in the ordering that is all we want to know.

2.2.2 *Bounded rationality and satisficing*

This approach begins with a critique of the rationalistic approach which is much easier to summarize now than it was in the days (in the mid 1950s) before the computer-analogy way of thinking had developed, when Herbert Simon[1] first suggested it. The critique is practical rather than philosophical, and can now be seen to flow directly from the fact that the human mind has a limited short-term processing capacity relative to its total unconscious memory. Consequently, irrespective of the philosophical validity of a criterion of maximizing an only-partly-conscious function, it is certain that in practical actions, full optimization is impossible. We simply do not have the conscious calculating capacity.

In the light of the recent developments in ideas about simulating mental processes and search processes described above, one might re-state the Simon critique by saying that the brain may have the capacity to exploit a huge quantity of distributed data, but not in the manner of the optimization scenario. When we say that decisions are often made by intuition, we mean that they are informed by all kinds of clues and wisps of information and mental models contained in the distributed memory. Thus economic decisions, as much as any other, will be informed in a similar fashion to the decisions of a commuter driver: he will drive his car faster, for a given degree of safety, or more safely for a given degree of speed, than a person to whom the route is virgin. But, as we all know, (and as is inevitable if the

---

1 Simon (1957, 1959).

procedure is actually PDP-like) such processes are also inherently inefficient and inaccurate. It is therefore a travesty to imagine that the commuter-driver is operating an unconscious procedure that maximizes an "underlying" utility function containing arguments such as speed and safety.

The real bite of Herbert Simon's case, however, comes at the next step, which is simply based on the contemplation of the psychological question, "If I am faced with a decision problem which saturates my calculating power, what, apart from running away from it, do I do?" The answer is I employ arbitrary simplifications or heuristics (subroutines), the test of the usefulness of which is that they will tend towards answers that are "good enough", meaning good enough for survival. Simon called this "satisficing". Satisficing procedures are not arbitrary, they are derived from a cycle of reward and punishment: if the current performance of the decision-making process, as measured by conscious sensations of utility (e.g., in an organization, profits), is poor, search for more effective heuristics is stimulated. The process fades, however, as performance increases, so may never reach optimization (if any such concept, against this background, can be defined). Models based on actual observation of satisficing procedures should be substituted for rationalistic models for all positive, predictive work in economics.

In the early period, this critique was most influential in the field of microeconomics, and especially the field of the theory of the firm[1], but more recently Herbert Simon[2] has suggested important macroeconomic applications. For example he has suggested (in the author's opinion, quite wrongly, as will become apparent!) that the Keynesian theory depends basically on money-illusion (non-indexing of wage demands) in the labour market, a form of bounded rationality caused by suppliers of labour finding the process of numerical indexing beyond their powers of calculation. (If correct, it would be indeed a momentous application. But it doesn't seem to accord with observation, not in England anyway!)

---

1 See e.g. Cyert and March (1963).

2 Simon (1988).

2.2.3 *Mixing satisficing with maximizing*

It is possible to criticise both points of view at various levels. The result at times seems like a close-fought boxing match.

Round 1: At the deepest level, the rationalist can argue that it is quite inappropriate to attempt theory based on realistic models of the mind, when, in the present state of knowledge, we have no way of testing these. Given that situation, it is possible to derive important and interesting theorems from the axiomatic approach, without which, in effect, there would be no basis for any normative economics at all.

Round 2: The behaviourist retorts that, on the contrary, without some model of the mind, there is no basis for any predictive theory at all, and that that conclusion in turn throws doubt on the usefulness of any purely axiom-based normative speculations. Given that preferences are both learned (and hence continually changing) and unconscious, by what experiment could one infer that a person was not behaving rationally? Does the rational model claim predictive power, or does it not? If the answer is not, then what is its purpose?

Round 3: At the more practical level, the rationalist can attack the behaviourist with a criticism which is, in the author's opinion, effective, and if effective, painful. The realities of adaption and learning are strongly emphasized by behaviourists; satisficing is not just a theory about heuristics, it is a theory about the dynamics of heuristics. Consequently, a particular boundary placed by the typical mind on the rationality of an important economic decision today, by tomorrow may have moved. Taking for example Herbert Simon's suggestion concerning Keynes, mentioned above, there may be controversy as to the extent to which the correlations between nominal wage movements and lagged prices which were observed between 1918 and 1939 were directly causal, but surely there are very few people who would claim that the effect did not exist in the years since. The conclusion of this criticism is to attack the behaviouristic theory just where it is proud, that is to say this is a criticism of its predictive power.

Round 4: The behaviourist counter-punch consists in pointing out, absolutely correctly, that all empirical economics, and especially all empirical model building, involves at some point explicitly or implicitly assuming various rationality boundaries; in effect, these represent the boundaries of the domain of the model. The reason is that irrespective of whether or not the subjects of the model (the humans who live in it) should be characterised with bounded rationality, the calculating and general modelling power of the model builder is certainly bounded: unlike the subjects, the model builder can only operate in the field of the conscious minds of himself and his clients.

Round 5: The fight is declared a draw.

Comment: Both sides must accept that working economists make use of both rationalist and behaviourial concepts every day. On the one hand, the economic theorist sees that without some hypothetical scale of reference, such as is provided by the concept of the optimum, the house of theory lies on mud. On the other hand, the practical, model-building economist, forced to bound his rationality, knows he must employ cut-offs and heuristics. Nearly every economist, always knowing the limitations of the concept of Pareto optimality, falls back on it (at least for the idea of dominance) in the course of many discussions. Few economists engaged in the field of the theory of the firm are happy if they are never for one moment permitted to contemplate the concept of profit maximization. The next moment, this same theorist-of-the-firm, having postulated discovery of an optimum price, needs to translate the implications into an operational production plan. The question of inventories arises. Does he then proceed to complicate things further by bringing in a complex and elegant uncertainty-based theory of optimum inventory holding? Or does she (or he) at this point cut off the frontier of complexity by means of a simple and arbitrary target ratio of inventory to turnover?[1]

2.2.4 Expectations

An expectation is a forecast. If we define "rational" in the sense above, any rational decision-taking process requires forecasts for any decisions involving uncertain future events and pay-offs; the forecast is a temporary mental model of the action drama. A rational forecaster will by definition employ all currently available information, including not only data on past, hopefully pattern-revealing, experience but also a more permanent internal mental model that has proved generally successful in organizing the data for forecasting purposes. In this language, a rational expectations model is a model in which, as a matter of fact, economic agents are assumed to be actually doing that. The catch of course lies in the question of whether "all available information" includes only information in the human conscious mind? Does it include information "distributed" in the unconscious? Does it include information in computer banks which, for lack of time or money, the agent cannot process? Where does the mental model come from? If it is to be a paradigm of the economic system, it cannot be uniquely derived from data:[2] it is partly no more than a possible induction.

Given this basic language, the question of the "consistency" of the resulting forecasts, when incorporated into an economic model, immediately arises. Having built a model we may then, following Muth,[3] ask whether we are assuming that economic agents within the model are worse forecasters than an outside observer, e.g. the model builder, who knows the model. If we find that a major inconsistency exists, it is some cause for concern, since it conveys the impression that the model might not be robust: the model contains the opposite of a self-fulfilling prophecy.

But on the argument from evolution it is by no means clear that an inconsistent situation could not be self-sustaining. In real life the

---

1 A useful survey of the foregoing type of debate can be found in an authoritative article by James March in the *Bell Journal of Economics* (1978).

2 For an interesting investigation of this problem, see Stephen Spear (1989).

3 Muth (1961).

underlying structure of economic systems never remains constant long enough for the question to be tested. As a working principle, however, the desirability of "consistency", at least in the round, can be accepted. More precisely we can say that if one can see a substantial sense in which a particular model violates the Muth criterion, one should try to purge the model of the contradiction without at the same time also "perverting" it, i.e. without creating features that are out of spirit or empirically implausible.

Robert Lucas[1] popularized a peculiar sense of the adjective "rational" applied to expectations. "RE" is a procedure for forecasting future prices from current prices based on perfect learning from past experience.[2] Under imperfect competition, however, we cannot treat current prices as signals for future prices, for the signals are set by the signalees. Bluntly, it has to be said that to the present author imperfect competition seems quite fatal to Lucas's idea of rationality.[3] But as these words are written, there is no doubt some bright spark out there preparing a paper on imperfect competition under rational expectations.[4]

---

1 Lucas (1972).

2 Frank Hahn has recently written, "For a while rational expectation theorists believed they could skip the learning stage and concentrate their attention on situations where everything that could be learned had already been learned. But the large multiplicity of such situations as well as the possibility that some of these allowed agents to live in an essentially fictitious world has convinced pure theorists (if not all macroeconomists) that the learning stage cannot be skipped." Hahn (1990).

3 This is probably the reason why Robert Lucas has privately written to say that he does not see much connection between "monopoly" and macroeconomics! The answer from the present author is the present book. Surveys of answers from other economists are in Chapter 5.

4 Richard Startz's paper (1989), discussed in Chapter 5 below, opens with the statement, "Many economists believe that there are implicit assumptions in traditional macro models that agents behave irrationally, or that the models are internally inconsistent, or both. In this paper I provide a model of "Keynesian" behaviour in which agent's exhibit consistent, rational behaviour." It appears to the present author, however, that Startz is using the term rational in its normal or general sense, similar to ours, rather than in a peculiar sense.

The deeper criticism of this application of the concept of rationality is that in reality not even with the aid of huge conventional computer programmes and databanks will humans make their important forecasts by strictly deductive processes. As in the past, so in the future, they will forecast by hunch and intuition, as already discussed above. A sharper way of putting this is to say that decision-informing forecasts will often be inductive. They will use procedures that on the one hand sharply bound the accessed data set, on the other are capable under appropriate stimulus of jumping into a mode that involves exploiting a much larger sample of total memory. Heuristic procedures, in turn, will adapt. Possibly, but not necessarily, the adaptations will tend to evolve in the general direction of improving predictive ability. This is a modern way of supporting the approach to expectations formation found in Keynes's *General Theory* and pre-figured in his *Treatise on Probability*.[1]

"Adaptive" expectations is a general term for forecasts based on plausible projections of past events that may pass the test of consistency but are not absolutely required to do so. They can also be seen as the general result of bounded rationality, a form of satisficing. For example the device of predicting variables according to past trends, or more precisely as based on distributed lagged observations of past data, is a heuristic. Virtually all practical economic models contain such heuristics to some degree. We explained in Chapter 1 how the user can insert adaptive expectations into the Imp-Mac Model.

---

1 Keynes (1921, 1936).

2.3 Pros and cons of computer simulation

An adequate economic model will involve both complex time dependencies and non-linearities and these relationships will not be analytical but of experimental form. If the model is appreciably simplified it cannot be adequate, if it is realistically complex the problem of making very large numbers of computations of its behaviour will be extremely onerous.

— Arnold Tustin, a Prof of Electrical Engineering, in 1953.[1]

Previous outstanding applications of simulation methods to the microfoundations of macroeconomics, include the work of Irma Adelaman, the large (huge, magnificent! see box) micro-to-macro model of the Swedish economy directed by Gunnar Eliasson in Stockholm, the Barbara Bergmann / Robert Bennet Transactions Model of the US economy at the University of Maryland, and the Marimon / McGrattan / Sargent model of the Kiyotaki / Wright exchange model discussed below (for all, see References). "Conventional" large econometric macro models can also be seen as, or used as simulation models.

2.3.1 Simulation versus mathematical analysis

The distinction between the simulation approach and the economic theorist's traditional method of mathematical analysis has been well discussed by Barbara Bergmann.[2] In the field of imp-comp microfoundations scholars have either used a representative firm[3] or a kind of "high-level" mathematical analysis whose results are presented as solutions to simultaneous equations, then subjected to traditional comparative-static qualitative analysis. But real life occurs in real time; so real-life economic agents inevitably adjust in sequence: consequently one cannot be sure of the predictive power of comparative-static analyses on their own basic assumptions. By contrast, in the case of a sequential simulation model explicitly operating in imaginary real time, once she or he understands the

1 Tustin (1953).

2 In the opening pages of Bergmann (1986).

3 See e.g. Dixon (1987); Ng (1980, 1986).

programme she or he can in principle be sure that the resulting process is an actual prediction.

2.3.2 Realism versus opaqueness

As Barbara Bergmann has also pointed out,[1] the practical challenge of building a simulation model compels economists to face important questions they often ignore. In particular, having designed a simulated routine for taking certain decisions, in order that the model may run, one must then design procedures for the modelling the consequences of decisions, e.g if I have set a price in the expectation of creating a certain demand, at what rate do I adjust my actual production to the new expected demand? How do I manage the financial consequences, etc? **Until these "consequential" questions are answered there is no micro-macro interface.** And without a micro-macro interface, it is not sure that there is a macro model. Apart from general enlightenment, it was almost certainly a design history of this type that led the Swedish model builders (to the best of the author's knowledge, see again box above) to be the first in the world to build an econometric model containing the essential distinction between firms and quasi firms; driving themselves, in the process, into the administrative task of persuading and organizing the private firms to provide the necessary statistical returns.

The other side of the coin, of course, is that while the implications, and especially the normative implications, of good analytic models are usually relatively clear, the same cannot always be said of simulation studies. Not infrequently even the published descriptions appear labyrinthine: in particular, detective work is often required to find the underlying model of price formation.

We hope the Imp-Mac model and its presentation is less open to such criticism. But in that task we have an advantage not available to the workers of the world who build econometric models, namely that it is an essential feature of the Imp-Mac model that although we believe that the general assumptions, especially those that go to the heart of behaviour and the physical environment, are unusually realistic, there are no numbers based on econometric estimation: the numbers are chosen by the client. This factor is crucial in relation to the elasticities of demand for individual products, which, unlike

---

1 Bergmann (1986) op cit.

THE SWEDISH MICRO-TO-MACRO MODEL

Directed by Gunnar Eliasson (see Eliasson, 1979, et seq), the Swedish Micro-to-Macro econometric simulation model (already referred to in Chapter 1) is possibly both the most ambitious and most successful project of its kind in the history of modelling and applied economics generally. It relates in principle to *all* large and medium firms in the Swedish economy modelled both as firms (organizations) and quasi firms. Data concerning finance and investment are collected for the firms, and a special direct survey, running since 1975, also obtains operational data on production, employment and capacity utilization and profit margins, etc, for the identifiable *divisions* of firms. This is almost certainly one of the few, if not the only, example of economists making this distinction in practice. The firm and quasi firm data are combined with a partly disaggregated household sector, employing a standard econometric consumer-demand model, and an industrially segmented labour market, within which, during a run of the model, the pull of relative demand from firms' transfers labour between industrial sectors. At the macro level the model is conventionally Keynesian, but the response of firms to macro forces is uniquely sophisticated. Very briefly, the procedure is to identify four broad industrial sectors for which it has been possible to estimate relations akin to Marshallian demand and supply curves. These are periodically solved in simultaneous iterations through the whole model, to give predicted equilibrium prices for the sectors. Firms thus estimate their future profit margins by a scheme of partial adjustment to the historical margins. The expected margins and associated expected internal rates of return then drive the firms' decisions concerning production, investment, innovation and possible exit. The decision processes are largely satisficing procedures, but with the property of converging towards maximizing in certain important cases: for example, quasi firms maximize production subject to the target margin; this amounts to a step-wise price-taking profit maximization. Important satisficing procedures stimulate firms to respond to adverse conditions by searching for technical improvements. In consequence the model is as much concerned with the prediction of supply-side growth as it is with more familiar aspects of macroeconomics. Finally and again uniquely it takes account of entry and exit of firms and quasi firms.

elasticities relating to broad consumer or end-use categories, have proved in practice statistically impossible to observe. See again the Swedish model box. In our project, we have been able to model price setting only because we have not done any econometrics!

2.3.3 *When to use simulation*

There are four main indications for the treatment of a scientific problem with the "medicine" of simulation; the first is general complexity, the second something called "sequentiality", the third general dynamics, and the fourth the particular form of complexity represented in non-linearities, discontinuities and irregularities:

(i) **Complexity**

Computer programmes at "low level" break up complex procedures into large numbers of small operations, at heart the operations of addition and subtraction. A similar proposition is true of programmes written in user-friendly or high level languages; any one instruction is simple, yet the whole is complex. So in writing a desk-top simulation programme, one piles simplicity on simplicity to obtain synergistic increments of complexity. Then one piles complexity on complexity. Pelion on Ossa and Ossa on Olympus. When you have finished, like the Greek Gods, you are unlikely to be able to remember precisely what you have done. But provided the parts are sound, so, in principle, is the whole: if it works, it works. The tools of mathematics follow the same general approach, and in so doing achieve results of great intellectual power and artistry, but they cannot so easily manage, complexity in our sense of the term. This will not matter if the omitted complexities are of genuinely secondary significance, but that is by no means always the case. In this book we are in fact concerned with a type of economic problems where details of micro behaviour have major macro significance.

(ii) **Sequentiality**

By "sequentiality" we mean a quality in a theoretical problem where sequential analysis may be essential for obtaining sound results. If economic events are modelled in sequence, we have an "ordinal" dynamic. Although the imagined events occur in imaginary real time, results may depend less on the relative rates of change as such, but whether this event occurs before or after that event; e.g. if a reduction in the output of goods produces a fall in the demand for labour, which might in turn produce a fall in wages, there is no meaningful sense in which we can describe the initial event as producing a "simultaneous" fall in wages and prices. If it should happen that some other event should intervene along the way, the macroeconomic end result may be profoundly affected.

The idea that economic processes occur sequentially is not new, in fact it is probably as old as economics itself. Before the days of the computer, however, it was difficult to analyze sequential processes in detail, so that most scholars concentrated on seeking the conditions in which the processes would find steady state, followed by the usual comparative statics. Contemporary work in macro economics still tends to go the same route. In a macroeconomic model containing both real and nominal variables, for example, it is customary to analyse the equations to find conditions for a kind of steady state in which real variables are constant while prices and wages are changing at constant (proportional) rates. By contrast, using simulation, it is possible to set the model running in a steady state, to shock it appropriately, and observe events relating to all variables, nominal as well as real.

(iii) Irregularity

> **Theorists interested in optimization have been too willing to accept the legacy of the great eighteenth- and nineteenth-century mathematicians who painted a clean world of quadratic objective functions, ideal constraints and ever present derivatives. The real world is fraught with discontinuities and vast multimodal, noisy spaces.** – Goldberg.[1]

Mathematics is happy with systems that are smoothly non-linear but is less comfortable with sharp irregularities. The ecologists who are currently attempting to study important potential non-linearities in the greenhouse-warming problem invariably use simulation. There is no surprise in that. What is less widely known, at the time of writing, is that it has been found that a broad-brush type of model will not do. There are some feed-back processes (especially those connected with ice-cloud formation) which at first sight appeared

1 Goldberg (1989) p 3.

> unlikely to be strong. At second sight they appeared more significant, but, in the absence of direct observations of their parameters, were incorporated in the larger model on the basis of plausible numerical assumptions. At third sight it turned out that the entire global prediction is sensitive to such assumptions: quite small variations, within the range of current observation errors, shift the so greenhouse warming scenario between manageability and catastrophe.

2.3.4 The role of iteration

One reason for the comparative advantage of the computer in face of complexities and irregularities is its speed, which leads in turn to the power of iteration, i.e. repeating a series of test calculations until one has numbers that approximate a solution. High-level languages contain the notorious "loopy" notation which is especially useful in writing iteration procedures.

Suppose one is modelling a firm maximizing profits. If one can specify smooth demand- and cost-curve equations (functions) one can solve these simultaneously for the famous marginal-revenue-equals-marginal-cost solution, in such a way that the optimum price/quantity combination emerges on the left hand side of a reduced-form equation, the right hand side of which contains only coefficients of the original functions. Given numerical values of the coefficients, and no other information, one can immediately calculate the numerical values of the optimum price and quantity from the reduced-form equation directly. But suppose, instead, that a realistic specification for a project in hand does not suggest smooth functions. In the Imp-Mac model for example, firms are to optimize by simultaneously choosing price and an investment path that maximizes discounted future profits or benefits. However, it is not possible to employ a simple formula for discounting to infinity, because that assumes exponential growth rates, while in this problem the optimum path of future capacity does not lie on either a linear or an exponential path (i.e. the optimum proportionate growth rates at future times are not constant). The cause in turn lies in the realistic character of the investment-cost function and some other realistic assumptions. Consequently the firm must envisage the possibility of varying rates of capital utilization at different points through time, with implications for labour productivity and earnings. For such a problem, iteration is the only feasible solution.

2.3.5 The problem of communication

The enormous advantage of the language of mathematics is that for those who have learned it, it is universal. In simulation, by contrast, it appears that one must either be able to read the high-level language in which a programme is written, or take the author's word for the way the model actually works. The fact that certain numbers went in and others came out is not sufficient. At the time of writing, while there are many more people in the world who can read and write high-level programming languages than there are economic theorists, there are certainly more economic theorists (students, academics and other professionals) who can do mathematical economics than there are economists who can also do programming. This situation is changing more slowly in economics than in some other sciences.

Intellectually speaking, as compared with high-level mathematics, high-level programming languages are childish. They are, or should be, easy to learn to read. They take longer to learn to write because they are full of black holes, mostly discovered by doing. The problem, essentially, is cultural rather than practical. It is easier, but more time consuming, to learn a programming language than mathematics. In any event, since it is impossible to begin to construct any kind of economic model without a theoretical structure, there is no way that simulation can be a substitute for theory.

2.4 The computer, Walras and money

You might suppose each dealer to write down his demand, how much of each article he would take at each price...and these data having been furnished to a sort of *market machine*, the [equilibrium] price to be passionlessly evaluated. – Edgeworth[1] [italics added].

1 From *Mathematical Psychics*, 1881, as cited by the article on Edgeworth by Peter Newman in Eatwell et al (eds) (1987) op cit. Edgeworth's italics have been deleted and present author has added italics, made a simplifying omission and interpolated the word "equilibrium".

Because so much of modern economics resides in a paradigm which is conveniently called "neo-Walrasian", it is useful to employ the computer analogy to interpret this. It is an ideal-system where general equilibrium is discovered at a meeting of all the economic agents under the auspices of an imaginary person who calls for quantity bids in the manner of an auctioneer calling for price bids. Each agent has a utility function, a production function and initial endowment of human and material assets. All goods are tradeable. As between any pair of goods there is a hypothetical barter price or rate of exchange. No actual trade may take place until general equilibrium has been found. All conceivable forward contracts are also tradeable.

2.4.1 Tâtonnement as iteration

The auctioneer first sets a random set of barter prices and the players respond with bids of quantities to be traded given those prices, based on the principle of utility maximization. The auctioneer, being human, can neither sense the immediate solution nor adopt a super-efficient iteration routine, so he adopts a plausible scheme devised by Walras, to "grope" towards a solution. This procedure has him adjust prices in discrete steps guided by the light of progessively reduced excess demands and supplies. Given time, if the conditions for general equilibrium exist, he will find it.

Devised in the late 19th century, this story appears a century later essentially as an iterative simulation, albeit anthropomorphically described. Today we identify the economic agents as elements of a numerical array, and the data as either a set of associated functions or, if we want to investigate unsmooth cases, agents' production possibilities and preference sub-systems can be represented in purely numeric subsidiary tables. We then write a master loop which either follows Walras's simple rule or possibly uses a more sophisticated search procedure. So, in modern times, "groping" becomes "efficient search". If equilibrium does not exist, the computer will tell us so by cycling.

2.4.2 The hybrid economy

Against the computer analogy, the key feature of Leon Walras's original story, that no exchanges may take place until the auction is complete and general equilibrium has been found, no longer seems significant in the context of the iteration itself, because the computer will find the answer so quickly that no animate being will have time to trade. The practical significance of the concept of "false" trading, by contrast, emerges not in the Walrasian world, but in the real world which exists in real time, and where, in consequence, all trading is sequential and therefore inherently "false". Among many other complexities that result, is the feature at the heart of the Keynesian paradigm, namely positive feedback. In a Walrasian auction no agent need ever allow the problem of "marketing" to influence his or her bid. If she is a household, she observes the price of every commodity against leisure and somehow responds in such a way that her bids guarantee that the total amount of work required and desired would just buy all the goods desired. But in a general system of "false" trading, agents cannot presume the discovery of general equilibrium, they must accept the actual income they are currently earning from the goods and services they are actually able to sell, the most pervasive feature of the real life of real agents in real economies. That income, in turn, has been fed back from the actual macro production activity of the system. The amazing discovery (ironic) "that there is no auctioneer" was brilliantly exploited by Robert Clower[1] in the early period of his stimulating attempts to reconcile Keynes and Walras: in consequence, a "real-life" economy, in this sense, is often known as a "Clower-constrained" economy.

Much of neo-classical economics of the past thirty years has seemingly consisted of attempting to model economic systems in which the auctioneer is absent but the system ends up behaving as if he were present, or, alternatively, ends up deviating in specific ways only. When these models mix the Walrasian essence with various deviations, your author feels they should be called "hybrid". We all know that strictly neo-Walrasian economies cannot exist in the real world: if they did we would never see booms and slumps. Therefore the hybrid cases are the interesting ones.

Hybrid models are typically based on the type of assumptions we call "broad-brush": for example, a general statement that we have a "competitive" model (taken to mean "perfect competition in all markets") qualified by wage "stickiness" in the labour market. In the author's opinion, the typical specification often fails to provide the amount of detail required to know whether a realistic implementation of the model would actually perform as the comparative-static

---

1 Clower (1965).

analysis, whatever its results may be, implies. More generally, as soon as the auctioneer is gone, one faces just the recipe of complexity and sequentiality that indicates the need for investigation by means of simulation, in contrast to mathematical analysis.[1] There is also the view[2] that no-one has in fact succeeded in finding sound theoretical foundations for the hybrid economy. Either the auctioneer exists or he does not. If he does not we are in a non-Walrasian world and that is that.

2.4.3 The role of money

Another crucial aspect of the Walrasian iteration routine relates to the role of money. As is well known, it is difficult to pin down the "pure" role of money in a Walrasian context. A way of putting this problem is to say that if the imaginary iteration programme is inspected, it will be found to contain no concept of money because it has no need of one. Consequently, the presence of money in a Walrasian auction could be explained only on the assumption that the auctioneer is not in fact a computer, but a human. Intended as an abstraction, he lives!

He lives, and he has a problem. Being only human he cannot possibly do the calculations for one round of bidding in reasonable time. So, to reduce his problem by orders of magnitude, he insists that all bids are made in a numeraire. Where does this come from? Monetary theorists such as Robert Clower have made the rather obvious assumption that the auctioneer creates a paper credit for each player at the beginning of the auction. He requires them to bid subject to the convention that he will call only nominal prices and they will bid ultimately to spend exactly the amount, nor more and no less, of their credit. The anthropomorphic auctioneer has thus arbitrarily determined both the quantity of money and its velocity of circulation. So he has determined the general price level. By contrast, with constant data (and assuming convexity, etc,), however hard he tries, his general equilibrium will always produce the same real results; same quantities, same relative prices: neutrality of money.

1 The argument here is strongly influenced by Professor Ignazio Musu, University of Venice, author of Musu (1979).

2 See for example the general conclusions of Weintraub (1979).

A. C. PIGOU, PART I: DEFENDER OF THE FAITH

Pigou, Arthur Cecil. Born 1877, died 1959. Fellow of King's College, Cambridge. 1908, Chair of Political Economy, Cambridge. 1914, lectured to the present author's mother. 1941, lectured to the author. 1945 and 1946 tutored the author. In 1950, on the author's election to a King's College Fellowship he wrote, "Dear Marris, Congratulations. I must tell you I voted against you. Here are the reasons...". In 1956, on the author's getting married, he wrote, "Dear Marris, sorry to hear you've crashed. Herewith a book by Richard Stone which I ordered because he is a Fellow of the College, but it was so expensive that I'm passing it on to you as a wedding present. Please see the poem inside." The book was Stone's classic contribution to the econometrics of consumer demand. The poem read, "When he dines in college/She must dine alone/But she may console herself/By learning off by heart/All these great statistics/Made up by Mr. Stone." Before 1914 Pigou was a lively personality, politically active, passionate about Free Trade and Liberal Democracy. In later life, recluse, apparently apolitical, eccentric and a misogynist. Always a (probably non-physical) homosexual. From 1906 to 1920 in a series of publications culminating in Pigou (1920), as well as other seminal contributions to general economics (e.g. Pigou, 1910) he laid down the theorems which form the basis of most of today's environmental economics. In the period 1920-1945 (e.g. 1941, 1945) he concentrated on the problems of neo-classical macroeconomics. In terms of effect, if not in sharpness of mind or pen, Pigou possibly ranks with Adam Smith, Marshall, Pareto and Walras, among defenders of the market economy; in his case, to be suitably moderated by limited state intervention.

2.5 The Pigou effect

If at an intermediate round of bidding the auctioneer happens to notice that the aggregate nominal value of excess supplies for goods exceeds the corresponding aggregate of excess demands for goods, the bidders for goods will at that point, on paper, have underspent their credit; there is a paper depression. At the next round, the auctioneer, following his adjustment rule, will be found on average to have reduced nominal prices. The resulting bids for quantities of goods will be correspondingly higher; the paper depression is in process of being corrected.

A. C. PIGOU, PART II: COMMUNIST SPY?

In 1988, Mr John Costello, in a book about the British communist-spy conspiracies (Costello, 1988), claimed that in the period 1900-1910, Pigou exchanged coded correspondence with exiled Bolshevik revolutionaries including the man who later took the name Stalin. He further suggests that there is circumstantial evidence that Pigou continued his Communist underground activities in the 1920s, when the true character of Bolshevism was better known.

What an exciting story if true! A Master Mole who used the "cover" of publishing powerful economic theories in defence of capitalism. Then, in the evening of his life, in the 1950s, sitting, as was his wont, reading in a deckchair on the grass to the left and just inside the main gate of King's College, dressed like a tramp – shaggy mustache, floppy straw hat – how did he feel as he contemplated the increasingly awful revelations about his old secret pen-friend Stalin?

Sadly, there are some difficulties about this fabulous story. One is that Stalin did not become a prominent Bolshevik until after the death of Lenin in 1924: in 1905 he was a youthful minor provincial conspirator who rarely travelled abroad. Stalin did however attend a conference of Social Democrats in London in 1907; maybe Pigou travelled to London and fell in love with him then?

Another difficulty is that Mr. Costello has three different Pigous. On page 149 of his book we have "homosexual don ... left-wing economist, Arthur Pigou"; on page 176 we have "Sir Arthur Pigou". On page 640 we have "Pigou ... rising young welfare economist". Only the third character existed. He was not a left-wing economist because he published no left wing economics; he was not a "Sir" because he was not knighted. Never mind. Perhaps these doubts are false.

To the present author, who found him a dull and conservative teacher, Pigou the Spy is much more exciting than Pigou of the Pigou Effect. There are only two things which could make the present author believe in an afterlife, the first would be that the ghost of Bizet, who died from a heart attack provoked by the Paris critics' reception of "Carmen", is present at every rendition of this the world's most popular opera, and/or that a ghost of Pigou is sitting on a deckchair somewhere in the Universe giggling over Mr. Costello. Readers further interested should read Lord Noel Annan's recent extensive, brilliant and scholarly evaluation in the *New York Review* (Annan, 1989).

This proposition, when applied to a hybrid economy, is known as the "Pigou effect", after the author's old Prof., Arthur Pigou[1] (see box) who is credited with inventing it, but did not really believe in it, or as the "real-balance effect", by Don Patinkin[2] who, in the 1950s, both popularized and critically analysed it. Its significance lies in the idea that in a "real" economy, if an economic depression did occur, and if nominal prices were actually in practice as flexible as under an auctioneer, then the "effect" would work as a practical mechanism to stabilize the economy. If a depression occurs, wages and prices fall and holders of nominal money balances experience windfall gains causing them to feel more wealthy, demand more goods and more leisure, so simultaneously indirectly increasing the demand for labour and directly reducing its supply. Conversely, in the event of a boom leading to an excess demand for goods, wages and prices rise, nominal balances are devalued and the opposite adjustments occur.

The majority of contemporary papers on theoretical macroeconomics place strong emphasis on the "real" role of real balances as an inherent macro stabilizer. Of particular significance for the present book, this feature is almost always found in contemporary papers on macroeconomics with imp-comp microfoundations. It follows that this method of modelling depends strongly on the idea that real money balances are perceived by households as a major physical element in their wealth and welfare. The problem is, of course, to derive that implication for the hybrid economy when it does not exist in the pure (Walrasian) economy. The result has been a large literature, including the distinguished literature tending to show how money can improve economic welfare by assisting in the process of carrying value between overlapping generations, which is not cited here.

---

1 Pigou (1941, 1945).

2 Patinkin (1956).

2.5.1 Kiyotaki and Wright; McGratten, Marimon and Sargent

Very recently (i.e during the calendar year 1989), there have appeared two papers[1], the first by Nobuhiro Kiyotaki and Randall Wright, the second by Ramon Marimon, Ellen McGratten and Thomas Sargent (the one being the stimulus for the other) which, are singled out for discussion here partly because they are recent, partly because, in the second paper computer simulation is employed and partly because they attack the problem from what seems to the present author the right end, i.e. from a simplified production-and-exchange economy that is profoundly non-Walrasian, suffers inefficiency thereby, and learns to improve its situation somewhat, gaining welfare in the process, by learning to use money. Economic agents are producer-consumers with varied tastes and production capacities; typically they are specialized in the production of a particular commodity for which they have little taste. Indirect exchange is necessary for society to reap benefits from production, and takes place in a sequential process in which, at each step, a pair of agents meets at random and decides (by consensus) whether to trade or not to trade. Between steps, goods can be stored. At trading meetings, agents know both their own and their partners' inventories. In a complex way, based on an elegant application of the John Holland classifier system for simulating induction[2], the agents then develop rules, based on the observed inventory holdings, to determine whether and how to trade. By mathematical analysis in the case of K & W and by simulation in the case of Sargent et al, the resulting sequential process is then investigated for equilibrium properties, which turn out to be both varied and rich.

If there exists no commodity with the property that it has "physical" utility for no agent, i.e. there is no potential fiat money, the system will develop the use of "commodity money", meaning that one or more commodities will be held in inventories for the purpose of

---

1 Kiyotaki and Wright (1989) and Marimon et al (1989). There is a small background literature, some in working paper form, that it surveyed by Kiyotaki and Wright.

2 As well as the papers under discussion, see Holland (1986) and Goldberg (1989).

indirect exchange. These commodities develop endogenous moneyness. Thus we have, surely for the first time, a rigorous analytical or simulation investigation of the familiar real-life process by which, in the absence of fiat money, commodity monies historically emerge.

Then K & W introduced a supply of potential fiat money and investigate the cases where it will or will not endogenously come to be used as actual fiat money in the sense of being widely held as a medium of exchange. Thus ancient questions, such as when one kind of money will drive out other kinds or vice versa, are subjected to the analytical discipline.

They conclude that the introduction of fiat money into the system improve welfare by reducing the deadweight cost of holding otherwise useful commodities as money. In a nutshell, "real" money as a medium of exchange arises from its capacity to improve the physical efficiency of the economic system, in other words is like an increase in productivity. The effect is similar to an endowment of natural resources.

It follows (the present author speaking) that the introduction of fiat money helps a real-life society towards the pure Walrasian solution, makes it richer and makes its households desire more goods and more leisure. Human societies have been more or less conscious of this for about 2500 years. That is why the author finds the KWMMS conclusions congenial!

2.5.2 The electronic economy

The KWMMS economy is evidently quite primitive. That in fact is its beauty. It is also a disadvantage in that the primitiveness of the exchange system represents more than a simplifying assumption; it is also the basis of the resulting picture of the nature and function of money. What happens if we go to the opposite extreme and think about an economy that is not only more advanced than the KWMMS economy, but also more advanced than any contemporary economy: the totally electronic economy? Every economic agent has a fraudproof widget that can smoothly interact with other agents' widgets to transmit to a central data "bank" the details of any transaction, including of course transactions between organizations or between organizations and individuals. The bank keeps an instant running record of all debits, credits and resulting balances. Persons employed on labour contracts receive their salaries in the form of second-by-second positive credits.

Every person or duly constituted organization has a right to an overdraft, the limits on which are normalized by agreed measures of turnover and on which interest, calculated instantaneously, is paid on a rising scale as the limits are approached or passed. Interest is also received, similarly calculated, on positive balances, and the "authorities" (who need not be the political government) adjust the interest-rate structure so that, in ordinary circumstances, the central operating account balances. There should also be enough degrees of freedom to aim for a target whereby, under full employment conditions, aggregate credit balances normally equal aggregate overdrafts. The authorities have an instrument of macroeconomic policy in their power to vary the overdraft rules and interest rate structure, including in these their power to decide whether overdraft limits shall be indexed. This instrument would be thus analogous to but potentially more powerful than the traditional combination of short-term interest-rate manipulation and open market operations that constitute the contemporary text-book picture of monetary management.

The economy is a mixed, corporate economy, in which production and commerce is carried out by quoted companies, whose shares are widely held among the population. Typically the risk-discounted total return on holding shares is higher than the interest available on the transactions balances. Therefore economic agents have little incentive to maintain credit balances as a store of wealth. There is no "high-powered" or "outside" money, because none is required (high-powered money exists in practical economies precisely because, unlike in the case of the electronic economy, the monetary institutions, being commercial "banks" in an older sense,[1] require reserves).

---

1 How many readers know where the traditional word comes from? The answer is that in Medieval Italy small traders sat at tables, with a built-in seat behind and often an awning above, much as they do today in the main piazza in Verona. The seat was called a "banco" or "banca". Gradually the shop itself acquired the same name. The money changers of Venice, who, as is well known, were also money lenders, operated from just such benches, or "money shops", near the Rialto bridge. So the money shop was a "banca". If a member of the fraternity (the most famous of whom, of course, was Shylock) defaulted on his obligations, with damaging effect on the whole group, they expelled him from

But our electronic databank needs no reserves because it never has to pay out: it merely records transactions. Although it would not seem so to the inhabitants, to the economic theorist this is a strictly moneyless economy. From a monetary point of view it is exactly like the pure Walrasian economy.

At first sight, a moneyless economy can have no real-balance effects. Typically, when the price level changes, windfall real gains in the purchasing power of the invisible medium of exchange will be balanced by windfall losses. At second sight, the situation is less certain. Faced with economic shocks of various kinds, it is not at all sure that agents holding overdrafts will react in symmetrical fashion to agents holding credit balances. In addition, as already hinted, it will by no means always be the case, at any time, that the aggregate balances and overdrafts are actually equal. However, in smooth circumstances, around equilibrium, we can probably say that as a matter of "pure theory" the electronic economy either does not in effect possess real balances or experience real-balance effects.

2.5.3 The modern economy

The monetary systems of most modern developed capitalist countries produce surprisingly similar results, despite a fair amount of formal and informal institutional variation. In some respects the archetype is quite similar to the electronic economy, and, in some respects, during this last decade of the century, the similarity is increasing. In other respects large differences remain and will probably (hopefully?) persist. There are all kinds of endogenously-created buckets of money and near money, some extremely large, sloshing around within and between countries, with varying degrees of indiscipline. There is a range of widely held paper and near-paper assets (documents representing claims or options on physical commodities such as pork bellies, homes, yachts). If the author must state which modern economist has most vividly expressed the underlying perception of the real world that imbues the present book, he would say it was James Tobin,[1] with his picture of a general portfolio of household and organizational asset holding into which monetary changes insert

---

the market, and, to ensure that he could not return, ritually broke up his bench. Hence, "bankrupt".

1 E.g. Tobin (1982).

themselves in a fashion which is complex, and in which medium-term cyclical effects may crucially differ from long-term effects.

In consequence, despite heroic efforts, applied monetary economists have been unable to find robust econometric specifications of the key relationships (such as the demand for money as a function of transactions, prices and interest rates) which are essential to tidy theories of the effect of monetary forces on prices and economic activity. This does not at all mean that monetary forces are never important. On the contrary, it means that in some circumstances they can be extremely important, in others not. For example, it is difficult to imagine that a major destruction of positive real balances, not offset by spending from the windfall gains of debtors, did not play a major role in the depression of 1981-4. This was certainly the view of the world's best-known macroeconomist, Rudi Dornbusch.[1] But to believe that by no means implies believing that had the slump been associated with falling prices (instead of, as was the case, being caused by rising prices), a symmetrical Pigou effect would have worked in reverse.

1 As expressed e.g. in an unpublished lecture given in the House of Lords in London in 1986.

3 Modelling Imperfect Competition

This chapter is partly concerned to survey the microeconomic theory of imperfect competition per se, and partly to deal with certain specific problems that arise when it becomes a microfoundation for macroeconomics.

The great weight of published writing on imperfect competition is straightforwardly microeconomic. Typically attention is concentrated on something called an "industry", meaning a distinctive group of quasi firms whose products are close (or even perfect) substitutes so that if one changes price, with all other prices constant, the greater part of the change in this firm's quantity demanded comes from or goes to other firms in the industry. The elasticity of demand with respect to the products of other firms in the industry is high, to other products low. Consequently it is possible to identify an "industry demand curve" telling what happens if all the industry's quasi firms change price together. Sometimes there is also embedded in the industry concept the implicit assumption that the "members" as well as sharing similar products, share production technology and a local labour market.

Given the industry concept, a micro imp-comp model then requires two basic sub-models, a model of the competitive process (e.g. are firms price setters and if, so, in setting price, do they conjecture, as in the Imp-Mac model, that other firms' prices will be constant, or do they take specific account of reactions?) among existing members of the industry, and a model of the process, if any by which firms in the long run enter or exit from the industry. In microeconomics, it is tacitly assumed that a firm entering one industry is coming from some other industry or from the economy at large, and that a firm exiting is similarly going into some unspecified limbo: the question of whether entry involves the number of firms in the goods market as a whole is not addressed. The two sub-models interact to create a theory which will typically determine both the short and long run equilibrium of the industry; in the short run, with a given number of quasi firms, the price and quantity of each; in the long run, after any entry or exit movements have ceased, the same plus a steady-state number of firms and hence aggregate output of the "industry".

The goods market of an economy as a whole, however, is a network of "industries". Each product has an elasticity of demand with every other, but it is higher with some than with others. "Industries" are clusters of products with high elasticities. For a given economy there is no unique way of identifying such clusters; there is no unique industrial classification. When we proceed to set up imperfect competition as a microfoundation for macroeconomics, we may therefore find it desirable to characterise the whole system in a particular way, possibly with quite severe simplifying assumptions, as is the case, in fact, with the Imp-Mac model. These are the assumptions which we call the structural assumptions. In addition, in place of the question of entry into one industry from other industries, we made need assumptions concerning entry of quasi firms into the economy as a whole.

Consequently, whereas a micro theory of imperfect competition contains only two basic elements (sub-models of competitive process and entry, as mentioned), a corresponding microfoundations theory requires three, **structural assumptions, competitive process** and **entry assumptions.** These topics are dealt with below in that order. The third section, concerning entry, as well as surveying other economists' assumptions on the topic, also contains a tentative suggestion by the present author of a new dynamic theory of the process. (It is not the theory embodied in the Imp-Mac model, which, it will be remembered takes the number of firms as fixed; as will be seen, however, the new theory can be used to give the Imp-Mac assumptions a degree of justification.) Thus the reader is reminded that in the Imp-Mac model the three elements run as follows; the goods market is, in effect "de-structured", i.e. there are no industries; the competitive process is one in which price setting is based on the conjecture that all other prices are given; and the entry assumptions are that there is no entry.

3.1 The structure of the goods market

We shall in fact identify three types of goods market, the first of which we shall call the **Chamb-Rob** goods market, the second we shall call the **Sym-Het** goods market, and the third the **Cournot** goods market. The reasons for the names will be explained. The Chamb-Rob case is the general, realistic, one; a network of heterogenous "industries". Each of the other two is a simplification. In the first, Sym-Het, there are no industries. In the second, Cournot, there are industries but they are homogenous.

3.1.1 Chamb-Rob (Chamberlin-Robinson)

The name given to this case derives from the microeconomic theory of Edward Chamberlin and Joan Robinson published in the early 1930s.[1] It is the most general case and many of its significant features have already been described; the "industries" are actually clusters of quasi firms selling distinct close substitutes; in effect, clusters of products. The number of firms in an industry may be large or small. If it is small the case is called differentiated or heterogenous oligopoly. The elasticities of demand within an industry are generally assumed to be high but the same; in other words, if one firm changes price, with all others constant, not only is the main effect, as already stated above, confined within the industry, but it is spread in equal proportions among all other firms. "Outside" elasticities are low; if all

---

1 See Chamberlin (1933) and Robinson (1933). The title of the first spoke of "Monopolistic Competition", of the second of "Imperfect Competition". Chamberlin began working on the subject as a PhD student in the middle 1920s but was pipped at the post by Joan Robinson whose book came out earlier in the same year (1933) as his, an experience from which he never, it seems, recovered: he spent his life insisting that the two theories were different, whereas, in truth, in essentials (especially for the purposes of microfoundations of macroeconomics) they are the same. The two books differ mainly in style, emphasis and extensions. Chamberlin's work is richer and probably deeper, Joan Robinson's more succinct. Seen in 1990, Chamberlin's complaint against Joan Robinson appears newly ironic. It was of course impossible for her to have stolen Chamberlin's theory by means of some kind of trans-Atlantic witchcraft, but it does now seem clear that she was greatly helped by her more local power over R.F. Kahn (for more see Chapter 4 below) whose work on the subject also began in the middle 1920s, was completed by the end of 1928, but was published only posthumously for the first time in English in 1989!

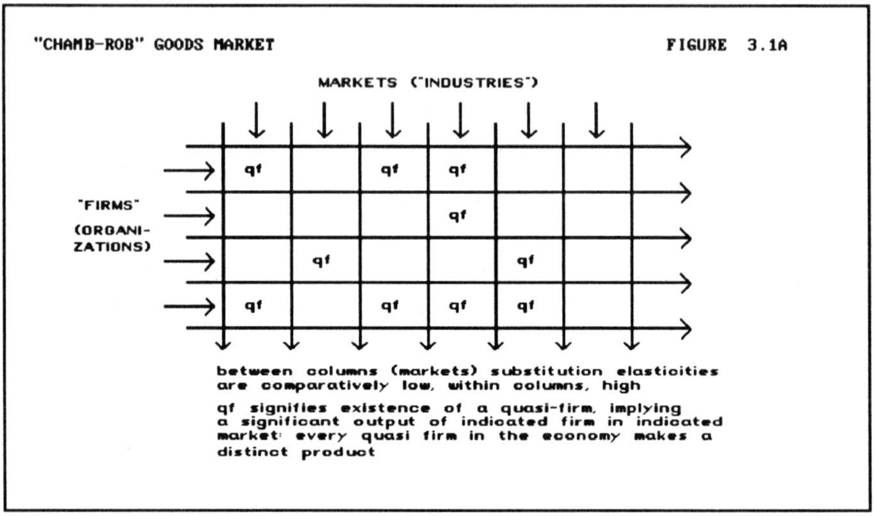

the quasi firms in an industry change price together, with prices and incomes in the rest of the economy constant, the total effect on the industry is small. A representation is given in *Figure 3.1A*.

It is not difficult to see that the explicit assumptions also imply that the quasi firms in an industry are similar in size, meaning that the value of the sales of the different products is similar. If the number of firms (products) is large, then their average size must be modest. In reality, in a modern economy, economic activity in the goods market tends to be highly concentrated. A small number of quasi firms in an industry will be responsible for a large proportion of the total value added of the industry. A small number of firms in the economy will be responsible for a large proportion of the value added of the economy. The first phenomenon is called, "industrial concentration" and the second, "business concentration". The first is measured down columns in a diagram such as Figure 3.1A: typically the largest four quasi firms in an industry will be responsible for something like half the value added. The second is a characteristic of the set of numbers representing the total values across rows: typically the largest hundred industrial firms will be responsible for something like half of a nation's industrial output. The effect of business concentration is to convert Chamberlin-Robinson industries, which contain on paper fairly large numbers of firms, effectively into cases where the competitive process is dominated by a small number.

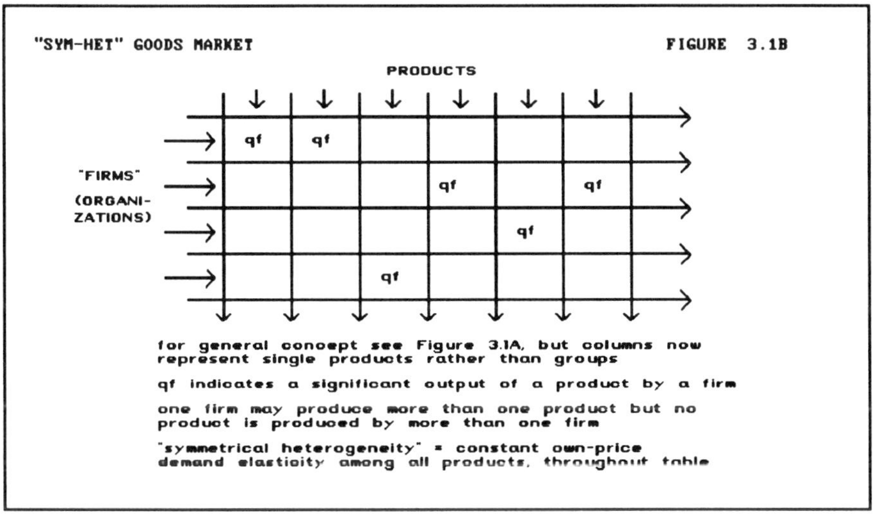

3.1.2 Sym-Het (symmetrical heterogeneity)

This case, which is in fact employed by other contemporary authors[1], is the one used in the Imp-Mac model. It is given its name because, as already described in Chapter 1, although products are heterogenous, they are symmetrically so. We have the Chamberlin-Robinson economy with only one industry; highly unrealistic, but highly convenient. Symmetry is represented in the assumption that the elasticity of demand with respect to a change in price by one quasi firm, with all other prices constant, is the same for every quasi firm, and invariant with respect to all changes in prices and real incomes. When any price changes, the effect on the demand for other products is spread evenly over all quasi firms (products) in the economy. The case is illustrated in *Figure 3.1B*.

The basic unrealism, in effect an internal contradiction, of the case lies in the fact that since we are modelling the whole goods market of a whole economy, the number of quasi firms and products must be large, but, if so, the symmetry assumption is not credible. On the other side of the coin, the basic convenience of the case has already been discussed in Chapter 1; general simplification and insulation of macroeconomic results from structural effects. In technical terms the

1 For example Blanchard and Kiyotaki (1987b), Mankiw (1988), Solow (1986b).

advantage lies in the relatively simple way the case, when employed as a microfoundation for macroeconomics in conditions of conjectural equilibrium (see also next section), defines the mathematical relationship, as set out in the next paragraph, between elasticity of demand, profit-maximizing mark-up and the real wage.

Define the **conjectural demand curve** of a quasi firm as the graph of quantities demanded if the firm varies price with other prices conjectured to be constant, and assume it is iso-elastic. The constant elasticity is the **conjectural elasticity.** Correspondingly define **conjectural marginal revenue.** In conjectural equilibrium, every quasi firm, on the assumption that every other firm's price is given, finds conjectural marginal revenue equal to marginal cost. Assume in addition every firm has the empirical cost curve (see Chapter 1 sub-section, 1.4.5) and is operating on the "flat" part of it.

For simplicity assume that opph = 1 and the nominal wage = 1. So average cost = marginal cost = 1. With the aid of a little elementary calculus we then arrive at the following:

p = price; q = quantity demanded
e = conjectural elasticity; k = constant

$$p = kq^{-(1/e)} \quad \text{[demand curve]}$$

$$R = pq = kq^{(1-1/e)} \quad \text{[revenue]}$$

$$dR/dq = (1-1/e)kq^{-1/e} \quad \text{[marginal revenue]}$$

$$= (1-1/e)p$$

$$(1-1/e)p = m \quad \text{[= marginal cost = av cost = 1]}$$

$$(1-1/e)p = 1$$

$$p = e/(e-1)$$

$$\textbf{mark-up} = p/m = 1/(e-1)$$

$$\textbf{margin} = (p-m)/p = 1/e$$

$$\textbf{real wage} = \text{[nominal wage / price]} = 1/p = (e-1)/e$$

The last three equations confirm the assertions made in this book's Introduction (page 9 et seq) concerning the relations between demand elasticity, mark-up, and real wage. Dropping the simplifying assumption that opph = 1 only modifies the message. For example, if opph, instead of 1, were 2, then the real wage, as compared with the formula above, would also be doubled. The formula for the mark-up is often referred to as the "Lerner" formula, after the outstanding economist, Abba P. Lerner, who, half a century ago, effectively invented it.[1]

The formulas show the considerable power of this model. On the assumptions, they have to be true. If firms are free to set prices, if demand elasticity and opph are constant, no matter what the nominal wage, the real wage must be as above. If a model appears to obtain different results, for example if the real wage appears to vary with output, somewhere along the line, one or more of these assumptions has been violated. Either elasticity is not constant, opph is not constant or quasi firms are not profit maximizing.

It is worth noting that if in the realistic Chamb-Rob case one could compute an appropriately weighted average of the within-industry elasticities, and assumed that all quasi firms in all industries set prices on the conjecture that other prices in their own industry would remain constant, the resulting general conjectural equilibrium would likely display macro results approximating to these formulae, with the weighted average elasticity taking the place of *e*. Consequently it is fair to say (and this is an important conclusion), that for the purposes of the microfoundations of macroeconomics, the "simplistic" Sym-Het economy is a fair representation of the "realistic" Chamb-Rob economy.

3.1.3 Cournot

The name of this case derives from a classic model[2] published by a great Frenchman, Auguste Cournot, the prophet of modern mathematical economics, a century and a half ago. Industries exist, but each firm within an industry sells the same product: by assumption, the concept of industry and the concept of product are amalgamated. If the number of firms is large, we have the internal conditions for perfect competition. But for reasons given in the Introduction, and further discussed in Chapter 1, such cases are rare. Consequently we may safely assume that it is a general characteristic of the industries

1 See Lerner (1944).

2 The model of "duopoly" found in Cournot (1838).

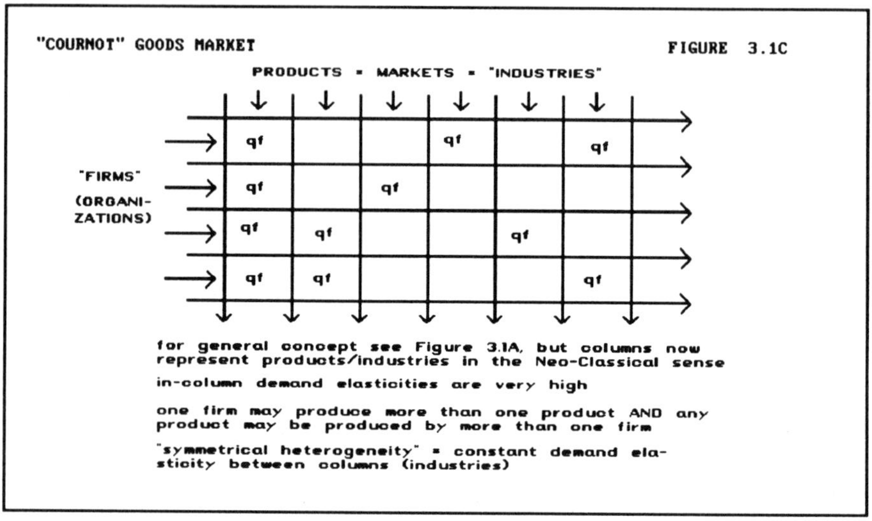

of a Cournot economy that the number of firms is small, in other words they are all oligopolies. The case is illustrated in *Figure 3.1C.*

For the purposes of microfoundations analysis the case has advantages and disadvantages. The advantages are three:

(i) There is a century-and-a-half-old line of economic theory on this type of oligopoly stretching back to Cournot himself in the 1830s and forward through Bertrand in the 1860s, and through Paolo Sylos Labini in the 1950s and finally reaching contemporary literature, most notably in the imp-comp models of Oliver Hart and Huw Dixon.[1]

(ii) If one can safely assume that the competitive process in this economy takes only the form of price taking, quantity setting, as will be discussed below, the model produces rather neat mathematical solutions in which results appear in terms of tangible concepts such as the number of sellers and the parameters of the industry demand curve; this in fact is the reason for (i), especially exploited by Oliver Hart.

1 Cournot (1838), Bertrand (1883), Labini (1956), Hart (1982), Dixon (1987).

(iii) It is a convenient theory for modelling the effects of collusion among sellers.

The disadvantages are two, the second following from the first:

(i) The assumption implied in advantage number (ii) above is invalid; there is no law to compel quantity setting. Consequently the stability or existence of any equilibrium founded on this assumption is seriously compromised.[1] This problem is more fully discussed in sub-section 3.2.4 below, which we must here anticipate a little. To put the matter at its crudest, there is nothing to prevent one seller at any time from deciding on all-out price-setting, price-cutting war; it follows that in this type of market one must either expect a war to end in only one firm surviving, or that stability is found in some form of quasi collusive or cooperative play, as will be discussed (3.3.3 et seq) below. Cournot was well aware of this and carefully analysed the cooperative case of joint profit maximization.

(ii) The theoretical implication of disadvantage (i) is confirmed is rarely observed in real economies. Typically, where a homogenous product is produced under such strong economies of scale that the number of sellers has been reduced to a handful, the same conditions make for instability: typically, the situation is in due course transformed into a total monopoly. The exceptions test the rule: they exist by favour of anti-trust regulation. There are indeed numerous important markets where a small number of giant quasi firms compete as oligopolies, but in nearly all these cases the products are not homogenous; close substitutes, yes, but homogenous, no.

We shall revert to this debate in the next section. In the meantime, by again anticipating the next section somewhat, it is possible to see a kind of equivalence between Cournot and Sym-Het. What would be

1 See Sonnenschein (1987) op cit.

the nature of a conjectural equilibrium in the Cournot economy? The answer depends on the nature of the competitive process and in particular on whether it is assumed to be price setting or "quantity setting" (see next sub-section below). Let us assume (somewhat reluctantly, it must be admitted) for the moment assume that the firms are indeed "quantity setters", that is to say that even though they are operating in an oligopoly, they can perceive a "ruling price" for the homogenous product, and believe (wrongly) they can place any amount they choose of the product at the price in question. Firms choose quantities to place on the market successively, and the total amounts they jointly supply locate a point on the industry demand curve, in other words a price that will clear the market of these quantities. Then the firms choose their quantities to maximize profits on the conjecture that other firms' quantities are constant.

What is the key elasticity, the quantity-setting conjectural elasticity, in this story? It is not the "industry" elasticity, which we may call E, because that relates to the effect of a price movement by all firms in the industry. It is the proportionate variation in the quantity sent to the market by one firm divided by the resulting change in market clearing price. If we know E, and also the numbers of firms in the industry, we can calculate it as follows.

Let the increase in quantity by the one firm be dq. Since no other firms are conjectured to change their quantities, this is also the increase in total-market quantity, which we can call Q, so $dQ = dq$. Similarly, since in this quantity setting model all firms always face the same price, if P is market price, and p is firm price, $p = P$, $dp = dP$ and $dp/p = dP/P$. Let P be market price and let the number of quasi firms be N. From the definition of elasticity the proportionate decline in price following dQ is

$dP/P = dQ/QE = dq/QE = dq/qNE$. Hence
$(dq/q)/(dP/dP) = NE$. But
$dp/p = dP/P$. Hence
$(dq/q)/(dp/dp) = NE$

What is the significance of this result? The answer is that we may think of ourselves as considering two alternative ways of simplifying a given Chamb-Rob economy, the Sym-Het way and the Cournot way. The Sym-Het way produces one parameter, e, the Cournot way two, E and N. If both resulting models hypothesized the corresponding conjectural equilibrium, it would produce the same mark-up and real wage if $e = NE$. Since all three numbers are to a considerable extent influenced by the way the model builder actually classifies the totality of quasi firms that makes up the whole goods market, he or she possess the practical discretion to ensure this.

3.2 The competitive process

By "competitive process" we mean the way quasi firms actually set prices or quantities. The Imp-Mac model assumes one way, a particular conjecture in a Sym-Het economy. There are many other possibilities, some of which we now survey.

The standard approaches are **conjectural** and the **game-theoretic.** For an excellent guide to the first, the reader is recommended the Cambridge University Press survey by James Friedman;[1] for the second, a masterly critique by A. J. Aumann,[2] himself a leading contributor of fundamental concepts in the field.

3.2.1 The conjectural approach

In the conjectural approach, the theorist postulates that the sellers in a market make their price or quantity moves according to some hypothesized conjecture concerning the reactions of their rivals. Typically, given that all sellers are assumed to be employing the same conjecture, the theorist follows are succession of moves, based on a constant conjecture, until there is a conjectural equilibrium in which no seller wishes to make any further move. The idea of a conjectural general equilibrium has been carried over to the economy as a whole by distinguished theorists led by Frank Hahn.[3]

3.2.2 The game-theoretic approach

In the game-theoretic approach, players are assumed to examine the general situation, and in particular to make note of the various likely consequences of their own actions on more than one hypothesis concerning their rivals' actions and reactions. "If I do this, he may do this or he may do that. Furthermore I know he knows I know this,

---

1 Friedman (1983).

2 See his article "Game Theory" in Eatwell et al (eds) (1987) op cit.

3 See Hahn (1978, 1980).

and he knows I know it". The game theorist then attempts to work out a way of playing the game that is, from the point of view of the typical player, most rational; in the broadest sense utility maximizing. Usually this involves "minimaxing", that is, examining each of the moves (known in game theory as "strategies", although closer in real life to "tactics") available to the player and noting the likely pay-off (e.g. profit) in the case where, if that move is made, the opponent selects from among all the moves open to him the one that does the most harm to the original player, i.e. produces for the original player minimum profit or maximum loss. Having thus analysed the situation, the original player is said to be "minimizing his maximum loss" if he chooses the move where this worst outcome is less bad than the worst outcome from any other move. The effect is to produce a guaranteed minimum from playing the game.

In the economics of sellers competition, the "game" is seen as a conflict between sentient, wilful, suppliers of a product, against the background (incomes, tastes) of passively-responsively, price-taking, consumers. Generally, games where a single player acts in a passive environment are called "games against nature" (e.g. I may have to take a decision about some outdoor activity without knowing whether it is going to rain: if I act on the assumption that it will rain, and it does not, I prospectively lose X; if I assume it will not rain, and it does, I prospectively lose Y: I minimax by comparing X and Y and taking the decision associated with the smallest of X or Y). In games of sellers' competition, the consumer plays the role of nature. In our games, it is common to assume that the state of nature, e.g. consumers' tastes, is known. By contrast, in the more general game against nature, the state of nature will usually be unknown.

A game of sellers' competition of this type is what is called "non-constant sum" as far as the sellers are concerned, in the sense that depending on the extent to which the sellers end up by "exploiting" the consumer there is a variable amount of booty (profit) to be obtained. If the sellers behave like pure monopolists they gain substantially. If they behave like perfect competitors, they gain less and consumers benefit more.

If we do conceptually include consumers in the game, under strict symmetrical heterogeneity, assuming an arbitrarily fixed number of products, the game is approximately constant sum. But when we recognize that the consumers are also householders, and own shares

GAME THEORY

For a select reading list on game theory see;-

Aumann (1961), Aumann and Drèze (1974)
Debreu and Scarf (1963), Harsanyi (1966)
Ichiishi (1991), Luce and Raiffa (1957)
Nash (1950, 1951), Scarf (1967), Shapley (1969)
Shubik (1959, 1967, 1984), Sonnenschein (1987)
Von Neumann and Morgenstern (1944)

In his two papers **Nash** established early post-Von-Neumann concepts that are still widely used. In the 1951 paper he suggested the idea of what in his honour is known as a **Nash equilibrium** in a competitive game the type of equilibrium used in the Imp-Mac model. More recently, **Aumann** (in Eatwell et al (eds), 1987, op cit) has suggested that this type of equilibrium should better be called a **strategic equilibrium.**

In his paper of the previous year Nash had pointed out that if, in contrast, the players were to find the **cooperative** solution to a game, this solution must include a division of the benefits of cooperation that is acceptable to all. He suggested it could be a **bargaining solution**, based on the prospective relative losses if cooperation broke down. Later, **Harsanyi** described and axiomatized a rational bargaining process which would lead to the Nash result.

The fact that the name of Nash is associated with two different fundamental concepts sometimes causes confusion. Another terminological problem for the general reader is the somewhat unhappy choice by Von Neumann and Morgenstern of the word "strategy" for "move" or "play" in a game. If a military analogy was desired, "tactic" would have been closer. Game-theory vocabulary was thereby deprived of a word for describing the concept of a plan (i.e. strategy) for determining moves (tactics) in an extended or continuing game.

The terminological "mishap", as usual, was probably not entirely fortuitous. Theory concerning extended games is necessarily unfruitful of hard theorems; and extended games necessarily turn into cooperative games requiring bargaining solutions which are in turn compromised by the difficulty of formulating a convincing general theory of threats. It sounds much more impressive to describe the short term Nash equilibrium (which in the long run is inherently unstable (see **Sonnenschein**, 1987) as a "strategic equilibrium" than as a "tactical equilibrium", despite the fact that in ordinary language the second expression gives a much better impression of what is happening.

in the firms, things are more elusive. This "total" game is not constant sum, because profits, distributed to households at the expense of wages paid to households, induce households to offer less work and demand more leisure (in contrast to other commodities) than would the same households maximizing their utility in a strict Walrasian economy.[1] It follows that the smaller the elasticity of demand or the greater the degree of collusion among firms, the greater loss to households compared with the "gains to firms". Since firms represent in effect the organization of households into teams for the purposes of production and investment, the concept of "gains to firms", however significant in the operational modelling of competition, has no significance for welfare, has no "real" value for society. Hence, in effect, when profits are increased by a greater imperfection of competition, what is happening is not a transfer of welfare but a deadweight loss to households, i.e. to society.

Since the pay-offs to the players in a non-constant-sum game are liable to be positive, it is better, in place of minimaxing, to speak of "maximining"; maximizing the minimum gain. The principle is the same.

3.2.3 Comparing the approaches

Conjectural theory and game theory are complementary. Game theory rationalizes the conjecture: I do not behave according to a certain conjecture because I believe that my opponent will necessarily conform to it, but because I have worked out that by behaving as if I thought my opponent will do that, I will maximin. To put the same point another way, if a conjectural model cannot be rationalized by game theory, it needs to be treated with caution. But game theory itself does not yield unique results so the game-theoretic test is not all-powerful.

Conjectural theory is helpful in practical applications, especially in the field of oligopoly theory. It gives us a way of describing what is happening. Game theory give us a way of discussing why it is happening. The greatest weakness of conjectural theory is that the achievement of a strategic equilibrium through a sequential process

---

1 The social-welfare implications of "excessive leisure" in the macroeconomy resulting from imp-comp microfoundations is discussed again in Chapter 5, subsections 5.4.3 (Startz) and 5.4.4 below.

KEY DATES IN IMP-COMP THEORY

The modern student of Imperfect Competition is confronted with important terms, such "Cournot Model", "Bertrand Model", "Nash Equilibrium", without (unless he or she be an exceptionally enthusiastic student of the history of thought) being in a position to know where they come from. The theoretical development of the field in fact progressed in fits and starts over a period starting precisely in the year 1838 and continuing to the present day. There were quiet or silent periods lasting as long as a quarter of a century or more - in the middle of the 19th century, in the first part of the present century and also, less obviously perhaps, from the mid 1950s to the mid 1970s. See the date pattern of references in the excellent survey of oligopoly theory by James Friedman (1983) whose own publications in this "semi-silent period" represent a distinguished exception.

1838 Cournot publishes "*Recherches....*", inventing the demand curve, profit maximization, theory of monopoly and homogenous oligopoly (quantity-setting), and anticipates theories of competitive equilibrium; this work largely unrecognized for next quarter century.

1877 Cournot dies, knowing that he has now been partly recognised.

1883 Bertrand (Paris) publishes review rubbishing Walras and Cournot (calling them "pseudo mathematicians"), and in passing invents the "Bertrand" (price-cutting) model of homogenous oligopoly, raising a question over the concept of competitive equilibrium that is much alive in 1980.

1928 Von Neuman published first paper on Theory of Games, but no impact on economics until after 1949, when, with Morgenstern he published "Theory of Games..."

1929 R.F. Kahn submits dissertation in Cambridge that effectively invented modern theory of imperfect competition, but this not published until 1989.

1933 Edward Chamberlin and Joan Robinson publish classic works on imperfect competition, in Joan Robinson's case, the result of extremely close collaboration with Kahn.

often involves assuming that players repeatedly act on a certain conjecture even though, after the first step, they have evidence that the conjecture is false. On the other hand, once "learning" is admitted, the very concept of equilibrium becomes elusive. In that dilemma, game theory can sometimes, but not always, help out.

In game theory it is traditional to distinguish between "competitive" and "cooperative" play. Traditionally a cooperative game is defined as one where the players can and do make legally binding and enforceable agreements to play in a certain joint way that jointly benefits them both. A competitive game is one where the binding-agreement condition is absent and/or at least one of the players chooses to ignore the possibility of agreement, i.e. to play "competitively". As is well known, it takes two to tango. Without enslaving someone, you cannot compel him to cooperate, even if cooperation is legal. In economic life, the commonest reason, of course, for the illegality of cooperative agreements is anti-trust law. The commonest source of the opposite situation, is the case of cooperation of workers against employers, and hence against consumers, and hence against themselves, encouraged, rather than restricted, by labour laws; a situation, in effect, explicitly embodied in the imp-comp microfoundations model of Oliver Hart,[1] to be discussed again in Chapter 5 below.

In a one-time game the distinction between competition and cooperation is clear. For example, two firms, which will never meet again (never compete in this or any other market) are tendering for a contract, under rules whereby if the two bids are close, the award will be split. In the first example we suppose that, although collusion is not a felony, there is a situation in civil law whereby no collusive pre-agreement in such a situation can be legally enforced. Ex-post blackmail of a cheater is unfeasible. Also assume away Mafia-like "enforcement". A "cooperative" joint high bid, splitting the contract lucratively, is thus ruled out because neither party can have any confidence that the other will keep to it. As in the case of thieves, there is no honour among competitors. They are forced to play "competitively", i.e. to assume that their opponent will do the worst. This means maximin, i.e. bid the lowest price at which, in the event

---

1 Hart (1982).

of a split contract, it would be just profitable to accept, rather than not participate at all.

This one-off game can be called a "finite" game. The conclusion that competition, in the game-theory sense now defined, is then inevitable, does not require the one-off condition to hold strictly. If the firms compete only occasionally, and the sums of money involved when they do are large, much the same result may obtain. More abstractly, one may virtually define a finite game as one where the players behave as if cooperation were unenforceable, either as a matter of practice or as a theoretical assumption.

As soon as the game is not finite, but rather "continuing" (the term is the author's; in the professional literature these games are classified as "extensive games[1]" or "supergames"), the picture changes greatly. Imagine that the two bidders mentioned above have to do it every week, or even every month. It is almost inevitable that they will learn to cooperate. Maybe the first few times, they both bid low. Then one, without so much as a wink, nod or telephone call, bids higher. The other bids low, and takes all. For the loser, in a continuing game, this is a loss but not a catastrophe: next week he reverts to bidding low, so the second player's gains prove transient. The second player has to be an idiot if he doesn't get the message. The first player knows this, so tries again. Eventually, to change the metaphor, the penny drops. From then on, week after week, both players will bid high, knowing that deviation by either will lead to a chain of events that must harm both.

This is quite a strong result, because it describes a lesson that is very profitable to learn. The learning process is not only a collective but also an individual interest. By the same token, provided the comparative economic strengths of the two players is constant (and both know it), a cooperative "equilibrium" reached in such a game is rather stable, in that it is in the interest of both players that in the event of one player foolishly starting a war, the other retaliates by following his price cut. Contrary to popular belief, provided the number of players is small, it is not at all inevitable that a price war must go all the way to the bottom. A player, by missing one retaliat-

1 See for example the title of the fundamental paper in the field by Selten (1975).

ory cut, makes a "peace" signal inviting the opponent to do likewise. Still they do not need the telephone.

If numbers are small, the game continuous, and entry in the form of other interlopers also excluded, the cooperative result is virtually inevitable, and virtually beyond the reach of legislation.

In real life, apart from entry, the most common cause of a breakdown of cooperation is a breakdown of the assumption of stable, known, comparative economic strength. Economic strength, basically equivalent to bargaining strength, can be measured by the relative costs to each side of an outbreak of war. One player may have discovered, or believe he has discovered, a superior, lower-cost, production function, or have gained an increase in financial liquidity that would enable him better to withstand a war of attrition, or etc. Even if he is not sure of his facts, he may feel the need for a trial of strength, to help establish facts and shareouts, just like birds with their flurries of fighting, rarely fatal, over territory.

So what we see in real life in finite small-numbered games is cooperation with outbreaks of war, and, in real-life industry, the potential entrant becomes a player in the game, preventing unlimited exploitation. (The general role of entry in Imp-Mac modelling is discussed in the next section.)

It follows that the question of whether an economic game is "competitive" or "cooperative" is virtually synonymous with the question of whether it is "finite" or "continuous".

3.2.4 Price setting versus quantity setting

A common feature of both conjectural and game theory is that whatever weapons the opposing players are assumed to use, they are the same. Cournot desired to see his players converging towards an equilibrium through a succession of moves. To model any such process mathematically it is necessary to simplify to the extent of assuming that that which is being changed or "moved" is something standard. In real business life all kinds of things happen; one firm cuts price, another retaliates with a new product or an advertising campaign, another by violence. Such things are beyond the capacities of formal theory, although Edward Chamberlin did, in fact, in a large-group context, heroically introduce the possibility of product variation and marketing expenditure.

If one is considering a single industry in a Chamb-Rob economy (see Figure 3.1A) and rules out advertising, product variation and the

Mafia, it seems fairly clear that the essential "weapon" is price. If, however, one desires to model a single industry in a Cournot economy, an industry that is where the product is homogenous but the sellers are few, as we have already mentioned, things are difficult. It is logically impossible for more than one price to rule for any significant length of time, because the player with the highest price would have all the customers. That suggests a quantity-setting model, after the analogy with perfect competition.

But what is really happening in a "quantity-setting" market consisting of maybe only two sellers? Each stands outside his shop with a pile of goods, apparently for sale at an unstated price. The eventual price is the price at which, given the market demand curve, the market will clear. In practical terms, as Bertrand pointed out (see box), the scenario is a legal impossibility. Either both sellers must already know the market clearing price, which means they must know the actual (not conjectural) quantity to be set by competitors, which means that the theory does not work out of equilibrium and cannot, therefore, represent a process for finding equilibrium, or there must be an auctioneer-like intermediary, or some arrangement for re-contracting.

However, if quantity setting can for some reason be assumed (imposed by law, with an intermediary?) then a strategic/conjectural equilibrium can be found where, on the assumption that other quantities are held constant, no seller desires to change quantity. As we shall see shortly, the resulting total market quantity will produce a market-clearing price which is significantly higher than marginal cost.

Alternatively, of course, price setting may occur. But then, as Bertrand pointed out, if in a homogenous market I really believe my rivals will not react to my price change, the implied conjectural elasticity of demand being extremely high (conjectural marginal revenue is approximately equal to price), I make a small cut in price, conjecturing a large increase in profits. Successively (no learning being permitted in this theory) other sellers do likewise until they have undercut each other to a point where they do not wish to cut further. Since this means that conjectural marginal revenue is going below marginal cost, it means that price must approximately equal marginal cost, in short, as Bertrand implied, the perfect competition solution.

MODELLING IMPERFECT COMPETITION FIGURE 3.2

ALTERNATIVE CONJECTURAL SCENARIOS

CONJECTURE	RELATING TO PRICE	RELATING TO QUANTITY
opponents will follow	both lead to Joint Profit Maximization $p = mE/(E-1)$ where m = marginal cost E = group demand elasticity	*[n.b. quantity-setting models apply to homogenous markets only]*
opponents will hold	leads to "Nash" strategic equilibrium, $p = me/(e-1)$ where e = own-price elasticity	leads to "Cournot" strategic equilibrium, $p = mNE/(NE-1)$ where E = group elasticity and N = number of players
opponents will move in opposite direction	both lead to "Quasi-Bertrand" the larger the opposing conjectured change relative to own intended change, the closer final $p = m$	

It follows that, as Hugo Sonnenschein has powerfully pointed out,[1] the quantity-setting Cournot result is not an equilibrium. Another way of putting the problem is to say that if we strictly confine ourselves to strategic equilibria, there is one for the case where quantity-setting is by some means imposed, and another where it is not. We already know the answer to this conundrum. We found it in the preceding sub-section. It is "cooperation". In a homogenous oligopoly, considered as a continuing game, no competitive strategic equilibrium exists. Once we have tacit cooperation, the question of price setting v quantity setting becomes irrelevant. The players find some place on the industry demand curve, simultaneously determining industry quantity and industry price. If they are approximately equal in strength, they will probably tacitly share the customers.

3.2.5 *Heterogenous oligopoly*

Consider a typical industry in this Chamb-Rob economy. Maybe 70% of its value added is in the hands of half a dozen quasi firms, hereinafter called firms, each of which produces a distinct product. We will assume that the large firms are similar in size and ignore the remaining firms. If one firm reduces price, while the others hold

1 Sonnenschein (1987) op cit. This is the argument already mentioned above in subsection 3.1.3.

constant, this firm will experience a substantial increase in sales volume at the expense of all its industry rivals, together with a smaller increase from consumers who divert expenditure from the products of other industries. Assume that the within-industry element of this demand system is iso-elastic. There will also be an extra-industry demand curve reflecting what would happen if all firms in the industry varied their prices together. This also is iso-elastic, but the constant group elasticity, of course, is smaller. The first is called e, the second E. The relation between the two will be affected by the number and size distribution of firms within the industry but, unlike in the homogenous case (where $e = NE$, see above), the link may not necessarily be simple.

Let all the firms have the same (empirical, i.e. flat) short run cost curve. Let the products be measured in commensurable units, and the demand system normalized so that for all products, when price is one, quantity demanded is one (the constant k above = 1). If N is the number of firms, when all prices are one, industry output is N.

3.2.6 *Price-setting conjectures*

Consider three conjectures concerning what will happen to other prices in the industry if I vary my price, e.g. change it by 20%,

"FOLLOW"	>	opponents will change 20% in same direction
"HOLD"	>	opponents will make no changes
"ENHANCE"	>	opponents will move in opposite direction by a large amount

The effect of FOLLOW is to make the conjectural elasticity E, of HOLD to make it e and of ENHANCE to make it very high (because in addition to their effect of my own price cut I am gaining large additional sales on account of the price rises by the others).

We now assume processes in which, starting from an arbitrary constellation of prices and resulting quantities, the firms sequentially and repeatedly follow one of the conjectures, learning nothing from experience. When for every firm the conjectural marginal revenue equals marginal cost, we have found a conjectural equilibrium. The three results are shown in *Figure 3.2.*

The top (FOLLOW) case, each player conjectures they have the power to lead the others along the industry demand curve until the marginal revenue indicated by E = marginal cost. In the final result (given our simplifying assumptions normalizing the internal demand curves) all firms will be charging the same price and selling the same quantity of the albeit different products. The price, and total industry quantity would the same as would be found by an organization which owned all the quasi firms and determined a strategy to maximize group (organizational) profits. Consequently this result may be called **Joint Profit Maximization (JPM).**

In the middle case, the firms jiggle about, according to the HOLD conjecture, until every one actually wants to hold, according to the marginal revenue indicated by e. Since e is greater than E, the final price is lower than under JPM.

The bottom case, which, in a price-setting context, and especially in a heterogenous price-setting context, is rather woolly theoretically, let alone its obvious implausibility, but is included for completeness. Whatever the elasticity is, because the effect on my quantity of my change is enhanced (reinforced) by the other changes, the conjectural elasticity is greater than e and therefore presumably high. Depending on how far the assumption is carried, we may again get $e/(e\text{-}1)$ close to 1 and a perfect competition result. We can call this a "quasi Bertrand" result because it approximates Bertrand, who, in reviewing Cournot, was concerned with a homogenous case.

3.3 Game-theory interpretations

Figure 3.3A describes the same basic situation (except that the number of players has been reduced to two) in a typical game-theory pay-off table, which is reasonably self-explanatory. A convenient way to interpret it is to imagine that the game is effectively finite because for some reason price changes can only be made infrequently. The game can be considered as a one-off affair lasting for the duration of the price-setting period. The influence of considerations concerning future rounds is ignored.

Therefore, if Firm A sets a price of 2.6, while Firm B sets 1.6, the allocation of demand according to the demand curves $Qa = Pa^{-e}Pb^{e}$ and $Qa = Pa^{-e}Pb^{e}$, with common marginal unit cost, m, with $e = 3$, and $m = 1.0$, produces net revenues of only 0.37 for Firm A and 2.57 (bottom row, second column) for B, which we can regard as their

GAME THEORY AND PRICE SETTING

FIGURE 3-3A

HETEROGENOUS DUOPOLY PAY-OFF TABLE
NET REVENUES: FIRM A, FIRM B

Common constant demand elasticity (e) = 3
Common constant unit marginal cost (m) = 1

Demand curves, Log(Qa) = e[Log(Pb)-Log(Pa)]
and Log(Qb) = e[Log(Pa)-Log(Pb)]
Net Revenue(a) = Qa(Pa-m) and Net Rev(b) = Qb(Pb-m)

Pa: Pb:	1.2	1.6	2	2.4
1.2	+0.20, +0.20	+0.47, +0.25	+0.93, +0.22	+1.60, +0.18
1.4	+0.25, +0.32	+0.60, +0.40	+1.17, +0.34	+2.02, +0.28
1.6	+0.25, +0.47	+0.60, +0.60	+1.17, +0.51	+2.03, +0.41
1.8	+0.24, +0.68	+0.56, +0.85	+1.10, +0.73	+1.90, +0.59
2	+0.22, +0.93	+0.51, +1.17	+1.00, +1.00	+1.73, +0.81
2.2	+0.19, +1.23	+0.46, +1.56	+0.90, +1.33	+1.56, +1.08
2.4	+0.17, +1.60	+0.41, +2.03	+0.81, +1.73	+1.40, +1.40
2.6	+0.16, +2.03	+0.37, +2.57	+0.73, +2.20	+1.26, +1.78

RECTANGLES = MAXIMIN PAY-OFFS CIRCLED AREA = STRATEGIC EQUILIBRIUM = "NASH" = CONJECTURAL EQUILIBRIUM
Equilibrium price = 1.5 (interpolation) = e/(e-1)

complete pay-offs from this game. Once Firm A has decided its price, not knowing the price to be set by Firm B, it cannot, on discovering the poor outcome, revise its price, it cannot cut to 1.6 in the hope of improving the result to .60.

It can be seen that if both firms set a price around 1.5 they are both maximining. If Firm A sets a price of 1.2 the worst outcome is 0.2. If B sets this price also the outcome is 0.20 for each. But if A sets 1.4, and B again does his worst by repeating 1.2, the result for A is 0.25 and so on. Eventually, as we consider higher prices for A, the worst outcome reaches a peak and declines. Around a price of 1.5 larger rectangle) it reaches a maximum. This for A is the maximin price. Owing to the symmetrical demand conditions,[1] the same price will also be found to be the maximin price for Firm B (small rectangle: the intermediate prices for Firm B had to be suppressed for lack of space). The common price, when both firms are maximining, is shown in the circle.

On the strict assumptions of the finite game, it is difficult to see how rational (in the loose sense of "sane") players reaching any result than the maximin result. It is not a question of "playing safe" or being

1 For simplicity, they imply that the "external" elasticity of demand for this internally heterogenous case is not merely small but zero.

GAME THEORY AND QUANTITY SETTING

FIGURE 3-3B

HOMOGENOUS QUANTITY-SETTING DUOPOLY PAY-OFF TABLE
NET REVENUES: FIRM A, FIRM B

Group demand elasticity (E) = 1.5
Common constant unit marginal cost (m) = 1
Group Demand Curve, Log P = (-1/E)Log[.25(Qa + Qb)]
Net Revenue(a) = Qa(P-m) and Net Rev(b) = Qb(P-m)

Qa:	Qb: .2	.6	1	1.4
.2	+0.73, +0.73	+0.38, +1.15	+0.25, +1.23	+0.17, +1.18
.4	+1.02, +0.51	+0.61, +0.91	+0.41, +1.01	+0.28, +0.98
.6	+1.15, +0.38	+0.74, +0.74	+0.51, +0.84	+0.35, +0.82
.8	+1.22, +0.30	+0.81, +0.61	+0.56, +0.70	+0.39, +0.69
1	+1.23, +0.25	+0.84, +0.51	+0.59, +0.59	+0.41, +0.57
1.2	+1.22, +0.20	+0.84, +0.42	+0.59, +0.49	+0.40, +0.47
1.4	+1.18, +0.17	+0.82, +0.35	+0.57, +0.41	+0.38, +0.38
1.6	+1.12, +0.14	+0.78, +0.29	+0.53, +0.33	+0.34, +0.30

RECTANGLES = MAXIMIN PAY-OFFS CIRCLED AREA = STRATEGIC EQUILIBRIUM = "COURNOT". PARALLELOGRAM = JOINT PROFIT MAX

Equilibrium joint quantity = approx 2, common price, 1.5 = NE/(NE-1)

risk averse. I cannot "gamble" on my opponent setting a higher price unless I have some special reason to believe that he will also want to take the same "gamble". Without some kind of communication, that would be, to say the least, very difficult. But if we do communicate, and I tell my opponent that I will set, say, 1.4, if I can hope that he will, in the absence of enforceable binding agreement or some kind of moral code or restraint, or prospect of a repeat of the game (all of which amount to effective cooperation, for the moment, by assumption, ruled out) it is now certain that, as an amoral profit-maximizer, the one price he will not set will be 1.4. If he knows I am going to set 1.4, he is in the position of any conventional maximizer, and will set not 1.4, which gives him a profit of 0.3 (bottom right corner), but 1.0, which gives him 0.41.

Notice that, unlike the conjectural equilibrium, the maximin result appears in terms of price levels, rather than price changes. It is this feature that gives it force.

To make comparison with the conjectural model we therefore need a starting point. That, in turn, implies that the game is played more than once. So let us arbitrarily assume that it has been played once, and found the maximin result, and will be played once more, only, for all time. By comparing Figures 3.2 and 3.3A the reader can be quickly satisfied that the conjecture "hold at price = 1.5" represents the conjectural equilibrium. On the mutually self-fulfilling conjecture of "hold", it is therefore stable.

Taken together, the two approaches, conjectural and game-theoretic, converge to the concept of the Nash or strategic equilibrium already discussed above. On the conjecture that strategies (price tactics) are constant, they will be constant. It is a powerful result for the finite game, but, given the dynamic essence of the scientific meaning of the word "equilibrium", it is also a somewhat elusive concept. If in order to move nearer to the normal idea of equilibrium we permit some repetition of the game, it is sometimes suggested that the Nash equilibrium could be seen as the product of a tacit, non-binding agreement, or "statement in advance" by the players that this is how they will play. If one believes that, one will play that. But it is not easy to give overwhelming reasons against the possibility that once one begins to relax the finite conditions of the game, the move towards the continuing situation also opens the possibility of this heterogenous oligopoly teaching itself to reach, by the kind of process already described above, a "cooperative" result somewhere in a South-Easterly direction in Figure 3.3A.

We can now turn back and complete our discussion of the "quantity-setting" scenario, using the conjectural approach, as on the right hand side of Figure 3.2, and the game-theoretic approach simultaneously. Clearly the concept only applies to a homogenous oligopoly. The results given in the Figure for the conjectural equilibrium are explained in the middle right hand segment: conjectural marginal revenue is the result of changing quantity, with other quantities constant, letting the market clear, and pricing the additional sales at the new market-clearing price. The calculation of it has already been explained and at the conjectural equilibrium it will, for both firms, be equal to marginal cost.

Figure 3.3B, a game-theory pay-off table framed in terms of quantity strategies, uses the data of Figure 3.3A modified according to the equivalence principles discussed earlier. We assume that internal elasticities are "infinite" and that there is an external elasticity (indicating the effects of group price changes) equal to the internal elasticity of Figure 3.3A divided by the number of players, in this case with two players, this gives an external elasticity (E) of $3/2 = 1.5$; the joint demand curve is multiplied by a constant (0.25) to obtain commensurability.

GAME THEORY AND THE BERTRAND PROBLEM

FIGURE 3-3C

HETEROGENOUS DUOPOLY PAY-OFF TABLE
NET REVENUES: FIRM A, FIRM B

Common constant demand elasticity (e) = 7
Common constant unit marginal cost (m) = 1

Demand curves, Log(Qa) = e[Log(Pb)-Log(Pa)]
and Log(Qb) = e[Log(Pa)-Log(Pb)]
Net Revenue(a) = Qa(Pa-m) and Net Rev(b) = Qb(Pb-m)

Pa: Pb:	1.2	1.6	2	2.4
1.2	+0.20, +0.20	+1.50, +0.08	+7.14, +0.03	+25.60, +0.01
1.4	+0.14, +0.59	+1.02, +0.24	+4.86, +0.08	+17.40, +0.03
1.6	+0.08, +1.50	+0.60, +0.60	+2.86, +0.21	+10.25, +0.08
1.8	+0.05, +3.42	+0.35, +1.37	+1.67, +0.48	+5.99, +0.19
2	+0.03, +7.14	+0.21, +2.86	+1.00, +1.00	+3.58, +0.39
2.2	+0.02,+13.92	+0.13, +5.58	+0.62, +1.95	+2.21, +0.76
2.4	+0.01,+25.60	+0.08,+10.25	+0.39, +3.58	+1.40, +1.40
2.6	+0.01,+44.83	+0.05,+17.95	+0.25, +6.27	+0.91, +2.45

DATA AS FIGURE 3.3A EXCEPT LARGE INCREASE IN ELASTICITY
NOTE HOW STRATEGIC EQUILIBRIUM MOVES TOWARDS PRICE
NEARER MARGINAL COST

The maximin result is shown in the same way as in the previous figure. Each firm supplies the quantity 1, making total quantity 2. With the aid of the inverted demand equation, we find that the corresponding common price is 1.5, which is the same as the equilibrium price in Figure 3.3A. This is the classic result of Cournot.

Cournot, however, was well aware of the potentiality of what we now call cooperation, and by implication defined a cooperative solution as one where joint profits were maximized. In Figure 3.3B this occurs at a joint quantity of 1.2 (0.6 each firm) and a common price of 3, yielding joint profits of 2.42 or 1.21 each, compared with 0.59 each in the competitive strategic equilibrium. The position is indicated by the parallelogram.

By reverting to the price-setting approach, we can use the game-theory type of analysis to demonstrate the critique of Bertrand as already summarised above, as in *Figure 3.3C*. The essential new feature is that the internal elasticity has been raised to a high level (7) thus approaching the conditions of homogeneity. Consequently, Figure 3.3C goes some of the way to telling us what happens if, with the comparable data that underlies all three figures, the players in Figure 3.3B turn from quantity setting to price setting. We see a new strategic equilibrium at a price of 1.2, so that, as compared with the quantity-taking strategic equilibrium of Figure 3.3B (which actually implies higher internal elasticity, i.e. "infinite"), the mark-up in the price-setting strategic equilibrium is reduced from 50% to 20%. A further increase in elasticity would push the result further in the same direction and, in the limit, with internal elasticity "infinity" we have price converging to marginal cost. This is also the conjectural result, of course; in the limit, according to the Lerner formula, as e becomes large the price/marginal cost ratio, $e/(e\text{-}1)$ converges to 1.

3.3.1 Cooperation

We have repeatedly pointed out that the resolution of the Bertrand paradox is "cooperation". In Figure 3.3C this would occur somewhere in the SW direction. Unfortunately we cannot make a direct comparison with the JPM result of Figure 3.3B because of the simplifying assumption, mentioned above, that in the heterogenous case in our data the "external" elasticity is implicitly zero, implying no upper boundary to profits. Wherever will be found the result, based on more realistic assumptions, that is where, in the absence of entry, such an industry will end up.

None of the versions of Figure 3.3 apply to the Sym-Het economy, or, to put the point more generally, to any heterogenous oligopoly where the number of players is large. We have already seen that this means more than that the number of firms be numerous, it means we are speaking of competition among a large group of quasi firms which are comparable in size. We have discussed why the picture is unrealistic, both for the industry and the economy.

The model is nevertheless very important, for the reason that it is the model used in the Imp-Mac model and also in a substantial part of the contemporary theoretical literature.

As far as conjectural analysis is concerned, there is nothing to add to the conclusion of Figure 3.2. Whether the numbers are large or small, given the "HOLD" conjecture, the result is the same (unlike on the right hand side of the figure, N does not apply in the result). With a large number of players, however, the conjecture is no longer arbitrary. Each player knows that the effects of his actions on others should be relatively small, therefore there is no reason to expect reactions.

IMP-COMP SCENARIO-SELECTION TREE FIGURE 3.4

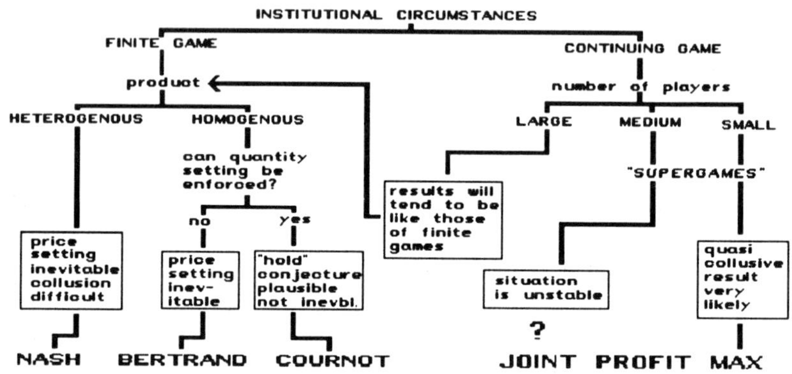

In the case of game theory we also have a rather strong result. Tacit cooperation is less likely, the other players are more like a random mass, the game could be seen as a game against nature. It is then relatively easy to see that the maximin play, i.e. the strategic equilibrium, is the same as the "hold" conjectural equilibrium, is very much the most plausible outcome.

3.3.2 *The "kinky" demand curve*

In the late 1930s, an idea developed, more or less simultaneously on both sides of the Atlantic,[1] that price would tend to be stable in small and medium sized heterogenous oligopolies because each quasi firm would expect that if it cut price, rivals would follow, but if it raised price, they would not. Thus the perceived demand curve was elastic upwards, inelastic downwards: at the point of change, it had a kink. Marginal revenue for a price increase above the kink would be low, below it, negatively, high. Therefore the kink price would seem the most profitable price over a range of marginal costs. In terms of Figure 3.2 above, this is an asymmetric conjecture where, one conjectures "follow" in one direction, "hold" in the other.

1 Hall and Hitch (1939), Sweezy (1939).

The problem with the idea of course is to determine the point at which the kink will form. Although the idea historically preceded the penetration of economics by game theory, its intellectual robustness may nevertheless be tested against game theory. How does it appear in a competitive-game context? If the kink is at the Nash strategic equilibrium, well and good; if not, the conjecture cannot be reconciled with competitive game theory: it then requires one to conjecture that rivals will behave irrationally.

Consequently, if the idea is to be reconciled with game-theory, the support must sought in the domain of co-operative play. In that light it appears not a bad way of describing the means by which price-setting players will be punished if they attempt to break away from the cooperative solution, whatever that may be. Thus the answer to the question, "where will the kink form?" is, "wherever, if one exists, lies the cooperative game-theoretic result for the type of market in question."

3.4 Oligopoly overview[1]

The upshot of our discussion is that similar basic circumstances lead to similar results, whichever theoretical approach is adopted. At first that appeared to be not the case as between the price-setting and quantity-setting interpretations of a small-group homogenous oligopoly, but then we saw that in those circumstances, in a continuing game, cooperation was almost inevitable. If it is a finite game, and quantity setting cannot be imposed, then the price-setting Bertrand result seems inevitable. This, indeed, was Bertrand's whole point. Stuffy though he may have been, we can now see, in the light of game theory, that Bertrand did, in fact, effectively destroy the Cournot case. Such is the mathematical charm of the case, however, that, a century and a half on, it remains in common use!

The author's philosophy for modelling the competitive process can therefore be summed up as "look for the circumstances". It is synthesized in the "tree" set out in *Figure 3.4.* It is a kind of algorithm based on practical, rather than theoretical questions. First

1 For a valuable in-depth survey of oligopoly-with-entry theory please see Patrizio Bianchi (1989).

we ask whether the actual circumstances are those of a finite or continuing game. Then we ask further questions depending on the first answer. If it is a continuing game with a small number of players, whatever the degree of heterogeneity of the product, cooperation, in the absence of entry deterrence, is the likely outcome. Hence we go down the right hand of the tree to JPM.

If, in a continuing game, the number of players is large, then cooperation is unlikely, and the game can as well be analysed as if it were a finite game. On the left hand main branch, therefore, we now ask whether the product is homogenous or heterogenous. In a finite game, without cooperation, maximining seems inevitable. If the players consider that price cutting may occur, they must maximin on the assumption that it will occur. Then the Bertrand result is inevitable. The great Cournot only survives if there is some outside constraint on price setting. If we are still in this part of the diagram, and the numbers are large, we have, or would have, perfect competition.

So finally, at the bottom right, we have the case of a finite game with a heterogenous product and a small number of players (Chamb-Rob economy), which, as the cross arrow shows, is also equivalent to the case of the continuing game with a heterogenous product and many players (Sym-Het economy). That is where we find Nash, Blanchard and Kiyotaki, Ng, Snower and the Imp-Mac model.

3.5 Entry

The whole of the foregoing discussion has been based on the assumption that the structure of the goods market is fixed, meaning that the list of quasi firms and the specification of their products is fixed. The fundamental implication of entry is that the profits of firms and quasi firms, apparently, under imperfect competition, determined by the nature of the "internal" competitive process, whatever that may be, are ultimately reconciled with the fact that entry, or the threat of it, may somehow reduce profits to zero or to some otherwise-determined norm. For the student of imp-comp microfoundations such a process may or may not have significant implications for cyclical theory. The connection is that if, in "normal" or "full employment" conditions, quasi firms make "zero" or "normal" profits, must a cyclical theory predict that economic recessions mainly take the form of shut-downs? Since we know that that is not true in real life, the question is rather important. We shall come back to it at the end of the section.

The subject is framed by two analytical distinctions, the distinction between the small-group case and the large-group case, and the distinction between the effects of entry and the causes of entry. Our discussion will be organized around the first distinction, making the second as it arises. We take the small group case first. More precisely, first we discuss entry into a single oligopolistic industry, followed by some speculation concerning the whole economy. Then, in dealing with the large group case, the whole Sym-Het economy being a "large group", no distinction between the industry and the economy is necessary.

We conclude the section and chapter with some speculations concerning the relation between entry, economic growth and macrodynamics that represent original ideas of the author.

3.5.1 Entry into the small group

We are dealing here with a field of economics (a large and very rich one) associated with "entry-deterrent" theory and with the theory of the "contestable" market.[1] The leading names in the first part of the field are Bain and Labini, in the second, Baumol, Panzer and Willig.

We begin with *Figure 3.5*. It is a model of a homogenous quantity-setting duopoly using basically the same data as Figure 3.3B except that the range of quantities for which results are given has been simplified, and the definition of pay-off transformed. The quantity tactics available to each firm now include the quantity zero, which is called "exit", meaning more precisely choosing not to be in the industry. When, however, a firm "exits", it does not earn nothing, rather it earns a level of profit in some other activity which for the moment we will assume to be an arbitrary number representing the best that could be achieved with the firm's transferable entrepreneurial, informational, organizational and material resources, which are

---

1 A reading list on entry deterrence and limit pricing would include Kaldor (1935), Bain (1956), Labini (1956), Modigliani (1958), Gaskins (1971) and Kamien and Schwartz (1975); on extensive games, Selten (1975, 1977): on pre-commitment, Eaton and Lipsey (1980); on contestable markets, Baumol, Panzer and Willig (1982). The relevant articles in the *New Palgrave* (Eatwell et al (eds), 1987 op cit) are Eaton on Entry, Kamien on Limit Pricing, and Willig on Contestable Markets.

GAME THEORY AND ENTRY-DETERRENCE — FIGURE 3.5

HOMOGENOUS QUANTITY-SETTING GAME WITH EXIT
EXCESS OF PAY-OFF OVER EXIT PAY OFF: FIRM A, FIRM B

Group demand elasticity (E) = 1.5
Common constant unit marginal cost (m) = 1
Exit Pay-off = .5

Group Demand Curve, Log P = (-1/E)Log[.25(Qa + Qb)]
Net Revenue(a) = Qa(P-m) and Net Rev(b) = Qb(P-m)

Qa:	Qb: EXIT	.4	.8	1.2
EXIT	+0.00, +0.00	+0.00, +0.96	+0.00, +1.04	+0.00, +0.98
.4	+0.96, +0.00	+0.27, +0.27	-0.01, +0.49	-0.16, +0.51
.8	+1.04, +0.00	+0.49, -0.01	+0.17, +0.17	-0.03, +0.20
1.2	+0.98, +0.00	+0.51, -0.16	+0.20, -0.03	-0.01, -0.01

B out, A in and deters entry — A out, B in and deters entry

both out — both in and cooperate — both in and play "Cournot"

assumed given and identical for both firms. This number is called the "exit pay-off", and in the example is set at 0.5. Then all the pay-offs are transformed by subtracting the exit pay-off. It is a finite game, with "exit" as a possible strategy for either player. There are no sunk costs of "entering" or "exiting", and no other barriers to entry or exit. The game is historyless, neither player can be called "incumbent".

We start at a moment when neither firm has entered and both are considering whether to do so, not knowing whether the other will enter or what it will do if it does. There is, however, not only some institutional force that restricts tactics to quantity setting but another that requires that a quantity, once set, is fixed for ever, so also the entry/exit decision. In effect we have exactly the finite, one-off game of Figure 3.3B, except that in the case where a player sets a quantity zero, in place of zero profit, he receives the exit pay-off.

Given the finite game, competitive play, i.e. maximining, is inevitable, and the reader will see that on the figures shown neither firm will enter. They cannot making a binding agreement for one to enter and share the profit, therefore each achieves maximin by acting on the assumption that the other will enter. For each the hypothetical pay-off for entry is the Cournot equilibrium, which, however, yields less than if they go elsewhere. Elsewhere, therefore, they both go. The good is not produced at all and presumably some other good is produced instead.

If, however, we lower slightly the assumed level of the exit pay-off, the reader does not need another print-out to see that bottom right cell would become the Cournot equilibrium. This yields better than exit, so both enter and the good is produced at a certain price. Duopoly, rather than an assumption, becomes a prediction.

We now drop the assumption that there is no "incumbent". One firm is already "in", and must set a quantity for all time. An outsider is considering entering, on the conjecture that the insider's quantity is fixed for all time. The insider knows this conjecture, and chooses a quantity that is for him not maximining but profit maximizing on the reverse assumption that the other firm, if it does enter, will choose his own profit-maximizing quantity given the conjecture. In a game-theoretic interpretation of the same idea, we simply impose the condition that the figure is exactly the same but the first row is deleted; Firm A is forced to be in the industry. Given the finite character of the game, he must maximin. This gives him a quantity of 1.2. Firm B, calculating this, can see that if he did enter his own best response would also be 1.2, with a net pay-off of -0.01, all other quantities (see bottom row) giving him an even worse result. If the numbers are exactly as set out, given his conjecture, Firm B will probably not enter. The effect is dramatic. Assuming that despite the fact that he is left alone, the ever-present threat holds him to this same quantity; Firm A's result now moves to the bottom left hand corner, and the industry quantity is halved. Consequently the resulting price is much higher. Equally dramatic is the effect of assuming, as above, that the exit pay-off is a little lower; we can create a situation where Firm A's maximin quantity remains the same, but the net pay-off to both firms will be more positive. So in the course of choosing his best tactic. Firm A is compelled to let Firm B in, and price comes tumbling down.

Now we drop two more assumptions, the assumption of constant returns and the assumption that there are only two players. If there are increasing returns to scale, it is less likely that for any given number of incumbent players, entry deterrence will be impossible. Start with one firm and assume that, despite increasing returns, the entry of one more firm cannot be deterred. There are now two firms in the industry, with reduced individual output and increased unit costs, nevertheless they make a profit above exit pay-off. On account of increasing returns, however, the addition of yet another firm will squeeze the post-entry "Cournot" profit level even further. Maybe another firm has to come in, but eventually the process will stop. This, in essence, was Sylos-Labini's model of the middle 1950s. The beauty of it is that by inspecting the cost functions and the demand curve of the industry, one can precisely predict final price, final output and the final number of firms. The problem is that it depends, in game-theoretic terms, on the assumption that the game is finite, thus ruling out the possibility of cooperation.[1]

3.5.2 *The heterogenous case*

Generally, the great bulk of entry-deterrent literature, however, rather than the homogenous case, deals with the heterogenous case. The pioneer (see above) was Bain, who assumed a historical sequence ending in a limit structure and a limit price, beginning with an initial structure of incumbent firms of a product probably intrinsically capable of differentiation and probably produced under increasing returns to scale. He did not assume a specific competitive process. He simply assumed that whether by instinct or collusion, if a profitable price existed for deterring further entry, the incumbents would wish to set it. In many modern industries there were however significant barriers to entry, not "artificial" but rather the result of

---

1 An attractive extension of the Sylos-Labini theory, called "pre-commitment", takes more specific account of the implications of the sunk costs of entry especially where there are major scale economies in connection with the optimal equipment in which capacity is to be invested. (The data in Figure 3.3B contains no scale economies.) First imagine a story where an arbitrary incumbent with given capacity already exists, then another firm enters, also with a given lump of capacity. If we know the two capacities and the relevant cost data we can work out the result of the game on any given assumption about how they play. For the sake of argument let it be Cournot. Depending on the numbers, the original firm may or may not be able to deter entry. Now take any given capacity level for the incumbent, let the potential entrant calculate the optimum scale of the lump of capacity for his entry that will maximize in the traditional sense, his maximin (Cournot) pay-off after entry. If this maximum maximin pay-off is greater than the exit pay-off, Firm B will enter, if not, not. Hence, for any arbitrary initial level of capacity by Firm A, we know, on these assumptions, not only what will happen to Firm B, but also to Firm A. Thus for any given capacity for Firm A there is an ultimate (maximin) pay-off. Now take the story yet one stage further back. Let Firm A be allowed to choose capacity to maximize its own ultimate return. Rather beautifully, this will determine everything, price, quantity and Firm B's capacity.

specific economic characteristics making it inherently expensive to launch a new product and attendant quasi firm. The greater the barriers the higher the limit price, an effect which could be observed by observing the industry's relative profitability. The barriers were then quantified in various ways, one of which was to assume that they were proxied by the degree of concentration. Hence the prediction was that profitability would be positively correlated with measures of industrial correlation.

3.5.3 "Contestable" markets

Among a group of existing incumbents in a given industry, we know that the "finite game" story is implausible. The repeating round of business life is part of the essence of the market process. "Entry" however, tends to be a lumpy affair, and is therefore more plausibly, but not necessarily, modelled by the finite game. We now therefore first discuss a "mixed" case or "semi-finite game", where the act of entry or "exit" is strictly one-time, but within an industry, at any time, incumbents are playing a continuing game. Then we shall examine the case where even the entry / exit strategy is available continuously: this case is in fact the case of the so-called contestable market.[1]

Although Figure 3.3B has quantity setting it can still be used to make a powerful point. Consider a "traditional" entry-deterrent story where there already happens to be an incumbent firm and a single outside firm is considering entry. If he does choose to enter, however, we arbitrarily assume that all his costs are sunk, he cannot at any reasonable cost, or within a reasonable time, subsequently exit. So, if entry occurs, both firms are locked in combat, and must play a continuing game. Then from all our previous discussion we know that it is virtually inevitable that they will learn to cooperate. Suppose that they already understand this. If so, because there is a greater benefit to be shared by the firms, it is more difficult to deter entry and entry is likely to occur.

Now assume the game is fully continuing; firms can enter and exit, costlessly at will. There are (for the moment) no economies of scale. Price-setting is permitted. The number of potential entrants is large. This is a game-theoretic picture of the concept of a "perfectly" contestable market. We see at once that although the game is

1 See, op cit, Baumol et al (1982) and Willig in Eatwell et al (eds) (1987).

continuing, cooperation is not predicted. Although the situation may end up as a small group, the lifting of the restriction on the number of potential entrants effectively enlarges the game, and to such an extent that the teaching process leading to cooperation cannot be relied upon. Hence we must look for a Nash/Cournot type of strategic equilibrium. Where will it be? Using again the expositional trick of relapsing into the quantity-setting example of Figure 3.3B, with the exit pay-off slightly raised, we know there is one solution, which we found with the finite game, at the bottom right position, labelled Cournot. Both firms are in the industry, earn approximately the exit pay-off, set a price of 1.5 and a joint quantity of 2.4.

But now, on the new assumptions, there is another possibility, not shown in the table. A single firm could produce 2.4, charge 1.5, and deter entry. If there were only a few potential entrants and/or important sunk costs of entry, this firm could possibly later raise price and deter entry by the threat that in the event of entry price would be lowered. But in the contestable market that cannot be. If the incumbent firm for so much as a moment raises price, an outsider dashes in, takes some profit and if necessary later dashes out. So the incumbent firm must hold price down to the level which yields no more than exit pay-off.

The problem with this fascinating paradigm is an internal contradiction which virtually parallels the internal contradiction in the perfect-competition paradigm that it aspires to replace. Without sunk costs, capacity cannot be created. It is inherent in the nature of economic life that quasi firms are bundles of interconnected specific human, informational and physical assets. Except in the rarest cases, diverting these to different uses involves major costs. If we keep literally to constant returns and also assume a homogenous product, there can be at any time any number of quasi firms in the market; the model is indeterminate between perfect competition and a single firm with perfect contestability. Hence it is inherently unstable. It only requires a gentle, but far extending, downward slope of some player's average cost curve to change the picture completely. Then this firm will take over the industry. Then a potential entrant will need to invest in a large scale of production to be a threat. Then it will have sunk costs.

How do the foregoing micro theories relate to macroeconomics? The answer is that none of them determine absolute price; in one way or another they all terminate in a margin or mark-up. It follows that if the theories are married to a macro theory, just as in the Imp-Mac model (which has no entry) when run without endogenous demand elasticity (see Chapter 1), a cyclical movement cannot affect prices unless it affects costs. The conclusion would seem to be that entry theory up to this point does not have major effects on the microfoundations of macroeconomics.

3.6 Large-group entry

We now turn to the case where the group of firms into which entry occurs is large, in effect a one-by-one process of entry into a whole Sym-Het economy.

3.6.1 The excess-capacity theorem

The starting point is the so-called "excess capacity" theorem, which emerged immediately and directly from the first imperfect competition literature of the early 1930s, was actively discussed for the next twenty years, fell out of fashion during the neo-classical revival, and has now been re-discovered at the Massachusetts Institute of Technology.

The first step is to define the average unit cost curve of the quasi firm to include an element of "normal" profit: if in the long run gross profits were inadequate, the firm would be shut down. Under perfect competition, this would have meant a downward move on the long-term supply curve of the "industry" in question. Under imperfect competition, it means the loss of a product.

Quasi firms are endowed, at least at the left hand end, with the empirical short-run cost curve (as output increases from low levels, opph increases). It is then assumed that there exists a mechanism by which high profits attract new entry of quasi firms (products) into this industry or, in the current literature, economy. So, unless the current profit-maximizing profit margin yields no more than a "normal" rate of return, one by one, there will be new entry of new products into the general population of quasi firms and products. For some reason real aggregate demand is fixed, so that consumers, on discovering that the new products have distinctive desirable qualities, can buy them only at the expense of other products. Consequently the demand curve of the representative pre-existing quasi firm shifts leftwards. We can conveniently assume it does so iso-elastically.

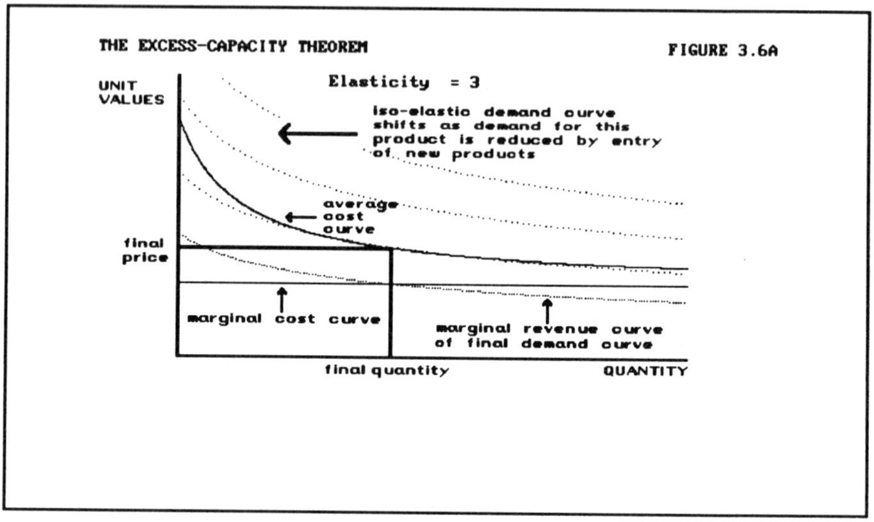

If entry continues far enough, all firms which are now in the economy will find that the profit-maximizing mark-up yields no more and no less than "normal" profit; entry will cease. To the equation for short-term conjectural equilibrium (price equals marginal cost plus profit-maximizing mark-up) there is now added condition for zero-entry long-term equilibrium, namely price equals "average cost" (including "normal profit"), giving us,

$$p = me/(e\text{-}1)$$
$$p = a \qquad [a = \text{"average cost"}]$$
$$a/m = e/(e\text{-}1)$$

See *Figure 3.6A*. The ratio, a/m, is the ratio of average to marginal cost. The fact that it must be greater than one indicates that in this solution average cost is declining, implying that increased production would reduce costs and has in consequence been called an indication of "excess" capacity.

As shown in *Figure 3.6B*, the degree of the excess varies against the elasticity of demand. If elasticity is very high, we approach perfect competition, and the excess disappears. If elasticity is low, the excess is large. Consequently the problem is seen as quantitatively related to the degree of imperfection of competition.

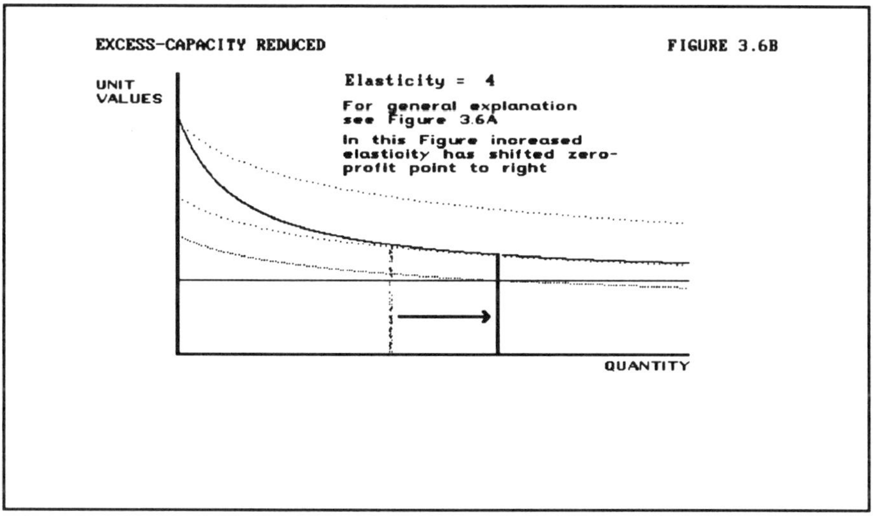

In the author's mind there is a grave problem with this hallowed result; if for some reason entry ceases at an earlier point, it might lie where the average cost curve was flat or nearly so. Where is "excess capacity" then? In the next sub-section we suggest an answer.

More generally, once we move from the Marshallian world into a world which distinguishes firms from quasi firms and is mainly concerned with cyclical macroeconomics, major conceptual problems appear, whose gravity, in the author's opinion, are inadequately respected in the contemporary literature. The gain or loss of products due to entry is a change in the structure of the economy. The decisions are made by firms, not quasi firms, and profits accrue to firms, not quasi firms. The rate of profit earned by a firm is intimately bound up with its rate of growth,[1] each reacting on the other. In turn, diversification (creating new products, new quasi firms) is an important means of corporate growth. So the theory of macro entry cannot be separated from the theory of macro growth. To put the point another way, the Marshallian concept of "normal" profit cannot easily be transformed into some concept that claims to drive the motivation of the high management of firms, in an economy at large, to take decisions on the founding or closing of quasi firms, a problem

1 Marris, R. (1980).

which involves the theory of motivation for creating new products in general. For firms, as organizations, profit has several functions, one of which is the finance and support of growth and another the finance and support of diversification; the two activities being closely, but not inseparably linked. Faster growth by firms in general, if matched by corresponding growth in the economy, tends to reduce excess capacity; only if diversification increases faster than the macro growth rate (implying subdivision of production without increase of production) does the tendency to excess capacity increase.

Before the chapter ends we will return to that crucial proposition.

3.7 A new theory of entry

It is well known that diversification plays a major role in the growth of firms. What about the economy? Do we expect the number of products to grow at the same rate as the economy, or slower, or faster? The last, evidently, is the case which will create excess capacity.

Consequently, in the opinion of the author, it is essential to consider the elements of a theory which can bring together the theory of growth and diversification of firms and the theory of macro growth. This we now attempt, combining a simplified version of a theory of the growth and diversification of the firm found in the present author's earlier work[1] with a simplified version of the theory of the relation between the growth of firms and the growth of the economy developed by Hiro Odagiri.[2]

It is firms who introduce new products, not quasi firms. Until the product is introduced, the quasi firm does not exist. A stylized picture of the growing firm is given in *Figure 3.7A*. It is an entity run by managers who may also be owners and who at the high level must consider decisions involving the possibility of expansion and or change of direction. Because it is in practice difficult to borrow more than a proportion of existing assets in a given period, internal financing is always crucial. Consequently a substantial operating profit is needed to finance strategic management, research, development and growth. One means for growth is diversification. Another is expanding sales

---

1 Marris, R. (1964b) Ch 4.

2 Odagiri (1981).

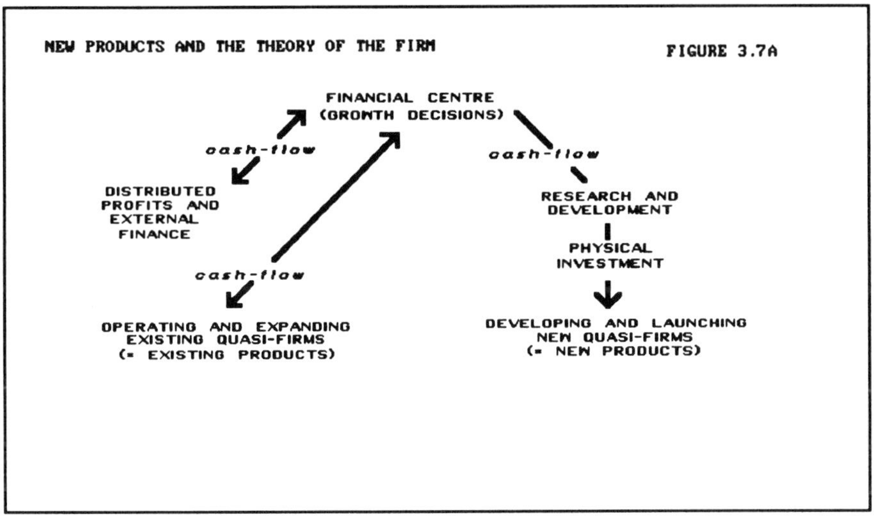

of existing products: if the demand curve is given, and price is already profit-maximizing, this requires that consumer income be growing. Finally, firms, large and small, not only innovate with respect to products but also with respect to production technology, and thus influence the economy-wide technological frontier.

It follows that profits motivate, facilitate and drive the growth of the firm and in so doing affect the growth potential of the economy. But, under imperfect competition, profitability is determined by the elasticity of demand. The latter, in turn, may well be increased by the introduction of new products. Consequently there is a circular interaction between demand elasticity, the desire for growth and the capacity for growth.

The total picture is depicted in *Figure 3.7B*. First consider elasticity of demand as pre-determined. The lower it is, ceteris paribus, the higher the rate of profit of the representative firm. Consequently the representative firm both desires and succeeds in growing faster, while satisfying its shareholders. Consequently the firm does more research and development, supporting this with higher conventional investment. Consequently the economy as a whole gains potential to grow faster. More precisely we say that we expect a lower elasticity of demand to be associated with a faster macro growth rate. Whether or not the number of products will tend to increase relative to the scale of the economy cannot be rigidly predicted. It is perfectly

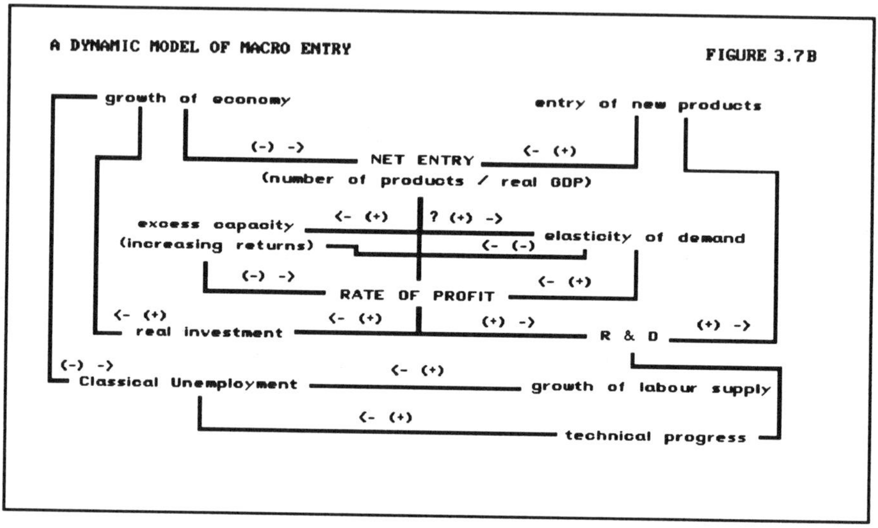

possible that "net entry" (excess of growth rate of products over growth rate of economy) is zero or even negative.

There are also two secondary loops, the effect of net entry on firstly demand elasticity and secondly on production costs. The point here is that if net entry does increase elasticity, it dampens the tendency to inefficiency of scale (see Figure 3.6B as already discussed, above). So that even if net entry occurs, we cannot be sure it will have its malignant effect. But if, despite all, the malignant effect does take place, then, for given elasticity, the rate of profit is reduced and so also in principle is the rate of growth of the economy. But the rate of creation of new products will also be slowed up, so we cannot be sure we have a "trap". In short, there seems no theoretical reason why an economy could not possess a potential steady state with constant macro growth rate and rate of profit, no net new product creation, no creeping excess capacity. Zero net product creation does not, however, mean no product creation; it means product creation at the same rate as the macro growth rate. Hence a positive macro growth rate, in this new theory, implies a growing number of quasi firms. The Imp-Mac model should have been, but has not been modified to meet this requirement.

4 What is meant by Keynesian?

One purpose of this chapter is to set out the author's view of what was wrong with the explanation of the Keynesian theory as given in the *General Theory* itself; another is to substantiate the claim we made in Chapter 1 that virtually all contemporary econometric macro models are basically Keynesian or more precisely neo-Keynesian. Before tackling these tasks, however, we need to face the problem that there are a number of theories which have acquired names ending in "-Keynesian", some of which, in the author's opinion, virtually deserve to be categorized as non-Keynesian. In the Introduction and in Chapter 1 we have given our own view of the essence of the Keynesian theory and by implication defined the scope of the term "neo-Keynesian" to mean developments on the Keynesian base. There is also the long established term "post-Keynesian" and more recently, almost since the present research project began, there has arisen an interesting school which has modestly taken the name "New Keynesian": further discussion of both of these schools is reserved for the next chapter, but we shall also need to make passing reference to them here.

4.1 Various kinds of non-Keynesian

4.1.1 "Stickies"

The view that the multiplier process essentially depends on the presence of some form of "stickiness" in prices in our opinion is non-Keynesian. By a "sticky" price we understand a price which is externally constrained to change relatively slowly, although, in the absence of the constraint, a profit-maximizing firm would wish to change it relatively quickly. (For further discussion see the section on the "New" Keynesians at the end of Chapter 5, below.)

Chapter 1 has made it clear why we are satisfied that however sticky some prices may be in real life, the Keynesian theory does not require this assumption. The contrary view, however, is widely held in the profession. For example Joe Stiglitz has written, "Conventional wisdom has it that a large part of the explanation of Keynesian unemployment is observed rigidities of wages and prices."[1] Joe's terminology was apposite: John Kenneth Galbraith, who invented the compelling term, "conventional wisdom", meant beliefs about the real world that were currently conventionally regarded as "wise" but which might well be completely wrong. In the present case, the "wise" belief is wrong unless combined with another arguably implausible belief, namely in the reality of a strong real balance effect. (See Chapter 2 above. The New Keynesian discussion in Chapter 5 below, just mentioned, is also relevant). But conventional believers are in good company, namely that of Maynard Keynes! In the obscure Chapter 17 of the *General Theory*, he uses the actual word, "sticky".[2] So perhaps the world's first non-Keynesian was Keynes himself!

4.1.2 Stabilizers

Both in the *General Theory* and in its immediate aftermath there were hints or developments respectively of features which would tend to enhance, on the one hand, or dampen, on the other, the potential instability of capitalist market economies. One kind postulates additional (destabilizing) positive feedback, another, (stabilizing) negative feed-back. An example of an additional destabilizer is the negative influence of a decline in output on the incentive to undertake private investment. This idea, explored in a brilliant paper by Nicholas Kaldor published in 1940,[3] produced a major literature of

1 Stiglitz (1984).

2 *General Theory* (Keynes, 1936), Ch 17, pp 238-239.

3 Kaldor (1940) postulated an additional behaviour relationship making private investment endogenous, and depending indirectly on current income as a proxy for future expectations. This curve of investment against current capacity utilization was S-shaped making three intersections with the savings function, one implying a stable, high level stationary state, another a stable low level state and the third state, between, unstable. But if the economy resided long at either the higher of the lower stable points, factors would accumulate to cause the curves to shift so that one of the stable equilibrium collapsed to instability, a crisis occurred, and the economy moved swiftly from one stable extreme to the

Keynesian trade cycle theory. An example of a stabilizer would be a tendency, if such exists, for income distribution to move counter-cyclically in favour of social groups with higher spending propensities, or for firms to maintain their employment or investment expenditure by dissaving previously accumulated profits. Such effects do not stabilize the system perfectly, but rather tend to hold fluctuations within limits. They have been called "built-in" stabilizers.

All good Keynesians believe that, depending on time, place and circumstances, there will be an inter-play of built-in stabilizers and de-stabilizers. Most practical macroeconometric models contain some of both. A loose analogy is the feature inherent in the basic design of the internal combustion engine which means that left to itself it will suck more fuel and go faster and faster. The "throttle" control restricts the fuel supply and gives a degree of stability. We all know, however, it is not necessarily sufficient, if we want constant speed, to set the throttle and leave it alone. This is because the suction depends on both the effort made and resistance encountered by the engine, a balance which is subject to constant disturbance by external factors such as road gradient. The result is that a car with a fixed throttle setting will be "partially unstable" much like a Keynesian economy.

What do we do if we want to completely stabilize the speed of a car without the need for constant throttle adjustments, e.g. in order to relieve a tired foot when driving from Cambridge Mass to San Diego? We add a "cruise control". This device measures the actual speed of the car, compares the result with the desired result, and adjusts the throttle by means of negative feedback. We can call this kind of mechanism an "inherent" stabilizer. Any macroeconomic model with an inherent stabilizer, in our view, is inherently non-Keynesian. Typically they are combinations of assumptions which by deduction produce the desired inherently stable result. One of the best known is the "Pigou" or "real balance" effect as discussed in the following two quotations,

> ...Keynes put forth the radical proposition that competitive market economies have no automatic mechanism that tends, in the absence of governmental policy guidance, to eliminate or prevent unemployment. After

---

other. This was thus the first Keynesian model of the trade cycle.

> a lengthy period of debate....it came to be widely agreed that this proposition was false as a matter of *pure economic theory...* . Even if the liquidity trap was *empirically* relevant, the real-balance effect would (as prices fall) automatically stimulate demand as needed [from supporting footnote; italics added]. – Bennet McCallum[1]

> I have said it some many times that I do not mind how you repeat it - the real-balance effect is very important in theory and very unimportant in practice. – Don Patinkin.[2]

We have already given, in Chapter 2, what we regard as overwhelming reasons on both theoretical and practical grounds for rejecting the Pigou or real balance mechanism as a proxy "cruise control" of a market economy. It is not necessary therefore to spell out our disagreement with Bennet MaCallum, except to raise an eyebrow over the idea of a scientific debate that goes one way in theory and another in practice.

Another type of inherent stabilizer, first proposed a decade and a half after his above-described debut in macroeconomics by Kaldor,[3] extends the hypothesis of a counter-cyclical movement in income distribution to a stronger theory where any lapse from full employment of capacity reduces the share of profits in the national income until full employment has been restored. This class of models is sometimes called "post-Keynesian", although as we shall see in Chapter 5, there are several other strands of economic theory, closely following Keynes, which also lay claim to that name. But the post-Keynesian Kaldor, in our view, is another surprising candidate for classification as non-Keynesian.

4.1.3 Neutral equilibrium

A further problem is posed by a famous proposition derived from Jean Baptiste Say, circa 1800.[4] In his original argument the celebrated French political economist told the story of a priest who decides he needs a new robe. He goes to the robe maker and places

1 MaCallum (1983)

2 Letter to the author, referring, of course, to Patinkin (1956).

3 Kaldor (1957).

4 Say (1803).

his order, and the robe maker orders some cloth, setting to work more cloth makers until eventually the income created returns (presumably via the ecclesiastical authorities) to create a precisely increased stipend for the priest. In the controversies and subsequent modifications which followed, the question arose as to whether or not Say was claiming a neutral equilibrium (output and employment self supporting at any level) or what would nowdays be called a full-employment equilibrium. The weight of scholarly opinion has come down in favour of the proposition that Say's main argument means a neutral equilibrium, so among history-of-thought buffs the controversial "vulgar" (full employment) version is seen as a red herring.[1] The most flattering interpretation runs that Say was simply replying to people who questioned, on demand side grounds, the possibility of economic growth. Say could be saying, in effect, if we could get from the one state to the other, the second state could be self-fulfilling.

Otherwise, Say's actual argument, taken as it stands, presents a problem of considerable contemporary relevance. Say can be said to be specifying an economy with no injections and no leakages; no fiscal deficit, no private investment, no saving. The familiar problems thus created can be illustrated by asking, "How did Say's priest pay?" Did he divert expenditure from something else (in which case the Law collapses instantly)? Did he take some money from under his bed, or persuade the robe maker to accept his credit (in either of which cases we are in a completely unstable economy with an infinite multiplier; $s = 0$, $1/s = \infty$). In any event, it is clear that an economic model containing the basic assumptions of a neutral equilibrium is yet another non-Keynesian.[2]

---

1 For an excellent account, see the book of Thomas Sowell on Say's Law (Sowell, 1972) or the same author's article on the subject in Eatwell et al (eds) (1972).

2 In a widely cited paper, Martin Weitzman (1981) argued that if it were not for the existence of short run economies of scale in the use of labour (the rising segment of the empirical opph curve) unemployed workers would be able to form small firms to re-employ themselves. But he was in effect assuming a neutral equilibrium; the demand necessary to buy the output of the new firms would be created by the act of forming them. For this reason Weitzman's theory, also, is to be classed as non-Keynesian, and hence not applicable to large-scale swings in the demand for labour such as occurred in the years immediately following his paper!

4.2 Econometric modelling

As already briefly mentioned in Chapter 1, in various places around the world, economic ministries, central banks, international organizations, research institutes and large corporations, there are "large" econometric macro models which are increasingly successful in providing convincing explanations, interpretations and reasonable forecasts of national and international macro events. Virtually all these models (including the Swedish micro-to-macro model discussed above in Chapter 2, section 2.3) are at heart neo-Keynesian models and none, to the author's knowledge, contains implicit non-Keynesian features such as discussed above. One reason, it seems, is that as soon as a person begins to write the equations of a practical econometric macro model, without a basically Keynesian approach, she or he finds they do not know where to begin. Another is that no policy-model builder who wants to stay in business is going to offer a model in which the labour market always clears: with the statistical unemployment rate varying internationally and through time between 2% and 15%, how can one justify a model where it is constrained to be always zero or some moderate positive number said to represent the "full employment" or "natural" rate?

Two people, since the Nobel Prizes for economics began, have received the accolade for work on or closely associated with large econometric macro models, Jan Tinbergen and Lawrence Klein. Both were total Keynesians. Klein's grandest project, the international "Link" model, despite his own regretted retirement, is currently extremely alive.[1]

It is an irony in the history of thought that Keynes was extremely intolerant of Tinbergen's early work, behaving arrogantly and foolishly.[2] In fact he and Richard Kahn shared a peculiar nose for

1 It is maintained by the secretariat of the United Nations in New York.

2 In 1938 he wrote to Kahn, "The League of Nations have persecuted me by sending two volumes of Tinbergen in proof and asking for comments. ...I think it all hocus - *worse* than Haberler. But everyone else is terribly impressed, it seems, by such a mess of unintelligible figurings. There is not the slightest explanation or justification of the underlying logic. The books are at your service - I don't recommend them." See Keynes/Moggridge, Vol 14, p. 289. On the other side of this discussion it must be pointed out that during his work in the Treasury in World War II, Keynes gave strong moral and practical support

doing nasty things to great people who were to make their names, and adorn their science, by econometric applications of the Keynesian theory. The present author was the first to tell Kahn the news of Tinbergen's election: he shrugged his shoulders and merely said, "I suppose it was inevitable". Another name hinted here is that of Richard Stone, whose early career was encouraged by Keynes but, after building the Cambridge University Department of Applied Economics to a world position it has never since regained, was squeezed out of the Directorship, by an administrative device (forcing him, quite improperly, to choose between the executive position and a Chair) originally conceived by Kahn, and to their shame, in due course supported by the economics Faculty. A quarter of a century then elapsed during which Stone, using his own research group, continued to do classic work, and duly received his Prize.

4.3 The trouble with the General Theory

The *General Theory* invented macroeconomics. More than 90 per cent of its words are concerned with questions other than quantity and price adjustments in micro markets. Its language is the language of aggregates. In that respect nothing like it had been seen since the works of the late eighteenth century economists (Cantillon, Quesnay) or of Malthus in the early nineteenth century.

4.3.1 Passages on microfoundations

The problem is that the book does contain some remarks on microfoundations, which are not only explicit, but occur in key passages. In consequence they have been much studied. A selection, representing a large proportion of the relevant wordage, is given in the boxes. Despite the huge amount of scholarly work of interpretation that has occurred, not too many people have come out bluntly with the proposition that the statements are internally contradictory, in short that if one takes them literally the *General Theory* doesn't work. Almost certainly the reason is the desire of many people to be

to the work of creating official National Income statistics in the form necessary to make macroeconomic theory applicable to real economies. This work in turn led to the creation of the United Nations standard system for National Income reporting which is with us to this day.

GENERAL-THEORY MICROFOUNDATIONS QUOTES I

(1) Page 24

"The amount of employment, both in the individual firm, and industry and in the aggregate, depends on the amount of proceeds which entrepreneurs expect to receive from the corresponding output. For entrepreneurs will endeavour to fix the amount of employment at the level which they expect to maximize the excess of proceeds over factor cost."

(2) Page 25

"Let Z be the aggregate supply price of output from employing N men, the relationship between Z and N being written $Z = \phi(N)$, which can be called the *Aggregate Supply Function*. Similarly, let D be the proceeds which entrepreneurs expect to receive from the employment of N men, the relationship between D and N being written $D = f(N)$, which can be called the *Aggregate Demand Function*.

Now if for a given value of N the expected proceeds are greater than the aggregate supply price, *i.e.* if D is greater than Z, there will be an incentive to entrepreneurs to increase employment beyond N....Thus the volume of employment is given by the intersection between the aggregate demand function and the aggregate supply function; for it is at this point that the entrepreneurs' expectations of profits will be maximised."

(4) Page 299-300

"The distinction between diminishing and constant returns partly depends on whether workers are remunerated in strict proportion to their efficiency. ...*if* the wage of a given grade of labourers is uniform irrespective of the efficiency of individuals, we shall have rising labour-costs. Moreover, *if* equipment is non-homogeneous and some part of it involves a greater prime cost per unit of output, we shall have increasing marginal prime costs over and above any increase due to labour costs. *Hence, in general,* supply price will increase as output from given employment is increased. Thus, increasing output will be associated with rising prices, apart from any change in the wage unit." [Italics added] simultaneously macro Keynesians and micro neo-classicals. A distinguished exception is to be found in a paper by Professor Ignazio Musu, of the University of Venice, published in Italian in 1979[1] and not to date re-published in English for the benefit of the rude Anglo-Saxons, which it surely should have been. What follows uses some of Professor Musu's arguments and adds others.

We may sum up the problems posed by the quotations in two questions. When aggregate demand shifts, what is supposed to happen in micro goods markets? And what in general is supposed to be going on in the labour market ?

Quotation (1) tells us that this is a profit-maximizing theory.

Quotation (2) employs a concept called "Aggregate Supply Price" which, the total quotation indicates, is an aggregate of quantities supplied multiplied by the corresponding supply prices. What is a "supply price"? It is a Marshallian micro concept existing only in the domain of price-taking perfect competition. It is the price that must be ruling on a market in order to "call forth" ("draw out") the quantity; it is the right hand argument in a supply function. The price is causing the quantity. So now, it seems, we know that the microfoundations of Keynes in the goods market are Marshallian perfect competition. (We notice that Keynes speaks of the maximization of "expectations" of profit, but, despite all that has been said and written on the point, the qualification is not significant; in the short run, it is quite clear, firms' expectations of profit on given conjectures are correct. That is to say the firms are correct in supposing that the economic environment is such that, if they wish to maximize profit, they should offer a certain amount of employment, which may not be full employment.)

Quotation (3), however, implies that the cause of "rising supply price" is, in effect, a rising labour-supply curve, an assumption that is inconsistent with a state of unemployment and general Marshallian conditions.

In the author's opinion, the following is a minimum account of things that are wrong with the foregoing picture.

1 Musu (1979).

As argued in the Introduction, it is unsatisfactory, to say the least, to represent a theory whose revolutionary message is demand constraint, as a theory of supply. For example, in the price-taking version, if there is a fall in Keynesian aggregate demand, the result appears as a downward vertical displacement of the price line; then firms, rather than reducing output on account of lack of demand, do so because, being price takers, they find it profitable to reduce supply. The complaint is not so much the assumption of high elasticity of demand but of price taking: once we move to price setting it is a short step to move to the general arena where elasticity of demand may be high, very high, or medium or low, and Keynes works well as a theory of demand constraint.

As also argued in the Introduction, perfect competition is unreal.[1] Assumptions of this type are justified as simplifications in economic theory if, and only if (a) the simplification is badly needed and (b) there are adequate grounds for believing that it is harmless. In default, one must assume that theory built on bad assumptions will be bad theory. The conditions for perfect goods markets include not only the familiar homogeneity of products and large numbers of sellers, but also absence of factors making for public regulation. Such a latter is instability. And markets with many sellers and homogeneous markets are almost all potentially unstable. Almost the only markets in the modern economic world that have the logic for the first two conditions are in fact unstable, to a degree that is either socially or economically unacceptable, and therefore mostly come to be regulated. These are markets for agricultural primary products. Elsewhere the logic of modern industry on the one hand, or of modern services-sectors on the other, predicts that wherever the first of the familiar conditions (product homogeneity) happens to be present, the other (many sellers) will be quickly destroyed, the short explanation being the inevitability of constant or increasing returns to scale. For all these reasons, excluding the case of paper assets, and

---

1 In an elegant contemporary paper, Victoria Chick (1991) argues that the standard conditions of perfect competition are not sufficient for lack of demand constraint. Her paper not only takes to pieces ("unbundles") the internal logic of imperfect competition but finds other examples from the *General Theory*'s small inventory of microfoundations passages which, in the present author's judgement, add yet further to the confusion.

GENERAL-THEORY MICROFOUNDATIONS QUOTES II

(5) Page 289

"We have shown that when effective demand is deficient there is under-employment of labour in the sense that there are men unemployed who would be willing to work at less than the existing real wage. Consequently, as effective demand increases, employment increases, though at a real wage equal to or less than the existing one .....[seven lines omitted, to clarify] - the decreasing return from applying more labour to given capital equipment [being] offset by the *acquiescence* of labour in a diminishing real wage." [Italics added].

(6) Page 13

"There may be *no* method available to labour as a whole whereby it can bring the wage-goods equivalent of the general level of money-wages into conformity with the marginal disutility of the current volume of employment. There may exist no expedient by which labour as a whole can reduce its *real* wage to a given figure by making revised *money* bargains with the entrepreneurs. This will be our contention."

(7) Page 259

"No one would wish to deny the proposition that a reduction in money-wages *accompanied by the same aggregate effective demand as before* will be associated with an increase in employment, the precise question at issue is whether the reduction in money wages will or will not be accompanied by the same aggregate effective demand as before measured in money...". [Keynes' italics]

(8) Pages 267 and 269

"There is..no ground for the belief that a flexible wage policy is capable of maintaining a state of continuous full employment...The economic system cannot be made self-adjusting on these lines." [267]..."If labour were to respond to conditions of gradually diminishing employment by offering its services at a gradually diminishing money-wage, this would not, as a rule, have the effect of reducing real wages. It is only in a highly authoritarian society, where sudden, substantial all-round changes could be decreed, that a flexible wage policy could function with success. One can image it in operation in Italy, Germany or Russia, but not in France, the United States or Great Britain." [269]

certain specially organized commodity markets (not including the bulk of oil transactions) "perfect" markets, for all practical purposes, do not exist. In some fields of economics, for example general-equilibrium microeconomics, the perfect-competition assumption in the past seemed needed on account of supposed mathematical difficulties encountered otherwise. In the case of the microfoundations of Keynes, however, the opposite situation holds: the perfect-competition assumption, as we see here, is at best awkward at worst, insupportable. It is therefore amazing to realize that the *General Theory*, essentially concerned with short period macro problems, should have been co-authored by a person, namely Richard Kahn, who ten years earlier had, in a most thorough and highly professional piece of research (empirically based on industrial case studies) firmly established the proposition that perfect competition was also an unsound, if not impossible, basis for, guess what, the economics of the short period![1]

Keynes is clearly using the neo-classical opph curve. We hope our previous discussion in Chapter 1 has already convinced the reader of the wrongness of that choice. If we substitute the empirical cost curve in the "General Theory" version of Keynes the adverse effects are severe. Part of the damage concerns cyclical stability, part the role of the real wage, as discussed by Keynes in quotation (5). Taking the first point first, it was, and is, an extremely attractive feature of the *General Theory* macroeconomics that they do not, as such, constitute a theory of instability. It was a theory of potential stability at any level of activity. Subsequently a huge literature built theories of oscillations (trade cycles) on this foundation; they were in effect theories of systematic movement between Keynesian states. But, and it is an enormous but, if we combine perfect competition with the empirical cost curve we must have hyper-instability. If we start from "full employment" just before the right hand end of the curve, the representative firm is making zero profits. A depression, manifesting itself in a fall in the price line, means that at any output above zero,

1 We return to the mystery shortly. The research project was Kahn (1929). In Kahn (1984) the author states that he did not draft any passages, and that his role was confined to long discussions and the writing of detailed comments in the margins of drafts.

profits are negative. Therefore profit-maximizing output is zero output. The economy comes to a total standstill!
Given the remaining quotations, what is the general picture of the labour market? The quotations do not say that a fall in the real wage could not cause increased macro demand and output, they say that in a market economy, the real wage cannot fall. Why? Because prices always follow nominal wages. Again, there is very loose drafting. Surely "acquiescence" is an unfortunate word for describing the process by which each worker at any time feels he is negotiating a real wage but, in the event, having no control over prices, ends up with something different? If that is passed over as artist's license, what about the ironic reference to totalitarian countries? Suppose we take it literally. The argument must relate to an economy where the government controlled both wages and prices, but not the output of firms. The latter, for one reason or another, are to accept government-made prices and wages and choose profit-maximizing output. In addition, the government conducts its macro affairs so that full-employment real aggregate demand is not guaranteed. Now, the sarcastic argument seems to run, such a government, desiring to increase aggregate output, rather than adjusting demand by fiscal means, decides to go for the same objective by decreeing a fall in wages with constant prices. Firms will undoubtedly desire to produce and sell more output; however, we are now in a literally fixed-price world, so the Keynesian macro equations tell us that the higher output cannot be sold. The totalitarian government has produced a state of absolute disequilibrium of the kind that has been in more recent years so elegantly investigated by Edmonde Malinvaud[1]. Did Keynes believe his own theory or did he not? An alternative interpretation is that the quotations are a loosely drafted exposition of another equally dangerous idea, namely that in general the real wage is endogenous, and should be forced down as effective demand rises, but if, by some means (e.g. foolish trade unions) the "workers" succeed in refusing to "acquiesce" in the process, output and employment could not rise because firms would not find it profitable to increase supply? What kind of procedure could be imagined here? If

1 Malinvaud (1977).

the unions index their nominal-wage claims on a real-wage target and compel employers to pay, employers may still raise prices, and, as we see in the Imp-Mac model, what follows will be a complex dynamic process which by no means rules out a rise in output. Or are we back in the totalitarian state, only now a true dictatorship of the proletariat? The workers control both prices and wages, and refuse to countenance a change in their ratio, so although the demand is there, firms (who apparently remain profit maximizers) refuse to respond?

One has a strong feeling, through it all, that the course of events was something as follows. The *General Theory* was fully worked out in its basic macro form, but then the authors were for some reason provoked to answer arguments emanating from many quarters that the solution to low-level equilibrium was a wage cut. Had they had in place (or at least beneath the walls) a set of reasonable imperfect competition microfoundations, they would have been home and dry. None of the awkward additional argument is necessary, and planned economies patently irrelevant.

The overall confusion may be summed up as saying that the quotations seem to imply a theory in which a decline in aggregate demand makes itself first felt by forcing down prices, inducing firms to reduce supply. If the nominal wage is literally fixed, although the interpretation seems at odds with the spirit of the book, it does apparently work. As soon as the possibility of a flexible nominal wage (without any real-balance effect) is admitted, however, the results depend on dynamics. A one-time fall in output followed by an indefinite downward movement of wages and prices is a possibility. But it would also seem possible to have an immediate, and then indefinite, fall in wages and prices with real output constant. In truth, it does not seem that any of Keynes' commentators made that interpretation. Sir John Hicks, for example, in a famous lecture given in Helsinki in the mid 1970s,[1] characterized Keynesian economics as "Fixprice". Notice that he did not say "Fixwage". Sir John continued to define his term in two ways, in the first of which he said it did not mean a system in which prices were literally fixed but rather that the causes of their variation were exogenous. The second definition, or amplification, implied that "Fixprice" systems, if not identical to, were

1 Hicks (1974).

at least close to being quasi imperfect-competition systems. If we re-read Sir John's "Fixprice" as "Fixwage", and continue to interpret Keynes as implying perfect competition in the goods market, he is formally correct. But if we go that way we cannot follow Sir John's other line of thought, that Fixprice means imperfect competition.[1]

4.4 Why did it happen?

As related in Chapter 1 the present author received bi-weekly personal lessons from R.F. Kahn (who died in June 1989) for a whole academic year. Later he became a close colleague and a member of the celebrated Cambridge post-Keynesian circle of the 1950s, but he was never a close friend, nor a member of the inner circle. Every Sunday in term Richard Kahn and Joan Robinson would take a long country walk, discussing economic theory, and there are a number of people still living who were on occasion invited to join them. By tacit agreement your author was never invited (it would not have been his cup of coffee) but by the same token it was sometimes agreed that if the walk ended near his house in Grantchester they would drop in (on occasion almost literally, over the fence) for tea. Through those forty years, Kahn's 1929 dissertation, called *The Economics of the Short Period*, lay unpublished in the King's College Library, available without permission only to Fellows of the College. Once or twice the present author asked the dissertation author about its contents, but the answers received, although not self-deprecatory, were of a character to discourage the initiative of walking 25 metres to the library and signing the document out. In these conversations Kahn mainly emphasized the statistical methods and content of the work, which it seemed might have been dated. Consequently, like 99.9% of the rest

---

1 Malcolm Sawyer, distinguished post-Keynesian scholar, argues (in Sawyer, 1991) that the power of the Keynesian theory lies in precisely the fact that it does not need the assumption of imperfect competition because it is also true under perfect competition, in other words a truly "general" or universal theory. Victoria Chick (1983) takes a similar position. For the reasons given above the present author simply has to disagree. To be even more awkward he would also ask why a theory is strengthened by claiming that in addition to working in the real world it would also work in an unreal one. A natural scientist would find this strange. But we all know that these authors are quite right in implying that among economists, things are different.

of the world's academic economists, the present author, although uniquely placed to do so, did not read the document until it was finally published in English, in October 1989, four months after Kahn's death and almost 60 years to the day since it was originally submitted.

For several different reasons, the revelation was little short of astounding. One feature was not a total surprise, namely that the dissertation set out the theory of imperfect competition, well before any other coherent published account, and two years before the book of Joan Robinson (which Kahn in any case probably largely composed during the Sunday afternoon events) or that of Edward Chamberlin, both of which came out in 1933. This means that Kahn was already fully absorbed of imperfect competition theory when, in 1931, he published the "multiplier" article, which, in laying the foundations for the *General Theory*, was probably the first rigorous paper on macroeconomic theory in the whole history of economic thought. (In 1932 he went on an academic tour of the US and while he was away Keynes published an article in the London weekly journal *The New Statesman* giving a popular description of the theorem, including realistic arithmetic examples, giving no acknowledgement to Kahn at all.)

The dramatically surprising features of the Kahn dissertation as read by the author in December 1989 were (1) the very high general quality of the writing, the scholarship, the theory, the maths, and the empirical work. The general standard is well ahead of the average quickly successful PhD dissertation in places like Oxford, Cambridge, Harvard or MIT today. None of Kahn's later published work has this combination of qualities in full; (2) the especially thoughtful, and considerably empirically-based, discussion of what actually happens when, in the short period, an imperfectly competitive firm experiences an adverse shift in the demand curve. What are the practicalities of reducing output: fewer shifts, less overtime, shorter basic hours, dismissals? What happens to costs in these different scenarios? Would that later economists making simplistic implicit assumptions about such matters were always so careful! (3) most extraordinary of all, the dissertation repeatedly supports, by logic and evidence, the empirical cost curve.

Why is (3) so especially extraordinary? In the first place, because Kahn, who even on his own modest account had semi-veto power over key theoretical passages in the *General Theory*, let pass the passage, quoted above, that seems to hang the whole theory on the neo-classical curve. In the second place because, in a correspondence that came sadly only briefly to life two years before his death, (see box) Kahn was continuing to display considerable ambiguity on the whole subject; in the letter of 2 May 1987 he will not say whether *he* thinks he invented the L-shaped curve (he did) and whether he is pleased or sorry. Notice how he diverts attention from the central issue by changing the subject to the "short-run supply curve" (which, with an L-shaped opph curve may still be upward sloping if the labour market is imperfect, but not in a general competitive model).

So what on earth was Kahn up to, in 1930-36 and for the rest of his life? More generally, did he already know, in the middle 1930s that the new (macro) economics must be placed on imperfectly competitive microfoundations? If so, why did he let Keynes go the other way? We shall never know the answer. What follows is merely a model that could fit the facts, others could also do so.

One generally agreed fact about Kahn is that, brilliant as he was, his mind was not prone to meta-theorizing. He did not see whole economies. He invented the multiplier because the question of the possible secondary effects (positive or negative) of public fiscal injections was much discussed at the time, and he, Kahn, knew about converging series. He did not wake up one morning and say "I invent, thee; consumption function". He just knew that those kinds of series had solutions if the appropriate coefficient (in this case marginal propensity to consume) was less than one.[1] For this reason it seems fairly generally agreed that it took Keynes to see the grander implications of Kahn's theorem. In the early 1930s, left to himself, Kahn wasn't about to invent modern macroeconomics (although, it can be argued, that in the multiplier article he implicitly did so). By the same token it is reasonable to suppose that he did not see something that now (with much hindsight) seems obvious, namely the essential link between a demand constrained macro theory and imperfectly competitive micro theory.

It has been suggested that the key to understanding Kahn lies in the hypothesis that he was under two psychological dominators, the

1 This passage is based on a conversation with Kahn.

A LETTER FROM KAHN

(He was 82; health declined shortly after and he died two years later.)

Lord Kahn, King's College, Cambridge, CB2 1ST (O223) 353311

My dear Robin 2 May 1987

I am delighted with your letter. Your line of thought naturally appeals to me. At the moment I am a bit heavily involved getting out my Fellowship Dissertation (in English) with, I think, an interesting new Introduction, a copy of which I shall send you when I receive the proofs [He never did – RM]; also another book of selected articles etc. I have not yet had time to read your enclosures. What I suggest is that a little later on, when I am clear of existing commitments (and of getting my Income Tax Return made), you come over and spend a night or two in College. There is a great deal I should like to discuss with you. [Sadly, none of this happened; if he had actually read my "line of thought", would he have been pleased or furious? – RM]

There was no disagreement between Maynard and me. According to Chamberlin I invented the "L" supply curve. Maynard invented from me the idea of thinking in terms of supply curves for capital goods and consumption goods. **It is *odd* that I failed to point out their shape.** After Lorie Tarshis and that other chap had pointed this out, it of course, added an *a fortiori* force to his argument. [His italics, my bold; it was odd indeed! - RM]

For my own part I think that the concept of the horizontal short period supply curve is exaggerated. I do not hold altogether with the ideas of Wynne Godley about the fixed write-up margin. What determines the size of this margin? And, of course, it varies between firms in accordance with their differences of prime costs.

In the *General Theory* Maynard was so anxious to get over to a reluctant audience his basic new ideas, that he indulged in simplifications, for which the book is unjustly criticised.

[30 lines on other topics omitted]

Yours ever (*Richard*)

deceased Maynard and the living Joan. Keynes (see Introduction) was a homosexual, Kahn, very much, a heterosexual, who had nevertheless been Keynes's very close friend. Keynes both needed him and dominated him. Then Kahn met Joan Robinson and they became lovers. Later he was not faithful to her and felt guilt towards her. But it was to her, not Keynes, that he presented the theory of imperfect competition. It was hardly surprising that Keynes said he was not very interested in that theory[1] (in truth he was not very interested in any microeconomics).

The course of events could therefore have been as follows. Keynes may have written the first drafts without any microfoundations passages. At that point Kahn may have raised the nagging question. Keynes agrees that something must be done, but there is no way that the "something" would be to introduce the emotionally loaded theory of imperfect competition. So, ingeniously and precariously, one or both of these great persons gave us the lash-up you see in the boxes of quotations from the *General Theory* above.

It is often said that there is a much simpler explanation, namely that outside partial equilibrium, imperfect competition is technically difficult to model, especially in the days before we had the theory of games (and notice how long, about 25 years, *that* took to sink in). To such as me, and maybe to you, dear reader, that sounds convincing. But we are not speaking of ordinary mortals, we are speaking of Keynes and Kahn. There is another problem with this type of explanation: as we shall see in Chapter 5, within a few months of the

---

1 Papers and letters in the Moggridge (1973-) edited collected works of Keynes, especially Vol XIV, show that Joan Robinson made several attempt to interest Keynes in the subject, especially in relation to the *General Theory*, but she never put the problem to him in the way it is seen by the present author. Another tell-tale is found in the defensive, almost rude language in which Keynes replied to the great Swedish economist Bertil Ohlin who had taken a very similar view to that of the present author and had commented "one sometimes wonders whether he [Keynes] never discussed imperfect competition with Mrs. Robinson". Keynes retorted that he could not see "what you [Ohlin] are driving at. The reference to imperfect competition is most perplexing. I cannot see how on earth it comes in. Mrs. Robinson, I may say, read my proofs without discovering any connection." All else apart, Keynes must have already known that the last sentence was at best a half truth. (See Keynes collected works Vol XIV, op ci,t pp 184-201, esp p 196.)

General Theory coming off the press, the way to solving the "very difficult" problem was clearly indicated by a then comparatively obscure Polish academic, named Michal Kalecki. If he could do it, why not they ?

Another and interesting light is thrown on the story by Maria Cristina Marcuzzo, of the Institute of Economic Science at Udine, Italy, who conducted a remarkable extended interview with Richard Kahn in the middle 1980s, not long before his death, which was then published, in both Italian and English.[1] In her introduction Professor Marcuzzo writes,

> In the *General Theory* the focus of Keynes' critique was to demonstrate that even accepting the...classical postulate [of] a downward sloping demand curve for labour as a function of the real wage, full employment may not be attained, because it is the demand side rather than the cost side which influences entrepreneurs' decisions on how much employment to offer. From the point of view of Keynes's argument, therefore, the hypothesis of diminishing returns to the firm was irrelevant. The advantage of retaining it, however, as for the hypothesis of perfect competition, allowed Keynes to use the accepted language of "classical" theory.

If one may comment by way of reply to an imaginary person representing a synthesis of the thought of Kahn, Keynes and Marcuzzo, one would say, "But, yes. The problem is that if that was the trick of persuasion intended by Keynes, he implicitly created a mechanism that was not the classical mechanism. The latter supposes that the real wage is the exogenous price for labour, raising which causes a backward move along a supposed demand curve for labour, derived from the demand curve for goods. Keynes's mechanism makes the real wage implicitly endogenous. Worse, his actual words "fudge" that issue. He implies that in a (perfectly competitive) market economy, workers cannot in fact change their real wage, but it might happen in a "totalitarian" economy where, the resulting mechanism would, by implication, provide an inherent stabilizer not available to the free market."

---

1 Marcuzzo (1988).

A more general comment is that although the "trick" (if this was it) had a dramatic short-term pay-off, in the long run it has proved a considerable liability. The truth is, that it is very difficult to model a profit-maximizing economy in which workers have any power over the real wage. In her actual record of Kahn's own words, Professor Marcuzzo brings out a final and fascinating twist to the mystery. Kahn, 40 years after the events in question, pointed out that in the very late 1930s, Keynes had entered into a dialogue in which he accepted the Dunlop/Tarshish evidence that real wages did not seem to move counter-cyclically; he therefore suggested that, instead, the mark-up of prices on wages must move counter-cyclically. Why? Because he was still assuming the neo-classical labour productivity curve! In short, a classic syllogism, "I believe A which implies either B or C. If you tell me that B is not true, then I infer C must be true!"

Even Cambridge economists are human. Personal relations can have historic consequences. While an undergraduate, in 1946, the author met Keynes in person, at a seminar, shortly before his tragically premature death, in company with a few other people such as P. Sraffa, J. Robinson, D. Robertson, R. Kahn (dons) and Harry G. Johnson, I. G. Patel (sometime Governor of the Bank of India, at the time of writing this book Director of the London School of Economics), and E. A. Russell (brilliant Australian economist who died young after a game of squash) (students). While Russell was standing in front of the fire speaking, Joan Robinson rather rudely gave Keynes a document, and Keynes rather rudely began reading it. So Russell just stopped speaking, and for a while there was silence. Then Keynes, at last aware, stopped reading, went pink to his collar and made a gesture of apology (a gentleman trapped into being rude to a student); Russell resumed his discourse. Graven on the author's memory of this incident is the aura of tension and irritation between Joan Robinson and Keynes. That is the relevance of this anecdote to the topic of the chapter which is now concluded. The point at issue is not just that Keynes was irritated by Joan Robinson, which he clearly was then and apparently had been for some time. The point at issue is that the irritation reflected a triangular psychological tension, which affected Kahn, which affected the history of economic thought.

5 History of Thought

Numerous, but by no means all present-day economists affect to be uninterested in the history of economic thought. The present author believes that, on the contrary, apart from the intrinsic excitement of all kinds of history, in the case of economics, if we do not know where our ideas came from, we cannot judge their value. The present chapter, however, is not exactly a conventional history. It is concerned with four topics, two of which are conventionally historical in that they relate to intellectual events between a quarter century and half a century old; the other two, however, relate to literature of the past decade.

The topics, in historical order, are, (i) the remarkable and to this day little known story of how the Polish economist Michal Kalecki interpretated the *General Theory* with imperfect competition within a few months of the book's publication, (ii) selected developments, including aspects of post-Keynesian economics, in the period 1950-1980, (iii) the literature on imperfectly competitive microfoundations of macroeconomics that has sprung up since 1980 and (iv), overlapping with (iii), the school, appearing around 1985, which has taken the name "New Keynesian".

This will be non-conventional history in another sense also; in discussing these works we do not even attempt to pretend to appear impartial; we are constantly plugging our own opinions.

5.1 Michal Kalecki

Michal Kalecki was born at the turn of the present century, and combined a deep Marxian influence with three other prominent features, namely love of his country, belief in liberty and a brilliant mind for original theories about capitalist economics. Obviously these were not a combination to make for an easy career, and an easy career he had not. In the 1930s he resigned his academic position in Warsaw in protest against actions of a reactionary government; in the 1950s, in New York, he resigned from a senior position in the United

THE POLES

How remarkable are the Polish people. Having no natural boundaries, their territory has been cyclically pushed, pulled, squeezed and expanded, following chronic aggression from West and East. Apart from their own short but heroic stand against the Nazis in 1939, and their more remarkable and tragically premature uprising against them (possibly treasonably encouraged by the Soviets) in 1945, they just happened to contribute materially to the outcome of WWII in two extremely important ways: they acquired a German cypher machine, did important work on it, and gave the results, and the machine, to the Alllies, thus laying the foundation of the subsequent intelligence operation that many believe to have been crucial; and their escaped fighter pilots were exceptionally skilled and courageous in the Battle of Britain, a battle in which every element counted. Finally on the political front, they were the nation who set the ball rolling for the process of democratization throughout Eastern Europe. In addition they gave us Chopin, Paderiewsky and many other great names in art, literature and science. In economics, before the iron curtain came down, they gave us Oscar Lange and Michal Kalecki. Ironically both of them were convinced socialists and died, in Poland, under Stalinist Communism, unhappy.

Nations Secretariat in protest against Senator McCarthy, and finally in the late 1960s, shortly before his death in 1970, back in Poland, he yet again resigned, this time in protest against the acts of a Communist government including a revival of academic anti-semitism.

As a jew, Kalecki survived World War II because its outbreak found him in England. He had been working in the field we now call macroeconomics since the late 1920s and had already gained a minor international reputation, although he had difficulty, not just linguistic, in making himself understood. At the beginning of 1936, the year of the publication of the *General Theory*, he had travelled on a Rockfeller Fellowship to Stockholm in order to work with the famous Swedish economists (who in the event found him aloof) and while still in Sweden received a copy of the *General Theory* hot from the press in London. He dashed off a review for the Economic Journal of Poland before proceeding on the next stage of his academic odyssey at the London School of Economics. The review appeared in Polish in Warsaw before the end of the year (those were the days), and at the LSE, this somewhat difficult person speaking broken English made himself felt as a person who understood Keynes's brand new theory very well indeed. This produced mixed reactions at an institution where, even to this day, the theory is not always fully understood. Kalecki proceeded to Cambridge where he met Joan Robinson, who thought he was fantastic. In due course, as the money ran out, Joan persuaded Keynes to find a small job for "my Pole", as she called him. Keynes's own reactions also seem to have been "mixed", partly it may be suspected for personal reasons and partly because it was increasingly emerging that in a series of publications between 1933 and 1936[1] Kalecki had been creating a body of theory of how the capitalist system works that had, to say the least, a very considerable affinity to the *General Theory*. In the author's opinion, in the history of economic thought, Kalecki's place is not a real rival to Keynes's, if only because, among a number of reasons, it is so often distracted by overt or hidden Marxian preoccupations: we recognize, however, that a different view (namely that Kalecki effectively anticipated Keynes) is perfectly tenable, although Kalecki never claimed that himself. In any event it is now clear that, because he was already accustomed to the macroeconomic way of thinking, he understood the *General Theory*, instantly, through and through, and more quickly and more thoroughly even than any other of its earliest and most perceptive reviewers.

All kinds of people had trouble with the *General Theory* in those days. The story is told that the venerable *Economist* newspaper sent it for review to Austin Robinson, Joan Robinson's spouse, later Professor of Economics at Cambridge and first President of the International Economic Association. "EAG" wrote a favourable review

---

1 Over his lifetime Kalecki published voluminously and in diverse places. In the 1930s much was in Polish, some in English, some in French. At different times he published essay collections with a varying coverage of his previous works. Bibliographers have not had an easy time, and those who rely on the essay collections have sometimes been trapped into ignoring things that at the time in question Kalecki did not wish to emphasize. One of the most effective bibliographical surveys, emphasizing the development of Kalecki's thought, is the one found in Targetti and Kinda-Haas (1982) op cit, where the complex web of publications on the 1930s is untangled. The claim that this work constitutes a macroeconomic theory of capitalism is theirs. In the reference list in the present book we have cited only the two Kalecki papers which are essential to our argument, i.e. the review of 1936 and the distribution paper of 1939.

preceded by some moderate criticism. Although *Economist* reviews were traditionally unsigned, it was agreed that this one should be signed, lest the public imagine that the paper agreed with the reviewer's opinion. However, when the piece, duly signed, appeared, the main favourable passages had apparently been cut out. Austin apologized to Keynes, explaining what had happened, who replied, "If you must write for the Yellow Press,[1] what do you expect?"

Kalecki had no such difficulties. The first words of his review read, "Mr. Keynes's book is, without any doubt, a turning point in the history of economics". Our theme here is that Kalecki understood especially well a crucial aspect of the subject, namely the problem of microfoundations. He did not need to devote much space to the revolutionary macro equations. He understood them already and almost took them as read.

Kalecki in recent times has become something of cult figure —conferences, books etc. The cult particularly concerns a large body of his opus, especially that with a Marxian flavour, that is not here our main concern. As one of his modern followers has well put it, Keynes was trying to make capitalism work; Kalecki, like Marx, trying to prove it can't. What he would have thought about world events since 1985 is a fruitless speculation. Our concern with Kalecki is more narrowly confined to the elements in his work that tend to show how the microfoundations of the *General Theory* ought to have been presented, right from the beginning. This remarkable perception was subsequently, however, largely suppressed by Kalecki himself and by the majority of his revivalists.

After intermingling with the great brains of Cambridge economics, not only Joan Robinson but also Sraffa, etc, Kalecki proceeded to Oxford, where during 1940 he had a job at the economics institute, and is reported to have maintained a discussion group of "radical" colleagues (what did they think of the Nazi-Soviet Pact of 1939, which

1 In those days in England, down-market newspapers were printed on cheap paper which turned yellow, so were collectively known as the "yellow" press. The present author is fond of this story. He likes to be in good company. *The Economist* did him a similar honour in an anonymous review which savaged "Managerial Capitalism" (1964b).

secretly carved up Poland?) In due course he went to Canada, then after the War became head of the World Economic Survey section of the United Nations secretariat, finally returning to his home country in 1955 to serve, controversially, under the Stalinist establishment. During his travels he published a wealth of rich work in English, including a remarkable paper in *Econometrica* in 1938. But that is less than half the story. The truly dramatic script lay buried, almost literally in the ruins of Warsaw, in the 1936 review of the *General Theory* which Kalecki never re-published in English, and rarely later discussed.[1] He also systematically de-emphasized his 1938 paper; and so, partly in consequence and partly for other reasons, most later students and re-publishers of Kalecki have either ignored or played down this aspect of his work.

Slightly over forty years later, the truth emerged as a result of a remarkable initiative by Dr Geoffrey Harcourt, Australian citizen, today President of Jesus College Cambridge, one of the world's leading scholars of "post-Keynesian" economic thought. During the course of his duties he became first the PhD supervisor and then the close friend of Ferdinando Targetti (now Professor Ordinarius of Economics at the University of Trento,[2] and recent author of a widely acclaimed edition of the works of Nicholas Kaldor), who was affianced to an extremely talented and extremely beautiful Polish economics graduate student, Dr "Bogna" Kinda-Haas. Knowing of the existence, but not all the content, of the Kalecki review, Harcourt suggested they jointly translate and edit it for publication in *Australian Economic Papers*. This was done and published in 1982, Professor's Targetti adding a valuable analysis of Kalecki's contribution to "Keynesian" economics. In the history of thought, it should have been a bombshell, but was not. The present author never saw the paper until 1988, when, during a visit to Trento, while strolling through the main piazza, an argument developed on the extent of Kalecki's

1 See Kalecki (1936, 1938).

2 The town in north-east Italy, which was the seat of the Council of Trent (1545-63), whose final failure to reconcile Protestants and Catholics sealed, as every schoolboy used to know, relative rates of economic growth of the nations of Europe (and, for that matter, of North and South America), for the next 500 years.

THE AMAZING DIAGRAM FIGURE 5.1

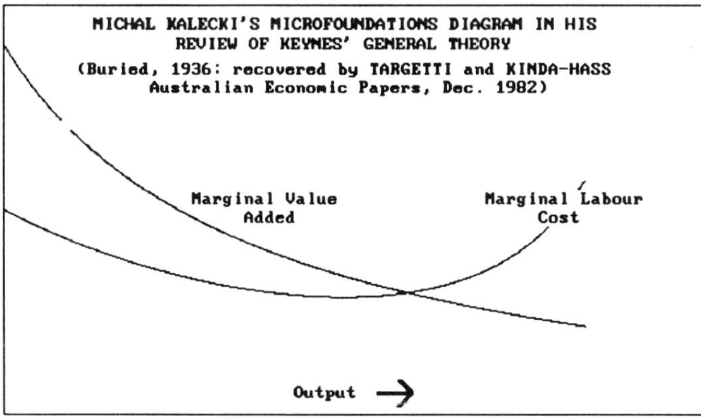

contribution. At a certain point Prof. Targetti ran back to his office, returning with an off-print. Reading as he walked, the present author's eyes fell on Kalecki's first diagram, and he nearly fell into Trento's celebrated baroque fountain.

The diagram is reproduced here as *Figure 5.1*. It is at least as interesting as any of the well known diagrams interpreting Keynes that appeared in the following decade. "Yet nobody knew it was there". In modern language, the diagram represents Kalecki's interpretation of the microfoundations of Keynes. It is totally based on imperfect competition, and uses the modern technique of presenting microeconomic curves blown up to macroeconomic scale. The marginal "value-added" curve is the marginal revenue curve of any firm, given (as we would now say) the conjecture that other firms' prices are constant, blown up to macro scale. Abstracting from all other prime costs, the marginal labour cost curve is the marginal cost curve, and is similarly blown up. The intersection of the two curves is a representation of profit-maximization, given the conjecture, and therefore corresponds in modern terminology to the large-group Nash strategic equilibrium.[1]

1 In the 1936 diagram, Kalecki does not specify iso-elasticity of the demand curve and implies a neo-classical opph curve. But in his 1938 paper he abandoned the

In the labour market, workers are price takers at a given nominal wage. For convenience assume the given wage is equal to one. Then at the point of intersection of the two curves, price on the vertical axis, expressed in "wage units" is the reciprocal of the real wage that must exist in the strategic equilibrium.

On scaling up from micro to macro the diagram neatly reconciles with macro aggregates and, in passing, sets the distribution of income! The area under the marginal revenue curve to the left of the intersection is nominal GDP, the corresponding area under the cost curve, aggregate nominal wages; the residual area is profit. But the figure does not actually tell us why the marginal revenue curve is where it is. It is in fact located by the Keynesian theory of macro income determination, which is not shown.

5.2 The theory that might have been

Had Kalecki proceeded, as he might well have done, to combine his own constructions of 1936 and 1938 with the type of theoretical and diagramatic treatment of the macro theory, that was already, between those two dates, becoming quite well known, how might the result have looked?

In *Figure 5.2*, we make our own attempt at an answer, a Kalecki diagram that might have been. The upper half of Figure 5.2 is micro, the lower "old-fashioned" Keynesian macro. The upper sector represents the condition for microeconomic stationarity, the lower sector the corresponding macro condition. The lower sector is the macroeconomic model, the upper its microfoundations. For stationarity the solutions in both halves of the diagram must coincide in the horizontal plane. The micro demand curves are a family of equations $\log q = E.(\log K - \log p)$ where q is micro quantity, p micro price, E elasticity of demand and K an income effect which will vary with the horizontal location of the Keynesian cross in the lower sector of the diagram. To map between the two sectors we require two steps, first a scale factor and second a connection between the locations of the micro demand curves on the one hand and the

---

neo-classical curve and made a strong case for, and used, the empirical curve.

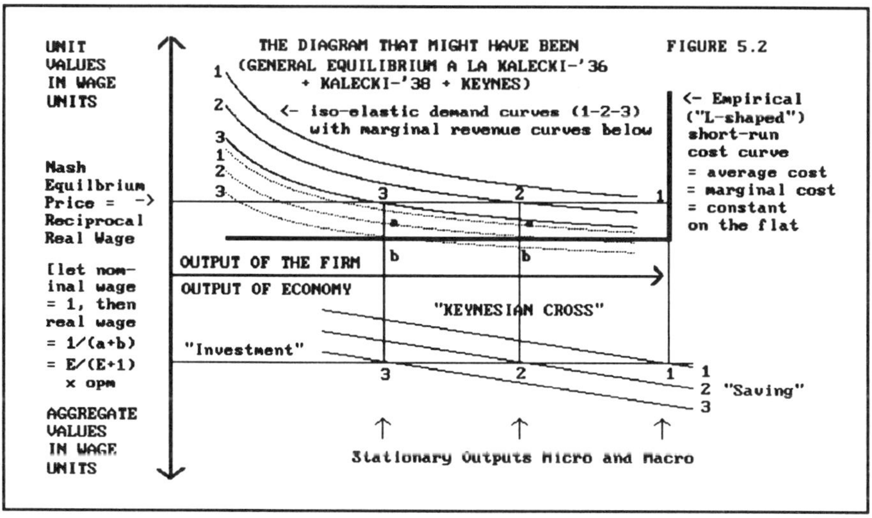

intersection of the Keynesian cross on the other. The first step is accomplished by assuming a fixed-structure economy with a constant number of quasi firms (i.e. no entry), the second by assuming that shifts in the Keynesian cross, e.g outward (3-2-1) due to e.g. downward variation in the propensity to save (1-2-3) materialize as income effects on the scale factor, *K*, in the micro demand curve, shifting it outward horizontally (3-2-1), producing successively higher micro equilibria (3-2-1).

What about wages? As the diagram is in wage units, nominal wages cannot affect it. Because we have assumed the completely flat version of the empirical opph curve, the real wage is invariant to changes in output and the demand for labour.

What about inflation? If effective demand rises (Keynesian cross for some reason moves to right), the path of stationarity, after passing through points of constant real price and real wage (nominal wages and prices could be doing anything, Phillips could be rampant, stagflation always possible) and then passes to the right of the vertical arm of the inverted L, everything changes: an inflationary process would set in with many possible scenarios. But, unless there is either a real-balance effect from the rise in nominal prices producing in the lower diagram either higher interest rates and lower investment, or higher consumption and a lower slope of the savings, or similar results due to the shift to profit, there is no dampening of effective demand and so, despite the rise in prices, real effective demand remains fixed at the intersection of the Keynesian cross (which has not moved) to the right of full employment. So the goods market does not clear at the new prices, and all kinds of things may happen, including indexing of nominal wages. The situation will continue until something, be it a distribution effect or a monetary effect, changes the lower-half diagram in real terms.

It is not an exaggeration to claim that Figure 5.2 presents the truly appropriate microfoundations for the *General Theory*, which are not, as we have seen, to be found in the book itself. But we have already remarked that after the 1938 paper Kalecki did not pursue the subject, so depriving himself of the opportunity to marry this paper with his 1936 review to produce something like Figure 5.2. Although it is not exactly material to the main theme of the present book, it is worth asking whether his decision was based on a conscious judgement that the implied theoretical line was a bad one. The answer, almost certainly, is partly yes and partly no. We do know that Kalecki was much impressed by a burgeoning literature on oligopoly and the effects of new entry into competition: Figure 5.2, as already mentioned, has a fixed number of firms. He increasingly argued that the capitalist competitive process was too complex, too uncertain and too indeterminate to model rigorously. Therefore it would be more scientific, rather than less, he implied, simply to assume that an average mark-up existed and was partially stable, without asking too many questions. In fact, in his later work,[1] he seemed virtually to define the profit mark-up as "the degree of monopoly"; a misleading and confusing usage, the formula is a theorem, not a definition. Nevertheless, Kalecki's argument at the time, and to some extent still today, seems strong. The case against it, however, is that either one must accept it and abandon the quest for rigorous microfoundations of macroeconomics altogether (in which case, as we have seen, in the long run one is in danger of being driven from the superstructure as well) or one ends up, as Kalecki did, with a virtually tautological formulation which is, to say the least, difficult to defend.

It is possible, however, that there were deeper reasons, of which the foregoing argument was to some extent a rationalization. In the

---

1 See Kalecki (1970-72), Sawyer (1985) and Osiatynski (1990).

author's opinion, the real explanation was political. It seems that Kalecki thought that to rationalize the working of the capitalist system from parameters of the consumer market (such as elasticity of demand) was somehow un-Marxist: it is certainly at odds with Marxian ideas of value.

Sublimated political ideology devastates the progress of our science. Kalecki's example, though a sharp one, and a "left-wing" one, must be compared with some of the things that have happened on the "other side". For example, surely we can now see that, most especially in the field of microfoundations, the "competitive revival" that seemed to almost take over our profession between 1960 and 1980 had similar adverse consequences.

5.3 The intervening years

As this is not a textbook, it is not appropriate to discuss in detail subsequent literature that, however important, per se, it may be, is tangential to our theme. But it is desirable to deal with three specific topics that arose between 1937 and 1980, namely "neo-classical Keynesianism", mark-up pricing and the Phillips curve and theories of distribution and growth.

5.3.1 "Neo-classical" Keynes

This sub-section heading is derived from the title of Sir John Hicks' celebrated review of the *General Theory* in 1937, "Mr. Keynes and the Classics",[1] wherein he invented "IS-LM", a construction which "true" Keynesians are said to be supposed to dislike. During the author's series of tutorials in 1946/7, Kahn never assigned the Hicks' article, and in the 1947 Cambridge Economics Finals no question required knowledge of it. In fact I never learned of IS-LM at all until after I had returned to Cambridge in the 1950s and already taught there for a while! The construction seems to me logically impeccable, but not profound, and only to be "disliked" perhaps for its potential propaganda qualities in favour of regarding the supply of money as of dominating importance. In my view "IS-LM" does no more, and no less, than extend the Keynesian theory in one of numerous directions that one may go to build a practical model.

1 As per, of course, Hicks (1937).

Figure 5.2, for example, can happily be converted, by anyone who so desires, into IS-LM format. The downward left-hand arm of the diagram could represent the real rate of interest, the lower sector would contain an IS curve (investment varies with interest, so every interest rate determines a Keynesian cross; IS is the path of these points), and an LM curve (given real balances, every real-income level creates a demand for real transactions balances which must be squeezed out of passive balances). The intersection of the two curves becomes the reconstructed Keynesian cross and the rest of the diagram is unchanged. Of course, the savings function is still there, hidden behind the reduced form which is the IS curve. The LM curve is a very reduced form indeed, behind which lies a large part of the theory of money, demand, supply and "market" clearing.

5.3.2 Mark-up and Phillips

The idea that, in practice, under conditions of pervasive oligopolistic uncertainty, firms set prices by means of a conventional *mark-up* on prime cost, emerged in the University of Oxford, at the end of World War II from one of the few occasions in the history of our science when business-persons were actually asked what they did (a major exception is found in the book *Pricing in Big Business* by Lanzillotti et al in the late 1950s:[1] the authors of the study were Robert Hall and Charles Hitch, and, apart from an excellent report, they threw in the theory of the "kinky" demand curve already discussed in Chapter 3 (sub-section 3.3.2).[2] Simultaneously on the other side of the Atlantic Paul Sweezy[3] made the same discovery.

William Phillips was a semi-genius New Zealand farmer's boy who did many things in economics, mostly at the London School, including inventing and measuring the Phillips curve, and was plucked from the profession by a heart attack in his middle fifties that killed him not long after: his premature death may have been partly the result of his experiences as a prisoner of war of Japan in World War II.

---

1 Lanzillotti et al (1958).

2 Hall and Hitch (1939).

3 Sweezy (1939).

"Mark" (up) and "Phillips" are closely connected in the post-Keynes history of Keynesianism.[1] We have seen that with iso-elasticity and profit maximization a constant mark-up is not an assumption but a theorem. With it, Keynes works, smoothly and rigorously. But in the 30 years after World War II, because Kalecki had hidden his marbles, and no-one else around (the present author included) had the wit to find them, all were at a disadvantage. We needed not only the general idea of mark-up pricing, but a theory to make it robust. The fundamental Keynesian microfoundations conundrum, "Why do changes in nominal demand go to quantities?" became the question, "Why does the mark-up stand up? Why may not changes in nominal demand, rather than going to quantities, go (as it were) to the mark-up?".

In such debate, the absence of a construction like Figure 5.2 is crippling. In Figure 5.2 we know why the mark-up is stable, and why demand-changes go to quantities: it is because that is the profit-maximizing thing to happen. It is no answer to say one "doesn't believe" in profit maximization. Apart from the fact that that answer is "non-available" to all who see themselves as "neo-classical" Keynesians, it is also non-available to persons, such as the present author, who as already seen in Chapter 2 has otherwise very great sympathy with the general philosophy of "bounded" rationality and the practical difficulty of maximizing. For where does the underlying

1 For an excellent synthetic treatment at the intermediate text-book level, the reader is recommended the book of Stephano Zamagni (1984, Ch 12). To the author's knowledge this is the only book in the world that at this level effectively explains and integrates the history of thought, methodology and philosophy of economics, the theory of price, utility, demand and supply, production, the firm and its growth, imperfect competition, income distribution, general equilibrium and welfare economics. The Italian edition was properly titled *Political Economy*; the English publishers' in their wisdom changed this to *Microeconomic Theory*, thereby probably adversely affecting the market. They may have feared that the original title would have tarred the book with the brushes of those who have appropriated "Political Economy" for radicalism. But in the result the prospective buyer, in being led away from the expectation of a neo-Marxian tract, is led towards the quite false expectation of a neo-classical one, and the richness of the book is lost. Such is the state of our "discipline" that it is possible that no solution to the kind of dilemma faced by Prof. Zamagni's publishers exists.

level of the mark-up come from? Answer, we do not know. Ours is not to reason why, we only estimate.

Turning now to the Phillips curve, because this topic may well be more familiar to some readers of the book than it is to the author, the length of this section will be inversely related to the importance of the subject in the history of applied and theoretical economics. The references are also selective, being confined to a single paper each by Phillips (1958), Lipsey (1960), Hines (1962) and Phelps (1968). As a result of the empirical research of the first three names, it was established that the rate of change of nominal wages may be significantly influenced by the level and/or rate of change of unemployment, by the recent rate of change of the consumer price index, and by proxies for the level of trade union militancy (this being the special contribution of Albert Hines). To a person who has the imperfectly competitive interpretation of Keynes, and of macroeconomics in general, i.e. the interpretation of Kalecki-'36 and the one propounded in the present book, "Phillips and all that" seems simple. As real aggregate demand rises, profit-maximizing firms desire to increase their output but not necessarily their prices. Individual labour suppliers or their "agents" (union leaders) correctly perceive an increase in the demand for that which they sell, i.e. labour. An individual who is behaving like a monopolist of her or his own labour (à la Blanchard and Kiyotaki, see below) or a union representing them (à la Oliver Hart, see below) does not react to such an experience like a profit-maximizing employer-producer. She, he or the agent-union, according to economic theory, will have a rising "cost curve" in the form of increased disutility of work, which must be compensated. Alternatively, if there is large-scale open unemployment, in a structured economy with a heterogeneous labour market, there will be a part of the economy (the smaller part) where there is still some excess labour demand: there always is. Hence, for one reason or another, if the pressure of demand in the labour market rises, the aspired real wage rises, pushing up nominal wages actually paid. Then profit-maximizing firms raise prices, wages are indexed, and we have the spiral. A similar interpretation is obtained, and was widely applied in the 1960s, using any of the non-profit-maximizing interpretations of mark-up pricing, as just discussed. The story told in the labour market can also be readily adapted to take account of wage bargaining. An increase in demand pressure patently increases the bargaining power of labour. In a bargaining theory other factors will also be important, for example the trend growth of productivity (makes unions demand more, employers more willing to pay).

Neo-classical economists, including "neo-classical Keynesians" have a more difficult time with the subject. Some of those who had this experience became extremely distinguished: your author has in mind his friend Ned Phelps. Anyone who has a theory that a rise in the aspired real wage, without intervention of any real-balance effect from associated nominal-wage movements, will directly cause a decline in the macro demand for labour, and vice versa, becomes worried as to how it can be that we see the Phillips correlations at all: when wages fall, for example, the demand for labour should rise, so the unemployment that is the causal factor in the Phillips relationship should never have had time to occur. Dynamic stories then appear necessary. They are not. Because its initial premise (that there is direct line of causation from macro wages to macro employment, without real-balance effect) is false, the problem is illusory.

In the late 1960s, under the influence of the world events described in the Introduction, in every OECD country the Phillips curves experienced persistent structural shift.[1] The constant (rate of change of nominal wages with constant consumer prices and minimum unemployment) began to increase; more significantly, the lag on prices became shorter and shorter. We shall see in the later analysis of the policy conclusions of Imp-Mac, that this is a particularly crippling development for the effective management of the mixed economy, essentially destabilizing. How it happened is quite obvious. Under the inflationary shocks of the time, people were learning.

This "creep" of the equations produced most "creepy" effects in scatter diagrams, loops, whirls, "vertical curves" and the like. Consequently the "curve" became somewhat discredited in applied work, but in more recent years has been generally rehabilitated in a form which has a simpler and more direct interpretation than the original form. Given that we are speaking of an aspired real wage manifesting itself through an indexed nominal wage, the most direct specification must be an equation in which the level of nominal wages

1 Marris R. (1979) and Alogoskoufis and Smith (1989).

appears on the left hand side, a measure of demand pressure and the lagged level of consumer prices on the right hand side. Divide both sides by the price level and in steady state this says that aspired real wages (not the same thing as achieved real wages, but, in steady state, converging to same) tend to rise with the pressure of demand.

Most of the econometric models around the world nowadays have a wage equation of this kind, the main source of differences being the left hand side variable which proxies demand pressure. Sometimes it is a measure not of direct pressure on the labour market, but of capacity utilization. As already indicated in Chapter 1, the Imp-Mac model follows the "modern" interpretation, albeit with a considerable range of user choice.

The foregoing can be summed up as follows.

(i) There was a simple interpretation of the Phillips curve which goes easily with the "Kalecki-imp-comp" interpretation of Keynes: effective demand expands, profit-maximizing firms desire to raise output, but not necessarily prices, and desire more labour; pressure on the labour market raises nominal wages, which causes the firms now again to raise prices, etc.

(ii) The modern interpretation, implicit in econometric models and optionally implicit in the Imp-Mac model, is that "real" pressure in the labour market pushes up the aspired real wage, a result which is expressed in upward pressure on the nominal wage, subsequently indexed. Given the indexing, the cleanest way to specify the story, and the one that is in fact used in modern econometric macro models and available in varying forms in the Imp-Mac model, writes,

$$W = a + lagged\ (b.P/P_o) + c.D$$

where W is absolute nominal wages, a constant with the dimensions of the measure of nominal wages, P/P_0 the price index and D a measure of demand.

5.3.3 *Distribution and growth*

This is another topic which has generated a large literature, some of which is relevant to the Imp-Mac model. It is theoretically a more amorphous field than the one discussed in the previous section. Less easily encapsulated, more easily dismissed. It begins with events in Cambridge in the 1950s. It is well known that from 1950 for nearly a quarter of a century Richard Kahn maintained a staff seminar, known as the Secret Seminar, in his rooms, meeting every Monday night in term time, admission by invitation only, from which it was quite an honour to be excluded. Qualifications for admission appeared to be brains and Keynesianism, but they could be traded off. A number of interesting visitors came in, Kenneth Arrow, Milton Friedman (before he invented monetarism), Robert Solow. Well-known excludees included Nobel Laureate James Buchanan (a visitor to Cambridge, but not invited to the seminar), M. J. Farrell, and Peter (now Lord) Bauer. The Secret Seminar saw first light on Joan Robinson's struggles with capital theory, including the moment - which for whatever its true importance in the history of theory has certainly created a literature - when Joan had a diagram on the blackboard and Ruth Cohen (stalwart of Cambridge Economics, member of a distinguished establishment family, subsequently Principal of Cambridge's leading womens' college, Newnham College) said there seemed to be a geometrical problem about it. Your author was present at that incident, and couldn't begin to understand what was going on. On another occasion, N. Kaldor appeared before the company with some equations which he said could form the basis for a theory for "turning Keynes upside down", i.e. making the distribution of income between wages and profits, via the mechanism of differential savings ratios, subservient to the need or assumption of full employment. On that evening he seemed to think he was missing an equation to solve the problem. Actually he was already over-determined. The late Harry Johnson and your author quickly helped him to sort that out, and for a while, in the stream of publications that resulted, received little footnotes of acknowledgement. More of the Kaldor theory shortly. Also at the Secret Seminar the present author first revealed the Economic Theory of Managerial Capitalism and Ruth Cohen again put her rather chalky finger on a very weak point. There was a theory of take-over from the point of view of the potentially acquired firm but little theory from the point of view of potentially acquiring firms, a possible means to growth. That chicken came home to roost 20 years later in the great take-over waves of the 1970s and 1980s.

Kaldor's theory, which will shortly be severely criticized, was originally to be explained in the following equation,

$$S = s_w(1\text{-}\sigma)Y + s_c\sigma Y = I$$

where S was national total savings, s_w workers' propensity to save σ the share of profits in the national income, Y the national income, s_c, the capitalists' propensity to save and I full employment investment. Given I, only one value of σ will satisfy it. Divide through by K, and we get only pure numbers. If we solve for σ, then on the right hand side we find the savings ratios, the capital output ratio and the growth rate. Now proceed to say that the growth rate must be Harrod's "natural" growth rate and we "know" the share of profits in the National Income "necessary" to avoid classical imbalance between growth rate of capital stock and growth rate of labour supply.

At this point another very important member of the Secret Seminar, Luigi Pasinetti (then a junior don, today Italy's most highly respected left-centre economist, current President of the Italian Economic Association, Professor at the Catholic University of Milan) steps in. He had previously been noticed only a few years earlier by the author when, visiting the UK on a cultural scholarship, he had begun to attend the Cambridge Economics graduate students' seminar, while also learning English. One day, in that seminar, Joan Robinson and "Sig" Prais, then a young Assistant Lecturer (today one of the UK's most elegant applied economists, Professor at the City of London University) were deadlocked in front of the students on the subject of yet again the so-called "Wicksell effect" in capital theory: they couldn't agree about its direction. From the back of the classroom came LP, and wrote a few lines of algebra on the blackboard, ending in a fraction. He said, "Mrs. Robinson is speaking about the denominator, Dr. Prais about the numerator of this fraction. So naturally they disagree".

Pasinetti gave a paper to the Secret Seminar pointing out that the Kaldor theory implied that "workers" were accumulating capital, and must therefore earn a return on same. If it be supposed they earned the same rate of return as the "capitalists", then, in order for the distribution of income between "workers" and "capitalists" to remain constant (if it was not the model was not in steady state), it was necessary to achieve a state of affairs where the rate of growth of the capital of the workers was equal to that of the capitalists; consequently both growth rates are equal to the national growth rate. Consequently in turn, the equation relating national growth rate to income distribution can be uniquely obtained from the corresponding equation relating to capitalists alone. Evidently, the growth rate of capitalist's capital is equal to their rate of return multiplied by their propensity to save. But the growth rate of capitalist's capital is also the national growth rate and their rate of return is also the national profit rate. Consequently, by substitution, we can state a relation of consistency in which the national growth rate equals the national profit rate multiplied by the capitalist's propensity to save. Alternatively, if the national growth rate is "given", the relation states that the national profit rate must equal the national growth rate divided by the capitalists's propensity to save: to support a given growth rate, a lower profit rate is necessary if capitalist's save well, and vice versa.

When published, in 1962, rather against the opposition of the then editors of the *Review of Economic Studies*, this paper caused an international sensation. Professor Pasinetti, as the references will show, has continued to expand on it and related themes ever since. As he was first the author's protégé, then his close colleague and always his warm friend, it is especially painful to have to explain his view of why the Kaldor theory, and hence the Pasinetti theory, has to be rejected for incorporation into the growth elements in the Imp-Mac model. Most people who have criticized the Pasinetti theory have been concerned about the nature of the equilibrium involved, and those who have criticized the Kaldor theory have attacked its less stringent requirements on grounds of uncertain causality. Your author makes no comment on those points, but is more concerned with two other, in his view devastating, points which he made (in print[1]) repeatedly at the time, and which, in his opinion have never been answered. Either one is extremely destructive. The first concerns the savings assumptions; the second concerns the microfoundations, or, to be blunt, as in Keynes, the lack of same.

It is known that households with different incomes do not have significantly different savings propensities, and there is no obvious reason why they should do. Kaldor, taxed with this, was wont to point out that profits were earned by companies, who were notorious for retaining higher profit shares than households would save from dividends. At this point he destroyed himself. He knew it (and put a lot of pressure on your author to lay off). Many others did not notice. The reason is that once one accepts the absolute reality of the modern corporation, and have incorporated that reality into one's theorizing, one must have a theory of the growth of the firm, and of the relation between that and the theory of corporate finance. In the absence, in the underlying Kaldor theory, of any well-specified causal chain, the Pasinetti equation can just as well be written the other way round. As such, in an economy with, say, a fixed number of firms, it must also be the equation of the rate of growth of the representative firm. Most likely, that growth rate will not be fixed by some outside natural rate, but will be endogenous to the growth efforts of firms, which in turn will at least influence, if not determine, the growth rate of the economy: this is the famous approach of Hiro Odagiri who designed the growth model for the Imp-Mac model. That being so, the retention ratio of the representative corporation will be determined by the directors of the corporation, endogenously, in the light of their growth aspirations, and traded off against financial-market constraints exercised by e.g shareholders or take-over raiders. But be that as it may, even without any endogeneity in the growth rate, the situation of the Kaldor theory remains hopeless. For it is quite impossible in theory, and equally impossible in the knowledge of real life, to imagine that the directors regard the corporate savings ratio as an exogenous constant, rather they know (and we know they know) that it something they must themselves decide.

1 Marris, R. (1964b, 1972). For an opposing outlook see Thirwall (1986, 1987).

On the question of microfoundations, Kaldor[1], not long before his death, criticized Keynes and Kahn for not having given the General Theory specific imperfectly competitive microfoundations. Unfortunately, he himself was the greatest culprit in such matters. In the 1930s,[2] he showed a deep understanding of the modelling problems of imperfect competition, but at no time in his life made significant contributions himself. In particular, as Keynes was said to have shown little interest in imperfect competition theory, so Kaldor showed little interest in formal oligopoly or game theory (despite the fact that when the latter first burst upon the world, Kaldor was not far beyond his fortieth birthday). Consequently, whenever he was taxed about the mechanism that ensured that the distribution of income between wages and profits always moved to ensure full employment, he resorted to casual hypothesizing.[3] Of course, he did not use arguments implying perfect competition. Rather he used to say, "Well, when demand rises towards capacity, it is natural to raise prices, that is, I mean to say, raise prices relative to wages".

Before considering this retort, it is desirable to remind ourselves of what is required to make the Kaldor-Pasinetti equation express a causal chain.

(i) The rate of utilization of existing capacity must be stable at approximately full employment, therefore, as capacity grows, it is necessary that income shall grow and total savings (leakages) shall grow so that the equality of saving and investment continues and the constant rate of utilization is thus sustained,

---

1 Kaldor (1983).

2 E.g. Kaldor (1934).

3 These remarks mostly refer to private correspondence with the author, when Kaldor was attempting (with some success, against better judgement) to tone down the criticism in Marris, R. (1972). The letters have not been kept, but the reader who wants to verify what is being said here can make the experiment of counting the number of words in the many thousands that Kaldor devoted to the topic of distribution and growth, which are devoted to microfoundations. She or he will find a ratio of about 1:100.

(ii) In order that, under (i) the long run growth rate of the capital stock be just sufficient to require a constant share of the available labour supply, the level of investment must at all times be such that the growth rate of the national capital stock is equal to the (exogenous) "natural" rate of growth, i.e. the sum of the (exogenous) demographic growth of labour supply and (exogenous) technical progress as reflected in opph,

(iii) Failure of condition (i) in a negative direction will create Keynesian unemployment, and of condition (ii) "classical" unemployment, the first of which also involves under utilization of the capital stock, the second of which does not. If therefore it is to be supposed that the required stabilities are to be maintained by a distribution mechanism, strictly, this mechanism must be of a kind that is activated by the appearance of unemployment of labour; a mechanism that is activated by under-employment of capacity will, however, act as proxy if we are concerned with deviations from equilibrium, as in equilibrium capital stock and labour supply must be in balance.

(iv) The adjustment mechanism must be an inherent, not merely "built-in" stabilizer;[1] in the event of a potential downward deviation from equilibrium, either the associated downward deviation in the profit margin must be so strong that the disturbance never occurs, or the margin must continue falling until there has been full cyclical recovery.

There are three types of theoretical route Kaldor might have considered, imperfect competition with flexible, i.e. counter-cyclical elasticity of demand, mark-up pricing theory or formal oligopoly theory. As regards the first, Kaldor never considered it and, as we have seen, both from the theoretical and empirical point of view, however interesting, it is far too weak a vessel to support the requirements stated at (iv). As regards the last, again Kaldor showed

---

1 For terminology, see Chapter 4, sub-section 4.2.1.

little interest, and, in the form originally stated by Labini,[1] it has no apparent cyclical implication. There would be a ray of hope from collusive oligopoly theory, however, if one could substantiate further the intuitive idea that collusive tendencies become stronger in the boom (unfortunately the theory of cooperative games, essentially the theory of bargaining over spoils among thieves, makes no such direct prediction), along the lines explored, in quite another context, by Joe Stiglitz.[2] It is perfectly possible that firms tend to collude more in the boom. But is also possible they do not, or at least do not always do so. In that case, pop goes the Kaldor theory!

In the middlde 1960s Kaldor had a very clever idea, known as the "neo-Pasinetti theorem" (Kaldor, 1966), much more typical of his older style, whose theoretical implications are of some relevance to the Imp-Mac model. This was based on taking (without, it has to be recorded, acknowledgement) a microeconomic concept originally invented by the present author, known as the "valuation ratio[3]" and applying it to macroeconomics. The valuation ratio of a corporation is the aggregate current market value of its issued shares, divided by the book value of the underlying assets. Starting from the Pasinetti interpretation of Kaldor, one may now more explicitly characterize the economy in question as a corporate economy, in which, by simplification, the only assets held by households are the shares in the firms. The "workers," capital becomes the households' capital, their portfolio, while the "capitalists," capital is the book value of the assets of the firms. Only if the average valuation ratio is unity are they equal. But so long as the valuation ratio remains constant, the Pasinetti condition that the two kinds of capital grow together is maintained. So a constant valuation ratio is a way of expressing the Pasinetti condition in a corporate economy. Let the firms grow at the natural rate, retaining just what is necessary for the purpose, and distributing the residual as dividends to households. Households now have two forms of income, and one might imagine that savings behaviour depended on the level of total income, its permanency,

1 See Chapter 3 above, ibid.

2 Stiglitz (1984).

3 Marris, R. (1964).

their sociology, etc. But Kaldor, in order to retain his battered distribution theory, insisted that for some unexplained sociological reason, the propensity to save from dividends would be different from the corresponding propensity from employment income. He also, and very correctly, assumed that as the economy accumulated capital, although the valuation ratio was constant, the amount of capital, earning power and dividend potential per shareholder household in the economy must be rising. In short there were continuous capital gains. These capital gains would be treated as income, and partially consumed. It is also required that the net savings of households be zero, for given that the firms are financing all the investment, household savings have nowhere to go (if they were net positive they would only push up the price of shares, violating the requirement of constant valuation ratio). It is therefore required that the savings of households from employment income and dividends, in total, just equal the consumption from capital gains. With given propensities this would happen only by coincidence. But with Kaldor's presumption of differential savings behaviour between wages and dividends, the saving from a given total income will vary with the distribution, between dividends and wages, of income. The latter in turn depends on the growth rate of the economy, which sets the financial needs of the firms, and their profit rate, which sets their financial supplies, the two factors thus determining the original available for distribution. Given the growth rate, the result depends on the profit rate. So, of course, here we are again. If we can postulate that there exists some mechanism for forcing the rate of profit to comply, we have a theory of profit. This idea was subsequently further, and misguidedly, in his opinion, pursued by another friend, and erstwhile student of the author, Adrian Wood.[1]

The good part of the Kaldor neo-Pasinetti theorem is the conceptual structure. The bad part is the implicit dependence on the type of adjustment mechanism that is destroyed, surely, by the arguments above.[2]

---

1 Wood (1975).

2 Luigi Pasinetti has seen this text, commented and suggested alterations. In substance the alterations have not been made. Instead we reproduce parts of his letter, paraphrased with as much fairness as we are capable.

5.3.4 The Odagiri solution

Operating on an entirely different plane of theoretical sophistication, Prof. Hiro Odagiri, who, as already mentioned, designed the growth model for the present work, published in 1981 his book *The Theory of Growth in a Corporate Economy.* This has a highly specific theory of the growth of the firm, making the growth rate of the firm and of the economy endogenous to the growth efforts of their managers, subject to various constraints including the constraint of the take-over threat. Price formation and distribution theory are neo-classical, so that the rate of profit is determined independently of distribution by means of a neo-classical long-run production function. The model is a full employment model, but unlike in the Kaldor theory, full employment is not an assumptions which also determines distribution.

The Odagiri model then does many things, which are not adequately detailed here, but inter alia it is married to an extended Pasinetti equation. Despite the independent determination of the rate of profit, the result as a whole is not overdetermined, because the growth rate itself has now become an endogenous variable. A long run Pasinetti equilibrium, with constant valuation ratio, is thus maintained. This short account still does less than justice to the book. As

---

> I think you are guilty of the Cambridge vice of arguding that colleagues' contentions are wrong and the really true and "Keynesian" point is the one *I* am going to present to you. (In the case of Kaldor, for example, rather than saying his choice of endogenous and exogenous variables was wrong, for which there is no support in your analysis, why do you not simply stress your own choice?) I am convinced that in future a resurgence of the theories of Keynes may come in a way that we may not even be able to imagine at present. The Cambridge vice makes resurgence more difficult. In the meantime I agree that Keynes failed to build microfoundations for his relationships, although he, with his pupils had the elements for doing so. But there is another line of economics, which consists of setting up macroeconomic relations that are true no matter what micro behaviour one may consider.

Let us agree to differ. The author believes that he has given his reasons for considering Kaldor to have been wrong, and that we cannot both have been right. He is also satisfied that there is no such thing as a macro relation that is true for any kind of macro behaviour. This book is concerned with the central Keynesian (not post-Keynesian) relation, namely the multiplier, and claims to show by reasoned argument that it works well on one kind of microfoundation and less well or not at all on others. If that is an example of vice, so be it!

will now be seen, the growth model designed by Prof. Odagiri for the Imp-Mac model, as already described in Chapter 1 above, represents a partial realization of his original scheme.

5.3.5 The disequilibrium school

We have already mentioned, and praised, the contribution of this school associated with the names of Barro, Benassy, Drèze, Grossman, Malinvaud, Muellbauer and Portes (see References). They also saw that the *General Theory* had a vital screw loose, but took a different instrument to it. They kept the static or structural aspects of the perfect competition paradigm but replaced the implied dynamics (or lack of same). What then made Keynes "work"? Answer, for one reason or another, prices and wages adjusted slowly in relation to quantities. Therefore given that agents were price takers, they would be adjusting quantities to prices which remained fixed for sufficiently long that the whole system behaved as a simple Keynesian model with "fixprice"; an engine for adjusting quantities. But, and it is a big but indeed, the effect of this approach is to make the whole Keynesian system one in which most markets, most of the time are not clearing. If one market is not clearing (e.g. households cannot sell the labour they have on offer, so employment is rationed), how does this affect behaviour in others? How do the mathematics of the whole anti-Walrasian situation work out? These turn out to be complex questions which Professor Malinvaud, in his original papers, addressed very elegantly.

The approach also reproaches the authors of the *General Theory* from another angle. Given that those authors did not specify imperfect competition, it would almost seem that they must have been implying some other kind of demand constraint, some kind of constraint on price movements, possibly dynamic. This leads inevitably to the analysis of disequilibrium states, which, however, Kahn and Keynes (more precisely, Keynes, copied by Kahn) disliked. In fact, when Professor Malinvaud was invited to give the Marshall Lectures in Cambridge (the annual distinguished visiting lectures), in the middle 1970s, Kahn was notably discomforted.

The theoretical work of the disequilibrium school was inevitably mainly concentrated on the macroeconomic implications of disequilibrium, rather than on what we here call microfoundations. Under imperfect competition, as is well known, the concept of market clearing takes on a different hue. A firm setting its own price will find itself not on its own demand curve only if there are special costs or inevitable time lags in making adjustments. In the Imp-Mac model, as already indicated, this happens. Firms adjust prices in turns, and in the meantime any resulting disequilibrium is taken up in movements of order books and stocks. These, however, do not have great behavioral significance, because when a person places an order, they pay money in advance, so there is no possibility of diverted expenditure, and the firms in turn place this money in a holding account, so there is no possibility of anticipated cash flow.

5.4 The imp-comp renaissance

As far as the author is aware nothing on the potentiality of imperfectly competitive microfoundations for Keynes, or for that matter of the imp-comp foundations of any macroeconomics, was published in the first forty years after Kalecki's for-Polish-eyes-only performance in 1936. Then, after 1975, came a series of developments which for various reasons are not easy to describe coherently. The significant work of the two distinguished Japanese scholars, described in the next subsection, was clearly Keynesian, and clearly "imp-comp". There followed, in the 1980s, a significant stream of literature (that is to say, a couple of books and a dozen articles) all of which was imp-comp but some of which, because in it, in one way or another, the labour market was forced to clear, was definitely non-Keynesian. Finally, at the end of the decade, there emerged the "New Keynesian" school that inevitably, but not always openly, implied imperfect competition. A bibliography is given in the box. Consequently the usual footnote references in the following text are omitted. The reader will notice that some titles speak of "Imperfect" and some of "Monopolistic" competition, the former being the term used by Joan Robinson, the latter by Chamberlin. While it is possible to argue that the original Robinson/Kahn and Chamberlin approaches were distinctive, it now seems that with the passage of time, any significance the different terms may once have held has faded. The choice of usage today seems mainly influenced by where the author graduated or was residing at the time of submitting his paper for publication. The general rule appears to be that some residents of Cambridge, Mass, where Chamberlin lived and died, use his term while most others do not. Consequently, in the potted bibliography given in the box, the fact that one title uses one term and another the other, gives the

BIBLIOGRAPHY OF IMP-COMP MICROFOUNDATIONS
(For publication details, see references)

1936 Kalecki review of the *General Theory*
1975 Nikaido, *Monopolistic Comp and Effective Demand*
1979 Negishi, *Microfoundations of Keynesian Macroeconomics*
1980 Ng, *Macroeconomics with Imperfect Competition*
1982 Benassy, "Developments in the Microfoundations of Macroeconomics"
1982 Hart, "A model of Imperfect Competition with Keynesian features"
1984 Snower, "Imperfect Competition and Crowding out"
1985 Layard and Nickell, "The causes of British Unemployment"
1985 Kiyotaki, "Macroeconomics of Monopolistic Competition"
1986 Benassy, *Macroeconomics: the neo-Walrasian approach*
1986 Ng, *Mesoeconomics*
1986 Solow, "Monopolistic Competition and the Multiplier"
1987 Blanchard and Kiyotaki, "The effects of Monopolistic Competition and Aggregate Demand"
1987 Dixon, "A model of Imperfect Competition with Walrasian features"
1988 Mankiw, "Imperfect Competition and the Keynesian Cross"
1989 Startz, "Imperfect Competition as a Foundation for Keynesian Macroeconomic Models"
1990 Startz, "Imperfect Competition and the New Keynesian Economics"

reader no clue to the type of imp-comp modelling, as discussed in Chapter 3 above, the paper in question employs.

5.4.1 Negishi and Nikaido

Professor Nikaido's book, published in 1975, was called *Monopolistic Competition and Effective Demand;* Professor Negishi's, published in 1979, *The Microfoundations of Keynesian Macroeconomics.* In our view Prof Nikaido, having started out in a very strong way, and much in the manner of Kalecki, with the representation of the Keynesian income effect in the micro demand curves, then seemed to lose his way in what looks like a Marxian form of macroeconomics. Professor Negishi employed the so-called "kinky" demand curve which we have discussed in Chapter 3 sub-section 3.3.4 above. It doesn't work in a competitive game, and therefore doesn't work in a large group heterogenous oligopoly. If it is a microfoundation for macroeconomics it must be in a chain of cooperating small-group heterogenous oligopolies. As a realistic description of the economy, it is good. But as a theoretical microfoundation, unless combined with a well-defined theory of entry, or other appropriate cooperative-game theoretical elements, for the reasons given in Chapter 3 (op cit) it continues to suffer from the difficulty that the location of the kink appears undetermined. Consequently, one cannot know whether the result is stable in a game theoretic-sense. Consequently, one cannot know whether it is a sound microfoundation.

At that time also, many economists approaching this field, Professor Negishi included, were concerned about the nature of the micro demand curve; was it "real" or only "perceived"? But, as we hope this whole book will demonstrate, in our view the distinction is unnecessary, at least at the conceptual level. Real-life firms have great difficulty in practice in estimating demand curves, because the conditions for controlled experiment do not exist. We, however, have no difficult in defining an objective conjectural demand curve which tells us, in principle, what will actually happen if this or that happens. Then, in the current fashion, we boldly assume that firms' estimates of this thing are unbiased.

5.4.2 The 1980s literature

As indicated, in the 1980s, things began to move more rigorously and more rapidly. Important and original movements of thought often have to start outside the great established institutions, and are then taken up, and then carried through vigorously. In 1980 Yew Kwang Ng published an article which effectively started the modern movement. But not being a resident of a town called Cambridge on either side of the Atlantic, and, if one has to be frank, possessing a certain profligacy in the presentation of equations, Y-K-N made less impact than his topic deserved. Within two years an extremely elegant contribution came from Cambridge England, by none other than Oliver Hart, of which we shall be seeing more shortly.

Very shortly, Oliver Hart was translated from a lowly position in East Anglia to a full Professorship at MIT. Over the next four years there came several more elegant contributions, from Oliver and others, not a few from MIT, which institution, having previously (almost) ignored the topic entirely, has now, as is the way of imperfect markets, acquired a partial monopoly of it. The result has several features, one of which is clarity and elegance, another is a tendency to try to avoid the "Keynesian" label even when it is appropriate. In alphabetical order the names are **Benassy, Blanchard, Dixon, Kiyotaki, Hart, Mankiw, Ng, Snower, Solow, Startz.** We now discuss them synoptically; the order and arrangement of the discussion signifies neither precedence nor valuation.

5.4.3 Benassy and Ng

These two scholars, who both came early on the scene, have more recently published comprehensive books. We cannot do justice to these books. Both are taxonomic, the former employing a representative-firm approach to the modelling problem, the later general-equilibrium mathematics. They are fine books, recommended for readers requiring full coverage of both Keynesian and non-Keynesian aspects of the general field. Benassy deals with the basic differences between Walrasian and non-Walrasian equilibria, the formal algebra of imp-comp equilibrium, and one topic not covered by any of the other contributors, namely the open economy. Ng has a particularly thorough treatment of the relations between cases with entry and cases without —with zero profits and without— and has an especially thorough treatment of the case where the economy has a certain degree of oligopolistic behaviour. He also has a penetrating study of the theoretical interactions between cyclical theory and entry theory.

5.4.4 Dixon and Mankiw

Dixon's paper, published in 1987, was called "A Simple Model of Imperfect Competition with Walrasian features", Mankiw's, published in 1988, was called "Imperfect Competition and the Keynesian Cross". Despite the differences implied in the titles, the two papers have a major common feature: they both assume a "Cournot" goods market as described in Chapter 3, subsection 3.1.3.

In Dixon's model the imp-comp picture is an original generalized version of Cournot quantity-setting oligopoly. Rather than three possible conjectures, there is a continuum, controlled by a user-selectable coefficient defined such that if one firm changes output by X, the others change by X multiplied by the coefficient. The coefficient ranges from -1 to +1. The result is a continuum of equilibria from joint profit maximization (coefficient = +1), through the strategic-equilibrium case ("hold") with the coefficient = 0, to Bertrand, with coefficient = -1. Despite what we have said about Cournot and quantity setting, we think this is neat. In respect of entry, Dixon assumes the "pre-commitment" game (see Chapter 3, long footnote in 3.3.1 above), thus avoiding the inevitability of co-operation. It is an interesting question whether one could not visualize a dynamic, capital-intensive economy as a succession of finite games of this type. If Dixon's coefficient is 0, and his group elasticity of demand is subject to our Chapter 3 "equivalence" assumption (see 3.1.3), at all times the profit-maximizing price/wage ratio is $NE/(NE\text{-}1)$, but under the equivalence assumption this becomes $e/(e\text{-}1)$ where e is the single-product elasticity if the same economy were modelled as a Sym-Het economy. Dixon assumes a free labour market with price taking on both sides. Any disequilibrium in the labour market therefore expresses itself in pressure on the nominal wage. Then he assumes a perfect Pigou effect, so the labour market always clears, and the economy finds an equilibrium in which the amount of "leisure" exceeds the socially optimal amount (because profits are too high and the real wage too low) in degree that increases with the profit margin, hence with the degree of collusion, hence with conjectural coefficient. Because a unique level of real balances is required for equilibrium, money is neutral. The originality and distinctiveness of Dixon, however, lies in his incorporation of explicit possibilities of oligopolistic collusion.

Mankiw, as already indicated, also assumes a Cournot structure, but models the oligopolistic process in less detail. This is the reason why he is bracketed with Dixon in the present discussion. On other grounds, however, his paper overlaps with Startz's, discussed below, which assumes a Sym-Het economy. Mankiw assumes that some kind of quantity-setting oligopoly game is played, leading to a profit margin which is fixed through the model. That is to say, the profit margin is a selectable parameter (once it is selected, of course, by implication, the real wage is endogenous). From here he deviates from Dixon quite considerably, because although there is public expenditure, the government always chooses to raise lump-sum taxes precisely equal to its expenditure (the so-called "government budget constraint") and furthermore, the household utility function does not permit of saving. There is, however, a "marginal propensity to consume", less than one, reflecting the fact that, faced with a potential increase in income, households will devote part of the gain to leisure.

In the absence of leakages or injections (all profits distributed to households, no household or government saving or dissaving) it is inevitable that any level of employment will generate just sufficient aggregate demand to buy the goods produced with it. These assumptions would lead one to expect a Say-like neutral equilibrium in which the labour market would not necessarily clear. Mankiw, however, makes the labour market clear by an apparently interesting route that is different from Dixon's but which gives the present author some difficulty. He argues that his implicit oligopolistic process will provide firms with a profit incentive to expand output so long as labour supply (determined by the real wage and the distributed profits) is forthcoming. Self-evidently, with a fixed profit margin, firms gain profit from expanding output, but the margin is the end-result, not an input, into the game of oligopoly. Firms may be playing collusively, but the concept of macroeconomic industrial collusion does not encompass a scenario where the nation's business leaders gather together and agree that if they simultaneously expanded output beyond their local conjectural optima, the result would be self-fulfilling. The usual name for that type of cure for "co-ordination failure" is "planning"! Another way of making the same point is that Dixon's 1987 model, which, as mentioned, has a more explicit oligopoly theory, does not obtain Mankiw's result.

The author nevertheless found Mankiw's paper, like Dixon's, elegant and succinct. This nice remark, of course, is a prelude to a nasty last word. The opposite of Keynesian is not Walrasian. To the present author, both Dixon and Mankiw seem to display insufficient appreciation of the fact that once any form of imperfect competition is introduced, Walras goes out of the window and cannot by any route climb back. With him goes, inter alia, the law of markets.

5.4.5 Blanchard and Kiyotaki

In this much praised paper, the goods market is Sym-Het, with large group imperfect competition, so that, whenever firms are profit maximizing. the ratio of price to wage, and hence the real wage is completely controlled by the Lerner formula. But they have a richly complex neo-classical-type production function, in which both capital and labour are specific to quasi firms, and most importantly, workers being heterogenous, if a single individual pushes up his or her relatively wage, substitution in production, for other workers, as well as small amounts of capital substitution, etc, will take place. In the labour market, every individual is a monopolist of their own specific labour. On account of the substitution effect, each faces a demand curve for their labour, and the entire labour market is modelled as monopolistic competition. Individuals perceive this, and attempt to adjust their real wage, and hence the amount of labour they do, until the marginal revenue from their wage-setting action is just sufficient to balance the marginal disutility of work. This is a micro adjustment process, operating on the nominal wage. With all workers doing this business and firms doing theirs (always substituting labour and setting goods prices for optimization) it is again necessary to bring in a strong Pigou effect actually to balance the labour required by firms for production, which is determined by aggregate demand, and the labour "offered" by workers at their optimizing positions on their perceived demand curves. As in the case of Dixon, the total effect makes money neutral (more precisely in the first part of their article; in the second part, which we do not discuss, there are adjustment costs for prices). To the present author's mind, it is the feature of each labour supplier being a monopolist of their own product that is most original and distinctive about B & K. It is a deep idea which does not depend for its interest on its practical realism for the everyday worker.

Figure 5.4 is inspired by an illuminating diagram given in the B & K paper. One may imagine some mechanism for determining aggregate demand in the manner of the lower half of Figure 5.2, where the mechanism was the Keynesian cross. In the authors' conception, it is real balances. The horizontal line is the real wage determined by the Lerner formula in the case of B & K, and the equivalent in the case of Dixon, and is horizontal because the present author has substituted the empirical cost curve. The strange line below, is intended to represent in the case of Dixon, a conventional supply curve of labour, based on the real wage, in a free labour market. It is not a true supply curve, but a path, because every level of aggregate demand and output determines a level of distributed profit which must affect the work/leisure choice. A point on the path states that if aggregate demand is at the level indicated in the horizontal plane, and firms are profit maximizing, then when households have received their profits and observed the real wage, this is the amount of labour they will supply. The same strange line can also serve for the rather subtle concept involved in B & K. At given aggregate demand, individuals perceive a point on the individual demand curve for their labour, a quantity demanded and the real wage as determined in the goods market. They then wish to optimize in the manner discussed. The "strange line" is the path of points where the real wage they would find optimum, and associated labour

THE REAL WAGE AND EQUILIBRIUM
(angles and scales exaggerated)

FIGURE 5.4

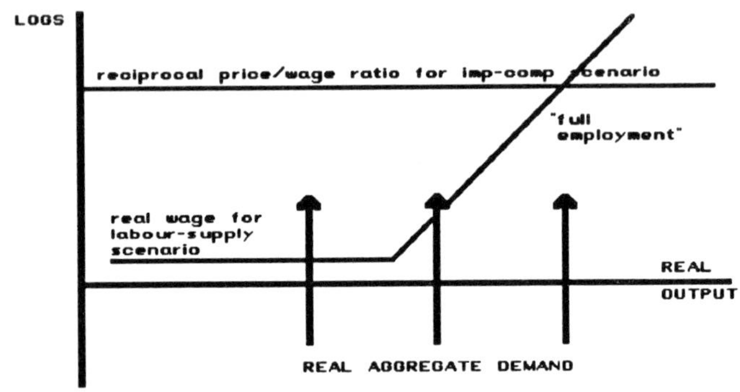

quantity, is consistent with the indicated macro aggregate demand.

In both Dixon and B & K the real wage consistent with the goods market scenario is at only one macro output equal to the real wage consistent with the labour market scenario. We have called this "full employment"; the authors would call it "equilibrium".

Without the Pigou effect there is no guarantee that the equilibrium will happen. In the Dixon case, if "labour market" real wage is below the "goods market" real wage, nominal wages will fall. Without a Pigou effect they will simply go on falling; the excess supply of labour will remain. This is the basic Keynesian story. In the B & K case something similar must be happening, the people are chasing after their optimizing positions; the excess supply is represented in an inability to reach them.

5.4.6 Hart

As B & K have a general system of large-group imperfect competition in both goods and labour markets, so Oliver Hart does something similar with Cournot. In the goods market he has the Cournot quantity-setting strategic equilibrium ("hold" conjecture). In the labour market however, he has unions, which restrain the quantity of labour supplied on the principle of maximizing the aggregate nominal wage of the union members: they perceive a demand curve for labour derived from the group demand curves for goods. There is a quasi real-balance effect[1], but not a full Pigou effect, because the union activity constrains the nominal wage. Consequently "money" is not neutral. Hart also permits the possibility of fiscal policy. Monetary policy or fiscal policy will expand aggregate demand, and unions will find it "profitable" to release more labour, until the total amount of labour employed is that amount which individuals voluntarily wish to supply given the real wage. Where does the latter come from? From the goods-market scenario. Hart, using Cournot, does not employ iso-elastic demand curves, so some of his results, mainly those concerning "Keynesian" expansion process, are a little difficult to interpret, but his great originality, apart from the generalization of Cournot (which of course your author does not like) is the modelling of unions.

5.4.7 Snower and Solow

Both these models have Sym-Het goods markets and both are distinguished by explicitly modelling entry. Solow's model is in two parts, long run and cyclical, the former being especially concerned with the excess-capacity theorem as discussed in Chapter 3 (sub-section 3.3.3) above. The cyclical model has a fixed number of firms making potentially positive profits, or alternatively surviving with

---

1 More precisely, there is a nonproduced good, changes in the price of which relative to the prices of produced goods, have, in the opinion of the present author, essentially Pigou-like effects in the Hart model. Oliver Hart, however, has written to say that he disagrees with the interpretation that the nonproduced good might as well be money, but if it is not, what is it? For the reader to make his own judgement, we give some quotes,

> ...(it is natural to think of the non-produced good as money, but such an interpretation may be misleading; see the remarks in Section VI)
> – *from Hart (1982) Section II.*
>
> ...what might correspond to the nonproduced good in reality[?] Possible candidates are land, old masters, etc. ...Another possible candidate is money. This is more complicated. In a static model there is no reason for agents to hold money. In a model with time, cash balances...might proxy future consumption. Note however that [we would be speaking about] real, not nominal balances.
> – *from Hart op cit Section VI.*

The question is, do we believe that macroeconomic fluctuations in a modern economy are driven by changes in the ratio of land to labour? Not, in the mind of the present author, an entirely rhetorical question, and not an uninteresting one, but also surely not, as Keynes would have said, a suitable question to answer mainly by means of the differential calculus.

"negative" profits through a depression. It has potentiality for both monetary and fiscal policy. It then deviates sharply from neutrality in respect of structural assumptions. Government goods are assumed to be sold with a lower demand elasticity than private goods, so that when government expenditure expands, average elasticity falls, and the profit-maximizing price/wage ratio rises, correspondingly the real wage falls. This is an interesting idea, but one could surely equally argue in the opposite direction. If government expenditure falls mainly on direct labour, for example, the whole effect will fall directly on the labour market. If government expenditure goes mainly to defence contractors, although they are frightful monopolists, the government is a monopsonist, and the outcome uncertain. No one doubts that defence contractors profits will go up, but must the military-industrial profit margin, negotiated between contractors and government, necessarily go up? Yes, it might, on the other hand it might not; so surely this is a secondary effect, more appropriate to an actual quantitative model?

Solow also assumes that in the short run profits are not distributed, and that losses are financed by borrowing. Consequently, the Keynesian multiplier is strongly affected by the profit mark-up and hence depends on elasticity of demand. Here again, numerous modellings are possible. In the Imp-Mac model the opposite occurs: in a non-growing economy all profits are distributed; in a growing economy distributed profits are a residual after private investment.

Snower has an excess-capacity entry submodel in which zero profits are maintained, by quick entry and exit of firms, at all times. As in Solow, firms face the same kind of imp-comp Sym-Het demand curves as found in the Imp-Mac and other models, but as in Solow, government expenditure is introduced into the system in such a way that when it increases, the profit-maximizing profit margin rises. In Snower's case, the reason for this is that, each firm receives an equal absolute share of government demand, which is represented as a linear addition to the firm's conjectural demand curve, in effect, as the present author understands, a "lump sum" element of zero price elasticity. Consequently, if government expenditure increases relatively to private expenditure, the conjectural elasticity of demand for the individual quasi firm's total output appears to decrease.

Snower then assumes that nominal wages are, in effect, indexed. An initial increase in nominal government expenditure therefore generates a wage-price spiral which eventually deflates the real economy either through government expenditure not being indexed or through a strong Pigou effect; in the end result, private consumption is reduced. The present author's comment on this "crowding out" conclusion is similar to his position on Solow. To him, the conclusion is not a theorem resulting from the introduction of imperfect competition but rather an artifact of particular detailed modelling assumptions that have no especial empirical support. For example, if the increase in government expenditure consisted of a proportional subsidy to personal consumption, as far as the author can see, the "Snower" price rise would not occur.

Another conclusion (of the author's) from these two models is that the entry assumptions make less difference to the general story than might have been expected. If Snower had assumed a fixed number of firms, but maintained the other assumptions listed above, he would, it seems, have reached the same or similar conclusions. Conversely, if he had omitted any one of those assumptions he would not have obtained his crowding out![1]

5.4.8 Startz

This paper[2] is discussed last because, in the opinion of the present author, its strongest feature is a particularly clear discussion of an aspect of all imp-comp macro models, namely "underemployment equilibrium". If and when the labour market clears, because the real wage is less than the marginal product of labour, and positive profits are distributed (making it possible for households to appear to be able to enjoy some consumption without doing any work) it clears at a socially sub-optimal level. Society is suffering the dreadful fate of

---

1 The author and Dennis Snower are close friends and colleagues. We have had written and oral discussions about his model, but have not reached agreement about its interpretation. Although the author is strongly convinced that the above discussion is correct, it is possible that he has yet misunderstood the implications of the Snower equations. Concerned readers are therefore referred to the published paper for purposes of judgement.

2 The reader is reminded of the special debt owed by the author to Richard Startz (see Acknowledgements).

enjoying an excessive[1] quantity of leisure. The question is, can fiscal policy or other demand-side shocks, change this equilibrium, e.g. improve it?

Unlike Mankiw's paper, Startz's assumes a Sym-Het, rather than a Cournot, economy, and therefore escapes the present author's already-stated general objections to Cournot as a microfoundation for macroeconomics. It is also distinguished by a particularly lucid verbal introduction which helps unravel the veil of maths.

> Consider a world of consumers who buy a good and sell their labour and firms who buy labour to produce the good. According to the traditional macroeconomic theory, a unit increase in autonomous demand results in a greater than unit increase in demand in final equilibrium. The usual reasoning is that increased demand by consumers causes firms to buy more labour and that the increased income allows consumers to buy more goods, and so forth so that a multiplier results. There is a simple fallacy in this argument when applied to a perfectly competitive world...... . Suppose that consumers increase demand by one unit, *which is to say that preferences change to increase goods' consumption by one unit and to reduce leisure by one over the wage rate*. The reason why the multiplier does not work in a perfectly competitive economy *with full employment* is that.....because the marginal rate of substitution and the marginal rate of transformation both equal the wage rate, the amount of added labour firms need to buy is exactly the extra amount consumers planned to sell...In contrast (under imp-comp] the equilibrium product price is "too high"; the consumers's *MRS* [marginal rate of substitution] is greater than society's *MRT* [marginal rate of transformation]. Suppose again that consumers increase goods' demand by one unit, reducing leisure demand by the consumer's *MRS*. The [firm] receives *MRS* units of leisure in payment, *MRT* of which is used to pay for production, and *MRS* - *MRT* of which is [distributed to households as

---

1 The excess may be defined as follows. Suppose every household has an identical pattern of preference ("utility function") between goods and leisure and was also equally endowed with skills etc. Suppose it was technically feasible (which patently it is not) to separate every household into an individual economy in such a way that it faced a perfect scaled-down copy of the production possibility frontier of the same macroeconomy: by magic, although labour is not divided, i.e. not specialised, the benefits of specialization are preserved. Therefore the households need not and do not trade. They simply do their own things and choose their places on the work/goods/leisure frontier. Having identical tastes, they all choose the same. The amount of work done at this choice, scaled up, is the macroeconomic socially optimal employment level. Lower employment implies socially excessive leisure.

profit.] .... This increased income causes them to increase their goods' demand so that .... there is a multiplier effect.

In a part of the quotation which has been condensed, Startz points out that if it were not for the distributed profits, consumers' utility would be constant. There is hence a plain implication that at the end of the day, it has increased. One is forced immediately to ask the question, how can we say anything about welfare when tastes have changed? Startz, as he develops his model, also obtains a balanced-budget multiplier. Both he, and Mankiw, decline to involve themselves deeply in the delicate question of the gain or loss to social welfare involved in transfers between government goods and consumer goods, so the welfare result remains ambiguous.[1] In good old "traditional" Keynesian economics, where depressions are caused by monetary imbalance between supply and demand, and in turn cause involuntary unemployment, few will disagree that if they happen, they create a clear and often massive welfare loss, often compounded in the future by loss of technical progress and growth. In Mankiw and Startz, we have fluctuations in output, but only ambiguously linked to fluctuations in welfare.

So how "truly" Keynesian are Mankiw's and Startz's contributions? There are, in effect, three types of macro-welfare situations of the modern economy.[2] Let **A** be the socially optimum employment level as defined in the footnote above, with the added condition that the government budget balances at a socially optimum level of government expenditure. Let **B** be the level of employment at which this same economy, with the same government expenditure, clears its labour market. We know this implies excessive leisure and hence

---

1 In a later working paper (Startz, 1990), Startz comes of the fence. He assumes that there is a socially optimal level of government expenditure, which is violated by the balanced-budget expansion. But the consequential loss of welfare due to excessive consumption of government goods is second order relative to the multiplier gain in production. Consequently, now (1991), Startz sees the fiscal expansion as unambiguously welfare expanding and hence his theory as that much more "Keynesian".

2 The theoretical microfoundations of the present discussion (the problem of "excessive" leisure in an imp-comp general equilibrium) has already been introduced in Chapter 3, subsection 3.2.2 above.

lower employment and output than at **A**. (We also know that the same level of government expenditure may no longer be socially optimal, but we let that pass.) Let **C** be the level of employment in a traditional Keynesian slump, with excess supply in the labour market, and hence smaller than **B**. Mankiw and Startz are bouncing around between **A** and **B**, traditional Keynesians, and (subject to its evasion of the question of what determines the labour supply) the Imp-Mac model, between **C** and **B**. To the extent that M and S bounce with positive feed back, that shocks go to quantities, and that, although the labour market always clears, this does not depend on an inherent stabilizer, they have some consistency with the concept of the essence of Keynes as discussed in the Introduction and the early part of Chapter 4, above. They deviate strongly, however, in that their shocks do not arise from changes in net injections to the circular flow of the medium of exchange. They also, it could be argued, deviate downwards in political relevance. We return to that question at the end of the next subsection.

5.4.9 Political economy of the 1980s imp-comp literature[1]

We conclude with some broader thoughts provoked by the preceding writers collectively. The paradox of Blanchard and Kiyotaki is that on the one hand it is perhaps the most patently unrealistic model of them all, since, being especially difficult to analyze out of equilibrium, it literally implies that we should actually observe a high degree of upward and downward nominal-wage flexibility, a large quantity of high-powered money as a store of wealth (to make real the Pigou effect) and a high degree of stability of employment. On the other hand, in contemporary times, the idea of conceiving every man and women monopolist of their own labour supply strikes a sympathetic chord. It seems to reconcile properly the micro sense that people do perceive a demand curve for their own labour, with the macro reality that a demand curve for labour as a whole does not exist. Why is this? The answer, I suggest, may be found in the evolution of the capitalist economy and in the way it is perceived. In the bad old days when Marx was writing, his picture of a homogenous, alienated, reserve army of industrial labour faced with a group of employers

11 Except "new" Keynesian, see below.

who may begin as small firms but end up, by the process of destructive competition, as oligopolists, was plausible. This gives us oligopoly in the goods market, perhaps somewhat homogenous, plus something like a "free" labour market, with both sides price takers. Industry is generally capital intensive. The real wage will depend inter alia on the degree of collusion, which is liable to go to a high level, but cannot go so high that the real wage is below subsistence. Tiptoeing past the question of stability, Pigou, etc (especially delicate if Pigou really was a secret Stalinist!), what have we here but the *Dixon model*, with coefficient = 1! But as we all know, the permanent immiseration of the proletariat did not occur, and Marx's predictions came to naught, because the workers were granted (rather than took) sufficient political and economic power that they could form unions and be represented in legislatures which passed laws tending to restrain extreme oligopolistic collusion in the goods market (in the US, at least, but Europe made up with stronger unions, etc). This looks like the *Hart model* (strategic equilibrium in goods market with Dixon coefficient = 0 plus unionized labour market).

So to what political economy does the B & K model belong? I suggest it is something that has sometimes been called the post-industrial society. Technical progress has been capital saving, equipment-type capital has become cheap and highly productive (computers), making humans highly productive, provided they acquire skills, which although not necessarily lengthy or extremely difficult to learn, require adaptability. At a given moment, we all (unfortunately, no, not all; 20-30% are left out) have certain skills, which are rather specific, and perceive a substitution demand curve for them. But we need to be flexible, however, in adapting them to the extremely rapid pace of technical change. What is clear, however, is at the end of the day, the labour market is not yet working, at least in Britain, according to the "predictions" of B & K. But maybe in some countries, e.g. the US, and in parts of Britain and Europe, it is, or is beginning to. We look for a Keynesian model with B & K microfoundations. The Imp-Mac model is not exactly that (it is too vague in the labour market) but it is consistent with it.

Finally there is the question of the post-industrial society in face of Mankiw and Startz. It is a not an unreasonable parody to describe their story as a cycle of migration between workstation and Jacuzzi. The venue is obviously southern California, and as is literally the case in not a few Californian households today, the migration does not require the "worker" to pass his or her front door. The present author does not intend to be purely rhetorical in asking how relevant this analysis is to events such as, for example, the world depression of 1980-85, or, for that matter, the one which may or may not be developing at the time these words are written. There are some intriguing questions. The utility of leisure is affected in a complex fashion (both competitive and complimentary) on the price and variety of available goods, but, in a realistic macro entry model (see Chapter 3, section 3.7) this factor is partly endogenous, raising a question over the uniqueness of the implied welfare optimum. Worse, the utility of leisure is evidently very much the product of a learning process, so results in this area are almost certainly path dependent.

5.5 The "new" Keynesians

What follows is essentially based on two papers, one by Robert Gordon, the other by Richard Startz (the latter's a later one than the one discussed above) both published late in 1990,[1] that came to the author's attention only a very short time before the present manuscript literally went to press. All the foregoing sections of this chapter had already been typeset and could not be significantly changed. Gregor Mankiw was also an early major and original contributor,[2] whose work strongly influences the surveys of Gordon and Startz. As the present book physically went to press, there was in fact announced for publication in mid-1991, a two-volume essay collection on new Keynesian economics edited by Gregor Mankiw and David Romer. This evidently prospectively important work is listed in our References but sadly, could not, of course, influence the present discussion. According to Gordon, the name "new" Keynesian was invented in the early 1980's but did not spread into general published use until after the turn of the decade. Needless to say, the present author, being British, did not read into the subject before he began work on the present project, also in the second half of the decade. Paul Samuelson is said to have described a vice of British economists as sitting down and trying to work something out for oneself because

1 Gordon (1990), Startz (1990).

2 Mankiw (1985).

this seems less effort than going to a library. The variation, in the present case, being that the library's competitor was the computer. The author is satisfied, however, (see below) that although there are major areas of overlap, the central ideas of the "new" Keynesians and of the Imp-Mac model are significantly different. He is equally sure that the strong empirical prologue to Gordon's paper represents a massive contribution to macroeconomic knowledge, new-Keynesian, old Keynesian, non-Keynesian, or whatever. Given this, and the fact that the paper was a *Journal of Economic Literature* survey, it will surely be widely read and need not be resurveyed here. What follows is essentially a comment.

As usual, there are significant problems of terminology, and as often we begin with a Latin qualifier. Gordon (second footnote, first page, of his article) distinguishes "new" from "neo", in the Keynesian context, by assigning "neo" to the so-called Samuelsonian neo-classical synthesis of "old" Keynesian economics. The reader who has followed the present book so far will know that this is unacceptable to its author, because he wishes to call his own work, which is inherently non neo-classical, neo-Keynesian. Gordon also concludes the same footnote with the statement, "...the word *new* rather than *neo* is used for recent work in the Keynesian tradition, so that it can be properly juxtaposed to the new classical approach." To the extent that this implies that all recent work in the Keynesian tradition belongs in the "new" tradition, we must equally beg to differ. Finally there is a difference between two brands of new Keynsian concept of price-stickiness, the first of which may be called "general" and the second "special" stickiness. The latter however is better known by the enticing name of "small menu costs".

5.5.1 "General" stickiness

The central feature of the "new" tradition, according to Gordon, is found in the role of "sticky" prices in the generation of macro output and employment fluctuations. Gordon, does not, however, define the term. He describes different kinds of stickiness but not stickiness in general. We gave our own definition, which we here repeat, in Chapter 4, "By a sticky price we understand a price which is externally constrained to change relatively slowly, although, in the absence of the constraint, a profit-maximizing firm would wish to change it relatively quickly." We should now add (the so-called "menu cost", see below) the case where there is a cost to changing the level of price rather than a constraint or cost related to the rate of change of price. The effect of our definition is to absolutely exclude from the concept of price stickiness the case where, in face of a change in nominal demand, without any rate-of-change or menu-cost constraints, a firm responds mainly by changing quantity, rather than price, because that is the profit-maximizing thing to do. As the reader should now well know, this case, the inevitable prediction of the Sym-Het economy with the empirical cost curve, is the paradigm case in this book. That is why we do not think the Imp-Mac model could be classified as new-Keynesian. But deep in his article, in a section discussing "monopoly", Gordon includes among his various categories of stickiness an interpretation of Blanchard and Kiyotaki (without menu costs) which is not those authors' own interpretation but rather the interpretation suggested by the present author in Figure 5.4 above: great minds do think alike. Figure 5.4 shows how B & K can be "neo-Keynesianized", and hence made consistent with our philosophy. Conversely, if the Court of economic terminology adjudicates that the new-Keynesian label properly includes this case, it has captured our paradigm. Naturally we appeal.

In our argument we emphasize that the question is not trivial. To stretch the scope of the adjective "sticky" in this way, apart from violating the language, creates a semantic fog. But at the end of the day it is not in fact clear whether Gordon sees himself as a "new "Keynesian or not. Some of his critical comments, when stripped to essentials, are severe, and some of his most firmly stated opinions are deeply sympathetic to our own outlook. One such passage has already been quoted in Chapter 1 (sub-section 1.2.4) above, and can here be reinforced with second, crucial, quotation,

> **Rational microeconomic agents care about the relation of their own price to their own costs, not to aggregate nominal demand. Unless a single agent believes that the actions of other agents will make its marginal costs mimic the behaviour of nominal demand with minimal lags, the aggregate price level cannot mimic nominal demand, and Keynesian fluctuations will result.**[1]

---

1 Gordon (1990) p 1139.

This is precisely the assumption of the Imp-Mac model. In it, the individual firm perceives his own quantity demanded as depending on its own nominal price and the nominal income of its customers, and, in the process of conjectural profit maximization, takes all other prices as constant. It is affected by macroeconomic price phenomena when, and only when, they work through wages. If we then look at Gordon's empirical/econometric classification of kinds of price stickiness, the Imp-Mac/Gordon parallel is further underlined.

Gordon breaks down general stickiness into an **inertia effect**, a **rate-of-change effect** and **hysteresis**, the latter being the opposite of the "level" effect. The inertia effect is simply serial correlation in prices, due, for example, to the indexing of wages. The rate-of-change effect (defined inversely) is a tendency for the current rate of change of prices not to follow ("mimic") the current change in nominal aggregate demand. The hysteresis effect is a tendency for the rate of change of prices to be insensitive to the current level of real demand: if nominal wages, à la Phillips, are sensitive to aggregate real demand, hysteresis is low.

The Imp-Mac model has **user-selectable inertia** in the form of user-selected wage indexing. It has **user-selectable rate-of-change effect**, working through the facility either to fix or to endogenize the elasticity of demand and to select the form and coefficient of the short-run opph curve. It has **user-selectable hysteresis**, or lack of same, via the two alternative wage models and the selection of the wage coefficient. Indeed the similarity between the adjustment processes embodied in these two research projects (Gordon's paper and the Imp-Mac model) carried out simultaneously, 3000 miles apart, without communication, is striking.

So is the alternative conclusion that Imp-Mac itself is, after all, "new-K-istic"? Not at all. In the Imp-Mac model, the user-selectable effects, which seem to parallel, as described, Robert Gordon's econometric categories, have essentially different implications. Unless the user, by not indexing government expenditure, introduces a strong real fiscal effect (thus imitating a strong Pigou effect), the user-selected effects influence the nature and course of inflation but *not* the behaviour of real output. This is the crucial difference lying at the heart of our assertion that the fundamental Keynesian theory has no need of the "stickiness" hypothesis. More precisely, this is our assertion unless and until we are suborned into calling a low rate-of-change effect due to simple profit maximization a form of "stickiness". The present author and the Imp-Mac model are not new-K; neither, in our assessment, is Robert Gordon. We are not "new" Keynesians but just good old Keynesians.

5.5.2 *"Special" stickiness: menu costs*

This is a very chic subject, whose fashionableness may partly be explained by seeing early life in a paper co-authored by George Akerlof,[1] a notoriously original mathematical economic theorist. The basic idea is a very simple one. Suppose a price-setting imp-comp firm faces, in addition to the usual demand and cost curves (for the sake of argument, an iso-elastic demand curve and the empirical cost curve), a special, lump sum cost, the co-called menu cost, triggered by any change in price from current price. Let the current price be profit maximizing. Let something happen to change the profit-maximizing price. Then it is perfectly possible that the loss of gross profit from not changing price is less than the menu cost. Ergo, when profit is defined net of menu cost, it is not, in fact, profitable to change price.

The smaller the elasticity of demand, for given menu cost, the more likely the result. With elasticity in the plausible range, the result is likely to occur even if the menu costs are "small" relatively to the dimensions of the problem. So prices are likely, on this account, to be sticky, and changes in nominal demand are likely to go to quantities. Hence, according to the theory, the explanation of fluctuations in aggregate output.

It is easy to agree that there are costs to changing prices, but there are nevertheless a number of economists, including, according to his article, Robert Gordon, who have difficulty in accepting that this theory has major practical explanatory power. One of Gordon's strongest criticisms is that there are also costs to quantity changes. The present author's difficulty, however, is of a different kind. For all the reasons discussed in the Introduction and ad nauseam through this book, a price-setting firm will not find that the price which (in the absence of menu costs) maximizes profits has changed simply because nominal demand has changed. Given Sym-Het and the empirical demand curve, the (without-menu-cost) profit-maximizing

---

1 Akerlof and Yellen (1985).

price changes only if either demand elasticity changes or nominal wages change. It is perfectly possible that the presence of actual menu costs could temporarily inhibit response to such events. The result will be temporary changes in the real wage and profits which could lead to indexing, inflation or all kinds of dynamical events. But in the meantime, if nominal demand changes, with or without elasticity change and with or without menu costs, the profit-maximizing quantity will change approximately in line with nominal demand, for the usual reasons. So the consequences of the menu-costs effect, interesting though they might be, will be, surely, secondary to the aggregate-output change that must occur in any case.

6 Technical Description of the Imp-Mac Programme

The essential purpose of the present chapter is to detail the technical specification of the Imp-Mac programme which has already been verbally described in Chapter 1: with some exceptions the two chapters match. The exceptions are, (i) in the present chapter we give a more detailed account of the nominal-wage modelling procedures; (ii) not all the variables and constants of the model were mentioned in Chapter 1; by contrast, in that respect, the present chapter is complete; (iii) the flow diagrams illustrating the cycle sequence given in Figures 1A and 1B in Chapter 1 were, as indicated at the time, slightly doctored for purposes of presentation; the doctoring did not affect any points of economic significance, but the authentic sequence is the one defined below.

It had originally been intended to meet the purposes of the chapter by setting out the vital parts of the Quickbasic programme code with an economic commentary on the facing pages. This idea was, with reluctance, abandoned, however, as the author became aware of the extent to which the economics profession has not over the past decade become comfortable with high-level microcomputer languages. On the other hand, for numerous reasons it is out of the question to describe the Imp-Mac model and programme in conventional algebra: to mention only a few of the reasons; it works sequentially, solves optimizing problems by iteration and contains non-linearities. Therefore, with reluctance we have been compelled to create a local notation, in fact a kind of self-explaining language, for the purpose of carrying out the expository task.

The contents of the chapter are as follows:

6.1 Nominal wage modelling

When initializing the main model, the user is given the choice of selecting from two alternative sub-models affecting the nominal wage, named wage models 1 and 2, respectively.

6.1.1 Wage model 1

If the firm is operating at or below the normal capacity utilization rate, the firm pays the wage norm. At higher rates of utilization it pays an increasing premium. There is no spread to other firms. The strength of the effect is controlled by a constant called the "wage coefficient". The effect is not iso-elastic, but the coefficient in fact represents the elasticity of the effect when the capacity utilization rate = 1. When firms are setting optimum prices they project forward their capacity utilization rates and appropriately take account of the projected effects on micro-wages via this wage model.

6.1.2 Wage model 2

In this model a macro variable called "macro labour utilization" is defined. It is the ratio of the current aggregate demand for labour to the demographic labour supply. Thus it is a pure number of dimensions similar to 1.0. The firm then pays:

(i) The wage norm;
(ii) A premium or discount on the wage norm which varies with the macro labour utilization rate with a sensitivity controlled by the same wage coefficient as defined in model 1;
(iii) A further premium if it has a rate of capacity utilization greater than 1.0, i.e. the same effect, with the same coefficient, as in model 1.

Since the same coefficient is used in both wage models, it follows that if a firm had a capacity utilization rate of 1.1, at a time when the macro labour utilization rate also happened to be 1.1, and if the selected coefficient were 0.5, (given that the arc-elasticity of wage-effects over the range between argument = 1 and argument = 1.1 is approximately equal to the coefficient) the nominal wage will be boosted 5% on account of the macro effect and a further 5% on account of the macro effect, i.e. by approximately 10.5%.

6.1.3 Wage indexing

One of the constants selected by the user when initiating a run is called "smooth length", another is called "wage index lag". The former variable is used in both the wage and some in some other model procedure for defining the length of time over which smoothed variables are smoothed. The latter variables lag the process of wage-indexing. During each model cycle the programme calculates a projected inflation rate and applies this to the macro nominal wage norm. The projected inflation rate is calculated per unit of model time, so, for example, if the rate is 0.0015, and if there are 20 units of model time per imaginary year (see box), the rate per imaginary year = 0.0015 x 20 x 100 = 3%. Then, at a certain point during the run cycle, the wage norm is increased in the proportion 0.0015.

The projected inflation rate itself is calculated by moving back in time the distance "smooth length", observing the deflator, then moving back a further distance, wage index lag, and calculating the average proportionate inflation rate, per unit of model time, and then calculating the exponential rate of change between the two dates.

6.1.4 Wage noise

If at run initiation user specifies "wage noise" then procedure applies small rectangularly distributed random shocks to macro nominal wage norm dispersed in proportion to selected coefficient. In the absence of bias, the expected value of the random shock is zero. If at run initiation user specifies "wage-inflation bias" expected value of random wage shocks = bias, else = 0.

6.1.5 Adjusted wage norm

In the terminology and actual working of the model, the term "wage norm" is applied to the norm after application of all the above effects except those embodied in the wage models. After application of the macro effect of wage model 2, if appropriate the norm is called "the adjusted wage norm". Alternatively, if wage model 2 has not been selected, the adjusted wage norm is identical to the unqualified wage norm. In either case, when the micro wage for an individual firm is calculated, the capital-utilization effect is applied to the concept called the adjusted wage norm, and the result is the actual hourly wage paid by the firm. In order that the user can distinguish the macro labour market effect from the other effects, both unqualified norm and adjusted norm are shown in the running display.

6.2 Notation

There are **20 editable constants**, plus handful of technical or "**internal**" constants which are set by the programme itself in the light of the user's selection of editable constants. There are **39** "**global**" variables which stand through the whole programme and in all its procedures, of which 19 are **macro variables, four shock variables** and **16 micro variables.** Micro variables relate to firms. By contrast, with a few exceptions, macro variables are generally aggregates of micro variables, the exceptions being variables, such as total consumer or government expenditure, which derive from the behaviour of non-disaggregated entities such as households or government. The aggregation of particular macro variables takes place within the programme cycle soon after the occurrence of potential changes in the corresponding micro data; this process is referred to as "**updating**" the macro variables. In addition to the global variables which stand through the whole programme and all procedures, there are also **local variables** defined only for purposes of operating or explaining particular procedures.

We shall also set out the **functions** which will be employed in the main description. In a computer model, the concept of a function has the same broad interpretation as in mathematical analysis, but is generally more explicitly numerical may also make use of "global" data not included in the arguments. Functions may also call other functions.

6.2.1 Notation conventions

Constants are represented by *three italic upper case* letters.

Global micro variables are represented by *two or three italic lower case* letters.

Global macro variables are represented by *two italic upper case* letters.

Functions are represented by *three roman upper or lower case* letters. Thus the statement, $x = FUN(y,z)$ means that the variable x is a number returned by a function named **FUN**, containing the numerical arguments y and z.

Local variables where possible follow the conventions for global variables but also in some case employ Greek-letter symbols and some symbols are used differently in different procedures.

Run cycles are numbered $1...\tau$ where τ, represents current cycle, and a cycle represents the execution of the nine main economic procedures listed below.

In listings, symbols marked # are defined per unit of **model time**, those marked ##, per **imaginary year**; **unmarked symbols** are pure numbers.

6.2.2 Operators

*	=	multiplication
/	=	division
Exp	=	exponentiation
Σ	=	summation (if no indication, over all firms)
$x[\tau]$	=	value of variable x at beginning of cycle τ
$g[x,T]$	=	average proportional growth-rate of x, between $\tau - T$ and τ.

6.2.3 Iteration (evaluation)

"Basic" and other programming languages have standard notations for defining "loops" or iterative procedures, which are widely familiar to programmers. There do not exist, however, corresponding general conventions in mathematical notation. We therefor employ our own terminology which is best explained by an example. Suppose we have a variable x which is an argument in a function $A(x)$ and in another function $B(x,k)$ where k is an already-known constant. We wish to set a certain value of x, evaluate $A(x)$ and $B[x,k]$, evaluate $z = A * B$ and repeat with a new slightly increased or decreased value of x until some condition is reached, which will typically be a condition on z. For example z may reach a maximum, a minimum[1] or become equal to a certain value, maybe the value of another known variable. Then, typically, we are likely to be interested in the value of x that existed when the condition was reached, possibly also in the value of z. In our terminology, this example would be defined as follows:

Evaluate, varying x in steps of δ until z = max
$z = A(x) * B(x,k)$
$Y = x$

In the final statement, the value of x is to be interpreted as the approximate value of that variable at the point where the "until" condition was met. In the actual computing procedure it is the value of x before adding the last step which resulted in satisfying the test condition. Thus Y is a different kind of variable from x. It is that value, and only that value, of x where the condition was met.[2] The same would apply if instead of, or in addition to, the last line we wrote "$Q = z$". Q would be the number representing the value of z when z had satisfied a certain condition, in this case maximization. Finally in some cases the steps may be endogenous to the procedure itself.[3]

---

1 In the cases of maxima or minima (always, in simulation work, necessarily essential local), in an actual programme, it may be necessary to set out specific tailor-made conditions for establishing convergence. Only where these sub-procedures could be economically significant is it desirable to specify them; in other cases they are not described.

2 The reason why we cannot use the ordinary mathematical notation $Y = x[\max z]$ is that the situation is usually more complicated than the example, or for other reason unamendable to that notation.

3 For example in order to permit the programme to run reasonably fast, it may be necessary to devise functions or other sub-procedures that adjust the rate at

In the type of case where an optimization is required in respect of two decision variables, i.e. the type of case where in programming language we need a loop that is "nested" within a main loop, we will write,

Evaluate, varying x and y until z = max

$$z = Z(x,y)$$
$$X,Y = x,y$$

The last line indicating that the optimum pair of values of the two variables, which we will call X and Y, is represented by the circumstance that we have taken a value of x, held it constant while maximizing the function with respect to y, noted the result, incremented x and continued to the maximum maximorum, x being the penultimate trial value of x and y being the penultimate value of y for the pass when that value of x was used.

6.2.4 *Cumulation*

We also use the loop procedure when we wish to obtain a cumulative aggregate of the values of z, over each of the successive values of x. The "until" condition is then usually a value of x itself, e.g. that it should have reached a certain level, say q. In such a case we will write:

Cumulate, varying x from p to q in steps of δ

$$z = A(x) * B(x,k)$$
$$Y = \Sigma z$$

It is to be understood that the summation sign here signifies aggregation over the successive values of z at each pass of the loop. Notice that unlike in the case of "evaluation", in the case of

---

which the incremental variable is changed in relation to the apparent rate of convergence of the test expression. If this method is adopted, it is likely that the size of the new step will need to be made to depend partly on the size of the previous step (e.g. in order to measure the rate of convergence). Consequently, before entering the loop, it may be necessary to lay down a numerical level for the size of the first step. Where this occurs in the Imp-Mac programme, being essentially a programming technicality, it is not indicated in the present exposition.

cumulation, order that the aggregation be fully defined, it is necessary to specify the starting value of x (namely p), the finishing value, q, and the variation step δ.

6.3 The constants

The model has 19 constants which can be edited (i.e. set) by the user before a run starts and one of which, base demand elasticity, can also be changed while the model is running; these are called "editable" constants. In addition there are certain constants cannot be. Two are fixed, three are derived from other constants, and one (employment-creation bias) is fixed at zero when the run starts but can, in fact, later be shocked. These are called "internal" constants.

6.3.1 *Editable constants*

We give a listing of symbols, names, default values and recommended range outside which the programme may not work. In the cases of constants representing lags, the selection of the value 0 does not indicate a zero lag, rather it indicates that the indexing is to be disabled altogether. The listing is followed by comments.

Notation	Constant	Default	Range
BED	base demand elasticity	3	2 to 7
DOG	demand-elast endogty	0	0 to 1
GEA	growth expectns adpty	0.3	0 to 1
GIL	govt indexing lag #	0	0 to *RNL*
IGR	initial growth rate % ##	0	-10 to +10
INF	inflation bias % ##	0	-10 to +10
IRT	initial return % ##	10	1 to 20
MAP	maxi adjust period #	40	10 to *RNL*
NFM	number of firms	5	5 to 20
OFR	optimizing frequency	4	see [1.3.2]
OPC	OPPH coefficient	1	0 to 3
PEN	Penrose coefficient	1	0 to 3
PSA	propensity to save	0.3	0.1 to 0.5
RLN	run length #	200	see note below
SML	smooth length ##	1	1 to 3
WAC	wage coefficient	0.5	0 to 3
WIL	wage index lag #	0	0 to *RNL*
WML	wage model	1	1 or 2
WNS	wage noise % ##	0	0 to 10

Reminder: # = per unit model time (cycles), ## = per imaginary year

N.B.: If (RNL*NFM) is too large relative to memory of hardware programme will freeze (see also comment on *RNL* below).

Comments on the above follow.

6.3.2 Comments on the editable constants

BED base demand elasticity

The all-firms iso-elastic demand elasticity unless modified by the demand-elasticity-endogeneity function defined in section 6.6 below.

DOG demand-elasticity edogeneity

The coefficient of the demand-elasticity-endogeneity function defined in section 6.6 below. If = 0, then demand elasticity is exogenous and internal constant *EDM* (defined in 6.3.3 below) is at all times = *BED*.

GEA growth-expectations adaptivity

Each firm's expected growth rate is a weighted average of (a) the average observed past growth rate of this firm's quantity demanded (adjusted to remove the effects of any relative-price change) and (b) the initial growth rate (*IGR*, see next constant but one); the weight of (a) is *GEA*, the weight of (b) is 1-*GEA*.

GIL government indexing lag

If this constant is set at e.g 10, then nominal government expenditure is made equal to $X * DF[\tau\text{-}10]$ where X signifies whatever value the model would have assigned to government expenditure if the user had completely disabled indexing (*GIL* = 0, see above) and *DF* (see below) signifies deflator; for the determination of X see main procedure number (4), below.

IGR initial growth rate

If this is set, at run initiation, at e.g. 3%, the demographic or "normal" labour supply will grow at the fixed rate of 3% per imaginary real year throughout the run; in the absence of shocks, government-led real aggregate demand will also grow at 3%, and the model will endogenize other variables, such as production and capital stock, to grow at 3% at constant wages and prices; hence, in the absence of subsequent user-interaction the model will respond with a steady-state 3% growth rate.

INF inflation bias

If this is set at 1%, other things being equal (including macro labour demand growing at the normal rate, i.e. at the initial growth rate), nominal wages will grow at 1%.

IRT initial return

The expected return which every firm will find under conditions of optimization at the start of the run and also during the run in the absence of disturbances from steady state.

MAP maximum capital-stock adjustment period

For the concept of capital-stock adjustment period see Chapter 1; it is a micro variable subject to optimization; when the model is in steady state the optimum value is low; if and when, however, following a shock, firms' discover that the optimum value has become high, owing to longer iteration processes, the programme will run relatively slowly until the capital stock has adjusted; by setting *MAP* at e.g. 10 the user can constrain the firms' choices and keep the programme running faster, at some cost, of course, in veracity.

OFR optimizing frequency

The number of times, per imaginary real year, that a firm becomes "in-turn" and has the opportunity to recalculate optimum price and adjustment period, and to adjust the production rate; at the time of run initiation, in selecting *OFR*, in association with the selection of *NFM*, the user determines the number of units of model time per imaginary real year, which number then becomes a constant with the symbol *MTY* (= *OFR* * *NFM*).

OPH OPPH coefficient

Coefficient controlling the shape of the OPPH-curve, the relation between output per person-hour and the capacity utilization rate; in all circumstances when the latter is 1 the former is one; if the coefficient is set > 0, the curve has the "empirical" shape; if capacity utilization is reduced from 1, opph is at first constant then gently falling, above 1, it is constant then sharply falling; an increase in the coefficient increases the steepness of both declining phases; if the coefficient is set > 1, the curve is neo-classical, declining smoothly throughout its length, with steepness increased by the coefficient, but always passing through the point 1,1.

PEN Penrose coefficient

Coefficient controlling the steepness of the investment-cost curve; an increase in the coefficient means that the premium on investment cost relative to capacity accrual, increases more rapidly (as compared with the case of a lower coefficient) once the desired proportionate rate of increase of capacity passes a threshold which is, in fact, in the programme set equal to the initial growth rate (below the threshold, whatever the value of the coefficient, the premium is zero).

PSA Propensity to save

Proportion of total household disposable income (wages plus distributed profits) not spent on consumer goods (hoarded as money).

RLN Run length

If set at e.g. 200 the run will automatically stop at $\tau = 200$; if the run is stopped earlier, by means of the "quit" facility (press Q or q) e.g at $\tau = 100$, then, in the programme memory, the "constant" run length becomes 100 and is saved as such in the event that the user chooses to save the data of the run in question on disc; the main reason of selecting a restricted value of Run length would be to economize memory (when a run is initiated a memory block of *NMF* * *RLN* * 16 * 2 bytes is reserved for micro variables, another of *RLN* * 20 * 2 for macro variables, approximately 20 * 2 for constants, and *RLN* * 4 * 2 for shocks).

SML Smooth length

Length of period of model time employed for smoothing or averaging certain variables, namely expected growth rate, indexed wages and, where required, the shocks; the actual application of *SML* differs from case to case, for details see the relevant procedures or for an example here see wage index lag, below.

WIL Wage index lag

If this is set at e.g. 20, then the projected inflation rate is calculated as average proportional increase in the deflator, per unit of model time, from τ - *WIL* - *SML* to τ - *WIL*; then, between τ and $\tau + 1$, the nominal wage norm, a macro variable affecting all firms, is increased in proportion to the projected inflation rate thus calculated.

WML Wage model

Set to 1 for wage model 1, 2 for model 2; for models see above.

WNS Wage noise

If set to zero, there is no wage noise; else the nominal wage norm faced by all firms is subjected to small proportionate stochastic disturbance, rectangularly distributed with mean = *INF* (see above); is *WNS* = e.g. 2, then the mean absolute proportionate disturbance is equivalent to 2% per imaginary year.

6.3.3 *Internal constants*

ECB employment-creation bias

This constant reflects the bias, if any, of firms' managements towards the creation of employment, possibly at the expense of profits. The number, in the range 0 to 1, whose full function will be further detailed, is fixed at zero at run initialization, but is "shockable", i.e. can be changed, after the run has started, to some other value.

EDM current demand elasticity

The objective elasticity of demand, with respect to own price, with all other prices constant, previously given the symbol ϵ. As already explained in Chapter 1, the model user has the choice of making either exogenous or endogenous. At run initiation it is set equal to the initial value of the user-selected shockable constant *BED* see (6.3.1 and 6.3.2 above). If the user does not desire the endogenizing facility he sets the relevant editable constant, namely *DOG* (6.3.1 and 6.3.2 above), to zero and *EDM* remains equal to *BED*. It will change during the run therefore, only if *BED* is shocked. Alternatively, the user sets *DOG* to a positive value and *EDM* will then deviate from *BED* counter-cyclically.

KYN, KPF "Keynes", Keynes per firm

"Keynes", fixed at the number 10,000, represents an arbitrary measure of the scale of the economy. It is macro physical output in the first cycle of a steady state. In this state labour hourly productivity = 1, so in this state "Keynes" also equals the demand for labour. Thereafter, the corresponding steady-state concept is $KYN * (1 + IRG)^{\tau}$. "Keynes per firm" = *KYN / NFM*.

MTY model time per year = *OFR* * *NFM*

SCO standard capital/output ratio

The capital/output ratio is not user selectable; it is always set at 30 in relation to per cycle production rate, equivalent to 30 / *MTPY* in the conventional definition related to production per year; with default values of number of firms (5) and firms' optimization frequency (4), *MTPY* = 20, hence by implication default *SCO*, in conventional definition, = 30/20 = 1.5 (i.e. in conventional economic writing the "capital/output ratio" would be said to be 1.5; implicitly, the conventional definition assumes normal utilization). Owing to the assumptions of the model, the numerical value of *SCO* has no effect on its economic behaviour.

6.4 Global micro variables

6.4.1 Initial values

The general character of the initial conditions has been discussed in Chapter 1. The main way of achieving the required initial micro conditions is first to guarantee Nash strategic equilibrium by endowing every firm with the nominal wage (which will be the same for them all) at just the level to optimize a price of 1, and at the same time to set all prices = 1 and all quantities = *KPF* ("Keynes" per firm). Then, during the first cycle, each firm's prices will be 1 and its production *KPF*; being endowed also with an appropriate capital stock, both capacity utilization rate and hourly labour productivity also = 1; hence for every firm employment = *KPF*. The foregoing, plus information concerning investment, gives sufficient information to calculate total wages and distributed profits. Given *PRS* (propensity to save) we have household savings. During the first cycle the programme then calculates government expenditure at exactly the level to ensure, via the standard Keynesian equation (main procedure (4) below), that real aggregate demand precisely equals *KYN*. The detailed micro requirements of the initialization procedure are, therefore, as follows;-

(i) optimum price = actual price = 1
(ii) quantity demanded at actual price = *KPF*
(iii) unsold stocks = unfilled orders
(iv) capacity utilization rate = 1
(v) output per person-hour = 1
(vi) nominal wage consistent with (iv) and (v)
(vii) production = employment = quantity demanded
(viii) capital stock = production x standard capital/output ratio
(ix) investment for growth at initial growth rate
(x) optimum capital-stock adjustment period = very short (no adjustment required)
(xi) expected growth rate = initial growth rate
(xii) expected return = initial return.

6.4.2 Listing of micro variables

Notation	Variable	Initial Value
ap	adjustment period #	2
cap	capacity	*KPF**SCO*
cuz	capacity utilization rate	1
dsp	distributed profit #	(*KPF*/*BDE*) - *inv*
egr	expected gr rt % ##	*IGR*
emp	employment #	*KPF*
ert	expected return % ##	*IRT*
inv	real investment #	see below
oph	output per person-hour	1
pri	price	1
pro	quantity produced #	*KPF*
qd	quantity demanded #	*KPF*
ufo	unfilled orders (phys)	*KPF**NFM*
ust	unsold stocks (phys)	*KPF**NFM*
nw	nominal wage	1 - (1/*BDE*)

Reminder: # = per unit model time (cycles), ## = per imaginary year.

6.4.3 Comments on micro variables

ap adjustment period

In steady state, actual capacity should always be precisely equal to required capacity, but owing to rounding errors this does not strictly happen; therefore it is found that the programme runs more smoothly if the minimum *ap* = 4 rather than 0; the iteration procedure for optimizing ap (see below).

cap capacity

In steady state capacity utilization rate = 1, therefore required capacity = initial output times standard capital/output ratio = *KPF* * *SCO*, as shown.

cuz capacity utilization rate

In steady state, capacity utilization rate = normal = 1.

dsp distributed profit

Steady state = strategic equilibrium = profit max; under Lerner formula when profit = max, share of profit in value of output = (1 / demand elasticity) = 1 / *BDE*.

egr expected growth rate %

In steady state each firm's expected growth rate = the "actual" underlying growth rate, namely the initial growth rate, *IGR*.

emp employment

With initial *oph* = 1, initial *emp* = initial production = initial demand = *KPF*.

ert expected return

In steady state actual expected return of all firms = initial return.

inv real investment cost

The real cost, including "Penrose" premium, if any, of increasing capacity (in order to obtain the corresponding nominal cost, must be multiplied by deflator); the initial value is obtained by plugging the appropriate values derived from the initial growth rate into the investment-cost function (*INV*) described below.

oph ouput per person-hour

This is a function, *OPH*(*cuz*) of the capacity utilization rate defined so that *OPH*(1) = 1; hence initial value of *oph* = 1.

pri price

Initializing this variable at unity is the key normalization of the model.

pro quantity produced

In steady state, = quantity demanded.

qd quantity demanded

All firms' demand curves are normalized for quantity demanded to equal *KPF* when price = 1.

ufo unfilled orders (phys)

At initialization firms are endowed with a backlog of orders such that if new orders ceased they could continue deliveries at the rate = to the current rate of demand for the length of a supercycle (see above).

ust unsold stocks (phys)

In steady state, = unfilled orders.

unw unit nominal wage per person-hour

Steady-state = strategic equilibrium = profit max; under Lerner formula (Chapter 3) when profit = max, share of wages in value of output = 1 - share of profits = 1 - (1 / demand elasticity) − 1/*BDF*; since the initial price = 1, the share of wages = actual wage.

6.5 Global macro variables

Notation	Name	Definition	Provisional Value
AN	adjusted wage norm	see [6.1.5]	*WN*
AW	aggregate nominal wage	(*nw***emp*)	*WN***KYN*
CA	capacity	Σ*cap*	*KYN***SCO*
DF	deflator	Σ(*p***qd*)/Σ*qd*	1
DP	distributed pft	Σ*dsp*	*KYN**(1/*BDE*) - *NI*
DR	discount rate	see Chapter 1	
ER	expected return	Σ(*cap***ert*)/Σ*cap*	*IRT*
GD	goods demand	Σ*qd*	*KYN*
GO	goods output	Σ*pro*	*KYN*
IG	initial growth path	*KYN***Exp*(*IGR**τ)	*KYN*
LD	labour demand	Σ*emp*	*KYN*
LZ	labour demand pressure	(*LD*/*IG*)-1	0
ND	nominal demand	Σ(*p***qd*)	*KYN*
NI	nominal investment	*DF**Σ*inv*	see above
NW	unit nominal wage	Σ(*nw***emp*)/Σ*emp*	*WN*
PI	projected inflation rate	see above [6.1.3]	0
RW	real wage	*AW*/*DF*	*AW*
UF	unfilled orders	Σ*ufo*	*NFM***KYN*
US	unsold stocks	Σ*uso*	*UF*
WN	wage norm	see above [6.1]	1-(1/*BDE*)

N. B. The variable *ER*, expected return, which does not appear on the right hand side of any equation in the model (i.e. is presented for interpretive purposes only) is in fact calculated as a moving average of length *SML* ("smooth length").

6.6 Functions

We now set out the main economic functions. Only functions with a significant economic role in the model are included. Functions whose purposes are strictly technical (e.g. relating to programme displays, user inter-face, numerical operations, etc) are omitted.

Capacity-utilization wage function *cuw(cuz,WAC)*

If *cuz* < = 1 then *cuw* = 1, else

$$cuw = cuz^{(WAC \cdot cuz)}$$

Note: the purpose of this function is to implement wage model 1.

Demand-elasticity-endogeneity function *EDM(BED,DOG,LZ)*

If absolute value of *LZ* > 1 or < 0.1 then *EDM* = *BED*, else

$$EDM = BED - (10*LZ*DOG)$$

If *EDM* < 1.5 then *EDM* = 1.5

Note: the purpose of this function is to implement the facility for making demand-elasticity endogenous; if the constant *DOG* is set to zero, there is no effect.

Investment-cost function *inv(a,b,PEN)*

a	=	capacity at model time τ
b	=	capacity required at $\tau + 1$
δc	=	required capacity growth
	=	$b - a$
cgr	=	normalized capacity growth rate
	=	$(\delta c / a) - IGR$
σ	=	$500 * PEN * cgr$
β	=	"Penrose premium"
	=	$(1 + cgr)^{\sigma} - 1$

If $cgr < -IGR$ then $inv = 0$

If $-IGR <= cgr <= 0$ then $inv = \delta c$

If $cgr > 0$ then $inv = a * (cgr + \beta)$

Note: the purpose of this function is to implement the "Penrose effect".

Macro labour-utilization wage function *luw(luz,WAC)*

$$luw = luz^{(WAC \cdot luz)}$$

Note: the purpose of this function is to implement wage model 2.

OPPH function ***oph(cuz,OPC)***

oph = ouput per person-hour
a = capacity at model time
α = .4 * *OPC* * (1 - *cuz*)
β = 10 * *OPC* * (1.4 - *cuz*)
(1) "Empirical" curve: *OPC* > 0
If *cuz* < = 1 then *oph* = cuz^{α}
If 1 < *cuz* < 1.4 then *oph* = 1
If *cuz* > 1.4 then *oph* = cuz^{β}
(2) "Neo-classical" curve: *OPC* < = 0
oph = 1 + *OPC* * {(*cuz* - 1) + $(cuz - 1)^2$}

Expected benefit function ***exb(tap,tp,tqd,rc,cap,egr,ECB,DR)***

tap = trial adjustment period (in iteration process)
tp = trial price
tqd = trial quantity demanded
rc = capital required to produce actual quantity demanded at τ with normal capacity utilization rate (= 1)
(1) Procedure during adjustment period[1]
π = a future model time, during adjustment period, measured from τ
α = $\tau + ap$
ac = actual capacity at τ
$pc[\pi]$ = planned capacity at π
$rc[\pi]$ = required capacity at π
gpc = planned growth rate of capacity during adjustment period
= $rc[\alpha] / cap)^{(1/tap)} - 1$
$unw[\pi]$ = unit nominal wage at π
ϕ = $(1 + DR)^{-\pi}$
Cumulate, varying π in steps of 1 τ to *ap*
$qd[\pi]$ = $tq * Exp(\pi * egr)$
$rc[\pi]$ = $rc * Exp(\pi * gpc)$

---

1 During the adjustment period, the planned capacity utilization rate, being in effect controlled by the ratio between required and planned capacity, is not constant. This in turn affects both nominal wage and labour productivity. Therefore the calculation must be done by iteration.

$$pc[\pi] = ac * (1 + gpc)^{\pi}$$
$$cuz[\pi] = rc[\pi] / pc[\pi]$$
$$oph[\pi] = oph(cuz[\pi], OPC)$$
$$emp[\pi] = qd[\pi] / oph[\pi]$$
$$unw[\pi] = AN * cuw(cuz[\pi], WAC)$$
$$c1, c2 = rc[\pi], .. * \{1 + gpc\}$$
$$inv[\pi] = inv(c1, c2, PEN) * DFL)$$
$$cf[\pi] = (tp * qd[\pi]) - (unw[\pi] * emp[\pi]) - inv[\pi]$$
$$dcd[\pi] = cf[\pi] * \phi$$
$$ded[\pi] = emp[\pi] * \phi$$
$$dcd = \Sigma dcd[\pi]$$
$$ded = \Sigma ded[\pi]$$

(2) Procedure after adjustment period[1]

$$\alpha = \tau + ap$$
$$\beta = ap + egr$$
$$\phi = (DR - egr)^{-1} * (1 + DR)^{-ap}$$
$$qd[\alpha] = tq * Exp(\beta)$$
$$rc[\alpha] = rc[\tau] * Exp(\beta)$$
$$emp[\alpha] = qd[\alpha]$$
$$c1, c2 = rc[\alpha], .. * \{1 + egr\}$$
$$inv[\alpha] = inv(c1, c2, PEN) * DFL)$$
$$cf[\alpha] = q[\alpha] * (tp - AN) - inv[\alpha])$$
$$dca = cf[\alpha] * \phi$$
$$dce = emp[\alpha] * \phi$$

---

1 After the adjustment period, actual capital equals required capital and hence both capital utilization rate and output per person-hour = 1. The wage paid by each firm is equal to their expectation of the wage norm; this expectation is assumed to be the current adjusted wage norm, that is, the current nominal wage as affected by macro but not by micro factors. We assume this not because we endow firms with a specific expectation that the current macro situation (which may be cyclically disturbed) will continue, but rather that they do not distinguish macro forces; they simply project the wage they know. On these and other appropriate assumptions we calculate the discounted benefits from the end of the adjustment period to infinity. As the assumptions imply a projected steady state, any growing variables can be projected to infinite at constant exponential rates, so the usual formula for infinite discounting can be employed. In general, this states that a variable X, growing at the rate g, discounted at the rate r, converges to an aggregate discounted value of $X / (r - g)$, the growth rate working like negative discount.

(3) Combine results during and after adj prd

$tdc = dcd + dca$

$tde = ded + dea$

(4) Transform discounted employment[1] and calculate expected benefit

$\alpha = (DR + IRT) * SCO$

$ade = tde * DFL * \alpha$

$exb = \{tdc * (1 - ECB)\} + (ade * ECB)\}$

Price-step function *prs(exa,exb,prc,tp)*

exa = test (old) value of expected benefit

exb = trial (new) value of expected benefit

$\alpha = (exb - exa) / exa$

prs = calculated (new) value of price-step

prc = current value of price-step

tp = trial price

$\beta = prc / tp$

$\epsilon = \alpha / \beta$

If $\epsilon > 0.2$ or < -0.2 then $prs = +/- .01$

If $\epsilon = 0$ then $prs = 1E\text{-}5$

Else $prs = \epsilon / MTPY$

Note: the purpose of this function is to accelerate iteration by relating the trial price change to the apparent rate of convergence of expected benefit to maximum; that is, by observing the elasticity of benefit with respect to price variation.

---

1 The purpose of the transformation is to make discounted employment commensurate with discounted cash flow; in initial steady state, with $DFL = 1$, as follows,

$$
\begin{aligned}
cap &= cfl / (DR + IRT) \\
cap &= pro * SCO \\
&= emp * SCO \\
emp &= cfl / \{(DR + IRT) * SCO\} \\
&= cfl / \alpha \\
tde &= emp / DR \\
&= (cfl / DR) / \alpha \\
tdc &= cfl / DR \\
tde &= tdc / \alpha \\
tdc &= tde * \alpha \\
&= ade
\end{aligned}
$$

6.7 Run initialization procedure

As described in Chapter 1, this procedure occurs only once each run, after the user has selected the editable constants, before the first cycle begins.

Set internal constants

KYN = 10000

KPF = *KYN* / *NFM*

MTY = *NFM* * *OFR*

SCO = 1.5 * *MTY*

Set global variables and fill order books

V(*j*,*1*) = macro variable *j* at time 1

v(*j*,*k*,1) = micro variable *j*, firm *k* at time 1

ods(*k*,τ) = orders of firm *k* booked at τ

For all *j*

V(*j*,1) = provisional value of macro variable *j* (see above)

For all *j* and *k*

v(*j*,*k*,1) = initial value of micro variable *j* (see above)

For all *k* and all τ from 1 to *NFM*

ods(*k*,τ) = *KPF*

Set discount rate (*DR*)

mec = discount rate to make *dcf* = *cap*

δ = 5E-4

TR = trial discount rate

ica = initial capacity, firm 1 (representative)

Evaluate, varying *TR* from *IGR* + δ until *dcf* >= *ica*

dcf = *exb*(1,1,*KPF*,*ica*,*ica*,*IGR*,*TR*)

mec = *TR*

DR = *mec* - *IRT*

6.8 The main cycle

We now detail the procedures, already described in Chapter 1, of the main cycle. When a procedure commences, some variables will be pre-determined; user selected constants, user-shocked constants or variables, and variables carried forward from the previous cycle or from a previous procedure in the same cycle.

Wherever possible the notation is simplified by omitting time indicators. But variables may change during a cycle, and the new value may be employed in a subsequent procedure during the same cycle. We therefore adopt the following default interpretations for different types of variables when the *[τ]* symbol is omitted; where it is not, it continues to signify the value of the variable at the beginning of the current cycle.

Shock variables

When a shock is introduced, using a procedure called "smooth shocks" appearing late in the cycle, the programme feeds the shock into the model through successive cycles on an S-shaped curve. Unless otherwise indicated the time definition for shockable constants and variables is the moment after the last time the programme passed the "smooth shocks" procedure just before the end of the preceding cycle.

Global micro variables

The value of a global micro variable appearing on the right hand side of an equation at a particular point in the cycle will be, according to circumstances, one of the following:

(a) the value determined by its appearance on the left hand side of an equation at a previous point in the same cycle
(b) the value carried forward at the end of the previous cycle
(c) the value at run initialization

Global macro variables

Different macro variables are updated at different points in the cycle, and these differences may be economically significant. The updated value is treated as relating to the time of the current cycle, until the end of the cycle, when, as already indicated, it is carried forward to the next cycle. The value of a global macro variable appearing on the right hand side of an equation at a particular point in the cycle will there be one of the following:

(a) the value determined by its last updating at a previous point in the same cycle
(b) the value carried forward at the end of the previous cycle

Local variables

Local variables relate only to the procedures or sub-procedures for which they have been defined. At a given point in a procedure the value of an RHS variable is the value determined at the last point it appeared as LHS in the same procedure. Local variables cease to exist at the end of their procedures and their symbols maybe re-assigned to other local variables in later procedures. Local variables may change not only within a procedure but within an equation. For example,

$x = x[\tau] + y$

means that immediately after the operation of this equation the value of x is equal to the value of the same variable at the beginning of the cycle, modified by the addition of another known variable, y, which could of course be a local or a global variable defined at a time also following our conventions.[1]

We now set out the main cycle procedures, in order of execution, in each case preceded, appropriately, by the corresponding lists of local variables.

Optimize price and adjustment period

ac	=	actual capacity at τ
	=	$cap[\tau]$
rc	=	required capacity at τ
	=	$SCO * qd[\tau]$
tp	=	trial price
tq	=	trial quantity demanded
tap	=	trial adjustment period
nci	=	nominal consumer demand for in-turn firm at τ
	=	pri[τ] * qd[τ]
nco	=	nominal consumer demand for other firms at τ
	=	$ND - nci$
pea	=	proportionate expenditure absorption by in-turn firm
p'	=	price-variation step
	=	initially 0.01, thereafter determined within procedure

—procedure continued on next page

1 Economists are, of course, familiar with a statements such as, $x[\tau+1] = x[\tau]+y$, but this notation this may not be appropriate in our programme. Why? Because x may be changed again, by a subsequent equation, before the end of the cycle. In our programme, a variable does not absolutely qualify to be called $x[\tau+1]$ until the programme reaches the procedure, at the end of the cycle, for carrying data forward into the next cycle.

Optimize price and adjustment period procedure continued

(1) In-turn firm does optimization

Evaluate, varying *tap* from 2 in steps of 2, *tp* from *pri* in steps of *p'* and *tq* from *qd* in steps of *q'*, until *exb* = max

$exb = exb(tp,tq,ap,rc,cap,DR,EGR,ECB)$
$exa = exb(tp-p',tq-q',tap,cap,DR,EGR,ECB)$
$p' = prs(exa,exb,p,tp)$
$q' = -p' * EDM$
$pr = tp$
$qd = tq$
$ap = tap$

(2) In-turn firm calculates optimized expected return

δ = 5E-4
TR = trial discount rate
nc = nominal capacity at τ
= $ac * DF$

Evaluate, varying *TR* from *DR* in steps of δ until $dcf >= nc$

$dcf = exb(ap,pri,qd,rc,ac,TR,EGR,0)$
$mec = TR$
$ert = mec - DR$

(3) Other firms, adjust quantities-demanded

$pea = \{(pri * qd) - nci\} / nco$
$qd = (1 - abs) * qd[\tau]$

(4) Update *GD* (real aggregate demand = Σqd)

Set firms' production

tst = target stock
= $qd * NFM$
smf = smoothing factor
= $\{1 + egr)^{NFM} - 1\} / NFM$

(1) All firms, set new production rates

$pro = (ufo + tst - uso) / smf$

(2) Update aggregate production ("goods output", *GO*)

Set firms' investment

ac = actual capital
= $cap[\tau]$
rc = required capital
= $qd * SCO$
dgr = desired growth rate of capacity
(1) Set investment and update capacity and capacity utilization rate
(a) Firms with adjustment period complete
$dgr = egr$
(b) Other firms
$dgr = \{(rc / ac)^{(1/ap)}\} * (1 + egr) - 1$
(c) All firms
$inv = inv(ac, ac*(1+dgr), PEN)$
$cap = ac * (1 + dgr)$
(2) Update aggregate capacity (*CA*) and aggregate nominal investment ($NI = DF * \Sigma inv$)

Do distribution calcs

(1) Update deflator (*DF*)
$DF = ND / GD = \Sigma(pri * qd) / \Sigma qd$
(2) Update projected inflation rate (*PI*)
AWL = absolute value of *WIL* (wage index lag)
$PI = g[DF, \tau\text{-}AWL\text{-}SML, \tau\text{-}AWL]$
(3) Update average real wage[1]
$RW = AW / (LD * DF)$
(4) Update demand-elasticity
$EDM = EMD(BED, DOG, LZ)$
(5) Index wage norm, apply noise and bias
RN = random number between 0 and 1
SC = scale factor
= $1 / (100 * MTPY)$

— procedure continued next page

1 Note: in addition, the model calculates and stores a 10-cycle moving average of the macro real wage, displayed in output, but not appearing in any equation and not included in the present chapter's list of variables.

Do distribution calcs procedure continued

NS = wage noise
= 4 * (*RN* - 0.5) * *WNS* * SC
IB = wage inflation bias
= *INF* * *SC*
If *WIL* > 0 then
WN = *WN*[τ] * (1 + *PI* + *NS* + *IB*)
else
WN = *WN*[τ] * (1 + *NS* + *IB*)
(6) update adjusted wage norm
LU = macro labour utilization indicator
= *LD* / *IG*
If wage model = 2 then
AN = *WN* * *luw*(*LU*,*WAC*)
else
AN = *WN*
(7) Update macro-average expected return (*ER*)
RR = raw (i.e unsmoothed) current average expected return
= Σ(*cap* * *ert*) / Σ*cap*
ER = (Σ *RR* [from τ-*SML* to τ]) / *SML*

Do micro labour calcs

(1) All firms
cuz = (*pro* * *SCO*) / *cap*
nw = *AN* * *cuw*(*cuz*,*WAC*)
oph = *oph*(*cuz*,*OPC*)
emp = *pro* / *oph*
(2) macro updates
LD = Σ*emp*
AW = Σ(*emp* * *nw*)
NW = *NW* / *LW*

Do firms' financial operations

$ods[t]$ = firms' orders booked in past model cycle t, not delivered at τ

$del[t]$ = physical delivery in current cycle of orders booked in cycle t

$rev[t]$ = cash transfers from holding account for delivery of orders booked in t

T = value of t (past) where order queue ends (no unfilled orders older than date)

nin = firm nominal investment

(1) all firms, manage order books

$uso = uso[\tau] + pro$

$ods[\tau] = qd$

Cumulate $del[t]$ and $rev[t]$ varying t from T, until,
either $t = \tau - NFM$ or $ufo = 0$

$ods[t] = ods[t] - del[t]$

$rev[t] = pri[t] * del[t]$

$uso[t] = uso[t] - del[t]$

$ufo[t] = ufo[t] - del[t]$

$rev = \Sigma rev[t]$

$uso = \Sigma uso[t]$

$ufo = \Sigma ufo[t]$

Note: when a variable appears with date t on both sides of an equation the value on the right hand side is that existing before the operation, the value on the left hand side the value after the operation.

(2) all firms, calculate distributed profits

$nin = inv * DF$

$dsp = rev - (emp * nw) - nin$

(3) macro updates

$NI = \Sigma nin$

$DP = \Sigma dsp$

$US = \Sigma uso$

$UF = \Sigma ufo$

Do macro shocks and macro feed-back

(1) calc "smoothed" (S-curve) shocks from raw data

$SH(i,t)$ = "raw" data shock-type i at time t

i = 1...4

t = $1 \ldots \tau$

1 = fiscal boost

2 = wage boost

3 = *BED* (base dem elast), level

4 = *ECB* (empl creation bias), level

Note: the array *SH* is set to zero, in the cases of shocks 1 and 2, and set at initial values in the cases of 3 and 4, until changed in-run by the user; when a change occurs the new value is repeatedly carried forward into the next cycle.

FB = fiscal boost

WB = wage boost

Cumulate, varying i from 1 to 4 in steps of 1, and t from τ in steps of -1 to τ-*SML*

$$FB = (\Sigma\ SH(1,t) \ /\ SML$$

$$\delta WB = \{\Sigma\ SH(2,t) - \Sigma\ SH(2,t\text{-}1)\} \ /\ SML$$

$$BED = \Sigma\ SH(3,t) \ /\ SML$$

$$ECB = \Sigma\ SH(4,t) \ /\ SML$$

$$WN[\tau+1] = WN * (1 + \delta WB)$$

(2) Do Keynesian macro equations
(reminder; *ND* = nominal aggregate demand)

GF = government factor

GE = government expenditure

AH = aggregate household income

CD = consumer demand

$$GF = (1 + IGR)^{\tau} * DF[\tau\text{-}GIL] * (1 + FB)$$

$$GE = PSA * \{(KYN * GF) - NI\}$$

$$AH = AW + DP$$

$$CD = (1 - PSA) * AH$$

$$ND = CD + GE + NI$$

Note: equation (2) makes government expenditure just equal to the amount required to create a steady state with aggregate real demand equal to *KYN* growing at *IGR*.

(3) Do macro-to-micro feedback (all firms adjust qds)

$$qd[\tau+1] = qd * ND \ /\ ND[\tau]$$

Calculate expected growth rates

obg = observed growth-rate, adjusted for relative-price effect
obg = *g[qd,SML]* + (*g[pri,SML]* - *g[DF,SML]* * *EDM*
egr = (*obg* * *GEA*) + *IGR* * (1 - *GEA*)
If *egr* > *IGR* then *egr* = *IGR*

End of cycle: inter-cycle ops

(1) Do displays
(2) Activate user interface for shocks, pause or data display
(3) If user keys **Q** or if τ = *RNL* then exit run
Else
 (i) Carry data forward from τ to $\tau + 1$
 (ii) Advance model time (add 1 to τ)
 (iii) Select new in-turn firm (fixed order)
 (iv) Start next cycle.

This completes the description.

7 Results and Conclusions

We are finally ready to give the reader examples of the Imp-Mac model in use. There is a large number of economically significant combinations of initial settings and subsequent shock patterns, and it is intended that users will be able to pursue their own particular interests. Deliberately, therefore, this final chapter is selective, and relatively short, though not, the author hopes, thereby unweighty. It is concentrated upon three main topics of major contemporary interest, namely the question of the "potency" of fiscal policy and analogous forces; the relation between wages and the demand for labour; and the theory and practice of stagflation.

The first topic, "fiscal potency" is used as a shorthand not only for the question of the expectations implied in the Keynesian theory, but also for the broader question of the way changes in nominal aggregate demand (whether actually caused by the government or some other source) affect micro quantities. In reality the two aspects are inseparable. Once you have the type of goods market assumed in the Imp-Mac model (see Chapter 1, subsection 1.2.4), if expectations are approximately consistent (in particular if firms believe that this is the kind market they are in), then firms will expect that, other than through effects on costs, that fiscal-type shocks will go to quantities, rather than to prices, because this is the prediction under these circumstances of profit maximization. In the present chapter we will demonstrate the working out of this theorem on alternative assumptions about concerning nominal wages and the labour market.[1]

The topic of the relationship between wages and the demand for labour is in fact several topics, with, of course, special interest in the

1 The theorem of fiscal "impotency" is sometimes extended to the case of "strong crowding out", whereby any government expenditure for one reason or another directly causes a primary reduction of some other form of expenditure, e.g. some monetary effect on private investment. As the reader must already be aware, rightly or wrongly, the general assumptions of the Imp-Mac model completely rule this out.

role of "real" wages. The basic problem under imperfect competition, as already discussed in Chapter 1, is that under the Lerner formula, the profit-maximizing profit margin appears to depend entirely on factors operating, not in the labour market, but in the goods market. Consequently, it appears that the real wage, in turn, is determined in the goods market, i.e. is not capable of influence from the push and pull of supply and demand in the labour market.

The problem is, if the real wage is thus "endogenous", how can it have an independent causal effect on the economic system in general or on the macro demand for labour in particular ? If, for example, as a result of some kind of shock (union-originated or otherwise) in the labour market, firms are compelled to pay higher nominal wages for a given quantity of labour, their initial profit-maximizing response, under imperfect competition, is to raise prices in proportion, so, in the event, the real wage seems not to change. In Chapter 4 we have already discussed Keynes's own apparently confusing thoughts on this point, which basically imply that a theory of causality from real wages requires that whoever or whatever it is that causes the shock must have command not only of nominal wages but also of prices, and hence, by further implication, have the power to prevent firms from carrying out their supposed lawful duty of profit maximizing. It is to be noted that this question is not the same question as the question of the cyclical behaviour of real wages. If either the elasticity of demand or the hourly productivity of labour vary cyclically, under imperfect competition, the real wage, precisely because it is endogenous, may (but will not necessarily; see discussion of Figure 7.2.5 below) also vary cyclically. But, by the same token, up to the present point in the argument, it is impossible to argue that the presence of some barrier to the "necessary" cyclical movement of the real wage can also affect the cycle itself, e.g. inhibit a cyclical recovery. Either a thing is endogenous, or it is not.

Economists who basically recognize the foregoing logic, but who remain nevertheless keen to further explore the problem of possible chains of causality between real wages and employment, pursue several different but potentialy related lines of thought. The first considers the possibility that if nominal wages are indexed, as fast as firms raise prices in response to wage increases, further wage increases occur, and that there could be a dynamic where, following an initial shock, on average, the real wage is permanently raised. In other words, in dynamic conditions, it might not be possible for firms to maintain an average price level, in relation to wages, that is indicated by optimization under static conditions. Given that this idea presents evident difficulties (in that, although it explains the immediate consequence of a shock, it does not explain why, as the effects work out through time, the dynamics are in fact such that the real wage is actually permanently raised), it can alternatively be relaunched as a theory of the effect of extreme, one-time shocks, e.g. the 1970s oil shocks.

Between 1975 and 1985, there is a variety of evidence that in both Western Europe and the United States, average real wages did "overrun", that is to say, the rate of growth of labour productivity having drastically slowed down, to say, a figure of *x*, real wages continued to rise at a rate, say *y*, which as higher than *x*, so that, in consequence, at the end of ten years the "cumulative" overrun was, say, *z*, this being the percentage excess of the actual level over the level that would have by this or that time obtained had *y*, instead of being greater than *x*, slowed down to equality with *x*. Unfortunately there is a statistical difficulty in measuring *z*. Part of the observed result in any such calculation may be due to structural shifts within the economy or sector studied. Clearly, in the case of total GDP, the case is serious, especially as it is well known that notably in the US there has been, since the middle 1970s, a strong trend to increase the proportion of employment and GDP accounted for by service occupations where wages are relatively low. Even within the sector defined as manufacturing, there could be problems. There is some consensus, however, that in the ten years after 1975, an overrun, measured by *z*, in manufacturing, in both W. Europe and the US, of about ten per cent, did occur with a subsequent slow relapse.

It is therefore interesting to accept a "moderate" over-run, in the OECD world as a whole, 1975-85, as a stylized fact. And it is an indisputable fact that there was a nominal-wage explosion around the world in the very early 1970s, before the first oil shock, and that the oil shocks themselves (1973 and 1980) had effects, inter alia, similar to extreme wage shocks. (See Figures 7.3.1 and 7.3.2 below. In the Imp-Mac model, lacking any non-labour inputs, we proxy oil shocks by wage shocks.) If we accept both sets of "facts" we are led to the logical proposition that either the indexing-dynamics theory must hold, or the one-time shock theory. Alternatively we must believe that by coincidence during the period in question either the average firm in the OECD world changed its motivation away from profit or that the goods market became more competitive in the sense that the average elasticity of demand increased.

In the runs below, we investigate these hypotheses, and reach certain conclusions, which, in order to preserve the tension, we shall not for the moment reveal. In the case of the two last-named, rather implausible, hypotheses, relating to managerial motivation and competition respectively, however, we shall confine ourselves merely to demonstrating how they could have worked, there being no evidence known to the author that they actually occurred.

Finally we shall demonstrate some runs to show how, with certain types of lag structures, apparent correlations between real wage and labour demand may appear statistically, when, from our direct knowledge of the actual structure of the Imp-Mac model, we know that no causality from the former to the latter exists. In order to help picture the results on runs relating to real wages, the graphic macro display shows not only the smoothed (moving average) real wage, but also a variable (which does not enter the model and is nowhere printed) described as the "amplified" real wage. This is an artificially contrived series where period-to-period differences have been amplified (multiplied by a factor), but the average value nevertheless held to the correct level. The reason for presenting this device is that otherwise the resolution of the "EGA" screen (by the time this book is published, it will be an antique) is inadequate to show the small movements which will be of interest in some of the analysis.

In the last section (7.3) we shall try and simulate or "imitate" the events of the 1970s and 80s. We shall explicitly aim to show that without additional assumptions, the Imp-Mac model can "explain" them. Because the Imp-Mac model (sadly) contains no provision for technical progress, the presence or absence of a real wage "overrun" will, however, have to be seen as question of a simple rise, or not, as the case may be, in the real wage. We can show the OECD economy set from 1970 on a growing path, and we shall see how the subsequent shocks are entirely sufficient to account for the major disruption in the growth path which then occurred, but, given the model's long-term fixed coefficients, we have to imagine (wrongly, of course) that the disrupted growth was of the kind where capacity, adequately led by demand, simply follows the growth of the demographic labour supply.

The implied theory of stagflation will be the one described in the Introduction, which may be briefly re-capitulated as follows. The world-wide inflationary impact of the Viet-Nam War caused the late-1960s wage explosion and early-1970s commodity-price boom. This produced some real-fiscal or real-balance effects which created a moderate recession in the US and some other countries, leading all countries to re-flate simultaneously creating a form of international fiscal overshooting, the peak effect of which came in 1972. On top came the first oil shock of late 1973, to which governments responded, in varying degree with indexed public expenditure and tight or untight money. The general effect was an erratic mixture of strong inflation and sharp recession, varying between countries, with a general tendency for the physical recession to be less sharp, and less long lived, than was the case in the subsequent depression of the 1980s. The cause of the difference, according to the author's theory, is to be found in the reaction of governments and the consequential effects on real aggregate demand. In the 1980s, governments, shaken, justifiably, by the inflationary experience of the 1970s, were much tighter with money, and in Europe, on the whole substantially less liberal in the indexing of public expenditure. In the US there was the famous Reagan and Volcker double act; extremely liberal public expenditure with very tight money, with complex results: whereas Figure 7.3.1, below, concerned with the 1970s, is mid-Atlantic, the picture of the 1980s given in Figure 7.3.2 below is centred somewhere around, say, Antwerp.

7.1 Fiscal potency and impotency

7.1.1 Recession and recovery under wage model 1

Figure 7.1.1 shows the result of a 10% negative fiscal shock followed 80 cycles later by an exactly opposite movement, restoring fiscal conditions to the initial conditions. The raw shock was imposed at model time 20, and had built up to its full effect by model time 40. The shock is not, of course, a 10% downward movement of government expenditure, rather it is a downward movement calculated by the computer to produce a 10% downward movement in Keynesian steady-state output, in effect, what happens is that we downshock the variables "Keynes" defined in Chapter 6. Although the shock itself

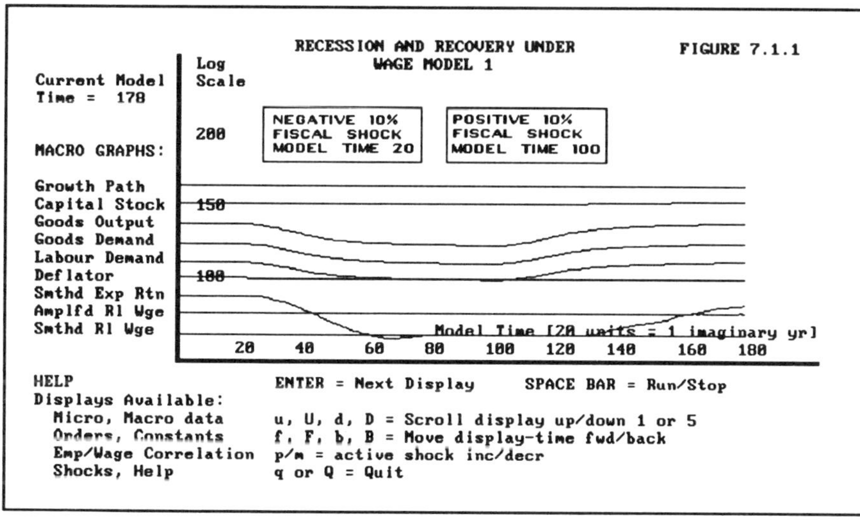

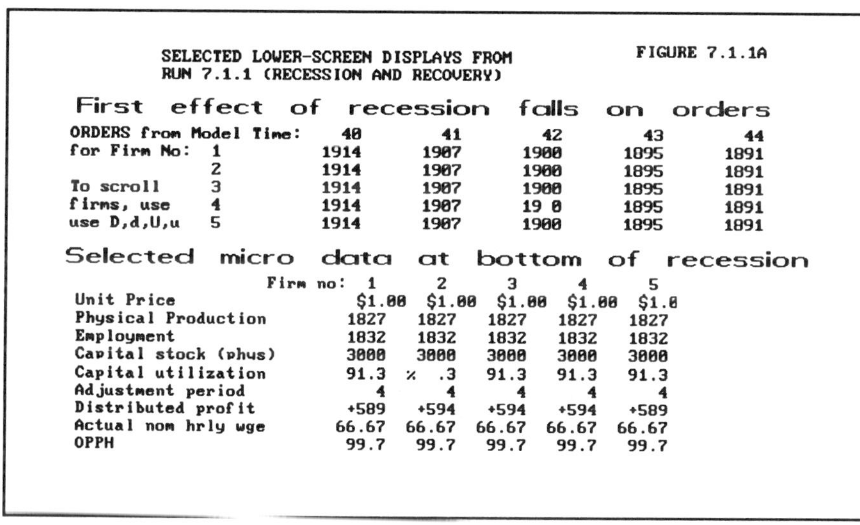

SELECTED LOWER-SCREEN DISPLAYS FROM RUN 7.1.1 (RECESSION AND RECOVERY) FIGURE 7.1.1A

First effect of recession falls on orders

ORDERS from Model Time:		40	41	42	43	44
for Firm No:	1	1914	1907	1900	1895	1891
	2	1914	1907	1900	1895	1891
To scroll	3	1914	1907	1900	1895	1891
firms, use	4	1914	1907	19 0	1895	1891
use D,d,U,u	5	1914	1907	1900	1895	1891

Selected micro data at bottom of recession

Firm no:	1	2	3	4	5
Unit Price	$1.00	$1.00	$1.00	$1.00	$1.0
Physical Production	1827	1827	1827	1827	1827
Employment	1832	1832	1832	1832	1832
Capital stock (phys)	3000	3000	3000	3000	3000
Capital utilization	91.3	% .3	91.3	91.3	91.3
Adjustment period	4	4	4	4	4
Distributed profit	+589	+594	+594	+594	+589
Actual nom hrly wge	66.67	66.67	66.67	66.67	66.67
OPPH	99.7	99.7	99.7	99.7	99.7

reaches its full effect by time 40, the full depression is not reached until some time later. This is the working out of the multiplier sequence, as discussed at the end of Chapter 6.

Because we are using wage model 1, there is no effect on nominal wages from the disturbance to the macro labour market. At the micro level, as *Figure 7.1.1A* shows, firms typically reduce the capacity utilization rate by the full amount of the depression, i.e. by about 10%. However, using the empirical opph curve, with a coefficient of 0.5, giving a rather modest slope to the increasing-returns phase of the curve, this has only a slight effect on opph. Prices, as will be seen, remain rock constant, despite the fact that each is being continuously re-checked for optimization. Prices remain constant because costs remain constant. As postulated in the Keynesian theory, the whole brunt of the recession falls on quantities. Now, however, rather than an assumption, we have a prediction. The author is vain enough to claim that this is the first time an explicit procedure has been presented for modelling the micro-macro interface of a Keynesian fluctuation so explicitly.

The upper half of Figure 7.1.1A shows the state of order books 25 cycles after the raw shock, i.e. about the time when the smoothed shock has reached its full height. The most recent orders are down the most. In this run, because there is no disturbance to wages and prices, the model does, as can be seen, settle down to a new low-level steady state, the traditional Keynesian low-level equilibrium. When this point is reached, the order books and stock levels will also stabilize, but, of course, at a lower constant level. All these events are then reversed in the recovery.

7.1.2 The effects of wage model 2

We now introduce wage model 2, that is, we introduce an effect from the macro labour market onto nominal wages. The detailed account of this model has been given in Chapter 6. In *Figure 7.1.2* and *Figure 7.1.3* the wage coefficient has been set to 1.0, which is sufficient to provide a marked, if not to say strong, effect. Intuitively, it is consistent with the general order of statistical results on macro wage equations: as can be seen from the equation of the capacity-utilization wage function set out in Chapter 6 (section 6.6), the coefficient approximates the elasticity of the curve around the point of zero macro wage pressure.) In both figures we have provided the same downshock as in Figure 7.1.1, but a heavier upshock, sufficient to imply 10% fiscal overshooting into the zone where the demand for labour substantially exceeds the normal demographic supply. But the results in the two figures are not the same. In Figure 7.1.1, the full force of the depression is felt, and also the full force of the overshoot. The overshoot results in a peak inflation rate of 4-5% per annum, due to the effect on wages of the pressure on the labour market. By contrast, in Figure 7.1.3, the effect of both the depression and the overshoot, in response to the same shocks, is halved, and

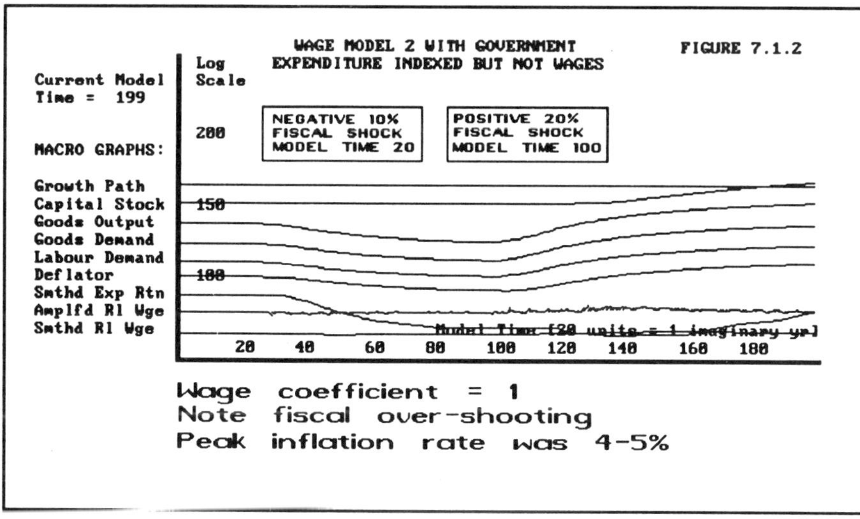

there is also less inflation. Why? The answer, of course, is the fact that in the second figure government expenditure is not indexed. Consider the "second shock", at time 100, when fiscal policy overshoots. The initial shock is a nominal shock. It creates a shift in firms' demand curves, which they find it profit maximizing, without raising prices, to follow. Orders increase and in due course firms find that the production-adjustment procedure[1] calls for higher output rates. In turn more labour is required. In aggregate the macro labour requirement exceeds the demographic supply and, although the necessary additional work is sucked from households, in the process the nominal wage is forced up. Now firms find that their profit-maximizing prices are higher, so higher prices are set. The government, however, having made its move in nominal terms, does no more, so the rising prices gradually reduce the real effect of the shock. Consequently the shock is less, consequently the labour-market effect is less, consequently the results on prices are less. A similar process can be seen at work in the opposite direction, after period 20: the economy is partially stabilized.

7.1.3 The "real fiscal effect"

---

1 "Set firms' production" in programme main cycle, see section 6.8 in Chapter 6 and/or subsection 1.34 in Chapter 1.

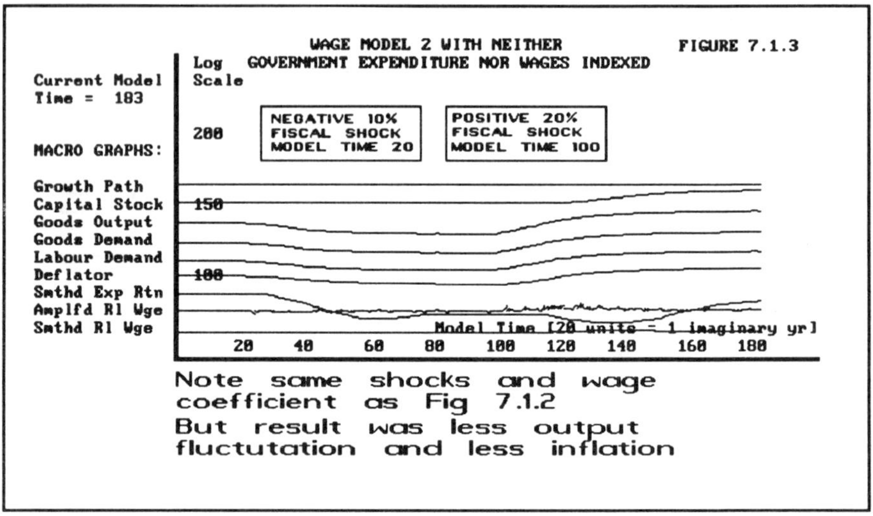

7.1.3 The "real fiscal effect"

In Figure 7.1.3 we are observing the operation of an "imperfect" Pigou-type effect, the "real fiscal effect". The significance of the result, however, does not depend on whether it stems from fiscal policy or from monetary policy. The essential point is that in both figures what we see are the result of policies, but different ones. If the government, fearing inflation, chooses to stabilize the nominal current injection of money, or the nominal stock of money, the basic result (quantitative and institutional differences apart) will be similar.

7.1.4 Economic growth lost and regained

In Figure 7.1.4 we give a general demonstration of how the Imp-Mac model works under economic growth and what happens when a growth path is lost and regained. The run begins with initial growth rate set to 5% per year, and, as will be seen, takes a few cycles to settle properly into the resulting steady state. By time 20, however, output, employment and capacity are growing at 5% and real investment is just equal to the physical rate of capacity increase required to support this growth without a "Penrose premium". The Penrose premium is zero because the firms are not attempting to grow faster than the initial growth rate, i.e. they are operating on the segment of the investment-cost function where the slope of the curve is unity (see "investment-cost function", in Chapter 6, section 6.6).

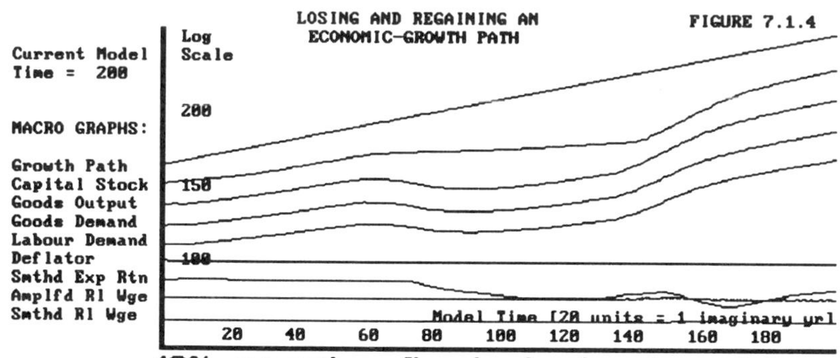

10% negative fiscal shock at model time 60, cancelled by 10% positive shock at time 100: growth had already resumed but on lower path

The economy is growing because the government, knowing that the demographic labour supply is growing, injects additional real demand at each time period to cause firms to discover that their demand curves are moving out at the appropriate rate. The coefficient of growth-expectations adaptivity has been set at 0.5, so it is not necessarily implied that firms know exactly what the government knows. Until a shock occurs the setting of this coefficient is not important, since, however it is set, firms, on calculating their expected growth rate, will always discover the correct rate, i.e. the initial growth rate, as pursued by the government.

At time 60 a 10% negative fiscal shock is imposed. Under partially adaptive expectations firms soon "write down" the expected growth rate and soon discover they have excess capacity. Under the model's assumptions of no capacity retirement and no capacity depreciation, investment falls to almost zero and capacity becomes almost constant. Capacity growth does not decline completely to zero because, the firms being only partially adaptive, retain in their expectations and calculate some influence from the initial growth rate and the implied prospects of recovery. If no further shocks were imposed, under the "rules of the game" of the model, steady-state growth would eventually recover, but along a permanently lower exponential world line with the original 5% growth rate. The demand for labour would remain permanently below the demographic supply, but be growing at the same rate, i.e. the proportional deficit in labour demand would not tend to increase.

The imposition of the positive shock at time 100, however, creates the possibility of regaining the old growth path, and thus also regaining a state of affairs where the demand for labour equals the demographic supply. Rather quickly, the situation changes from one of excess, to deficient, capacity. The "optimize price and adjustment period" procedures, on evaluating the situation, "decides" to lengthen the adjustment period, although by less than might have been intuitively expected. It is found that the long-term-discounted-cash-flow-maximizing strategy involves rather rapid investment, incurring marked Penrose penalties, so (as can be seen by comparing the paths of capacity and of production respectively) the period of deficient capacity and above-normal capacity utilization is relatively short.

7.2 Wages and the demand for labour

The general objectives of this section have been described above. We now discuss the specific topics in turn, namely the different effects of a wage shock under different conditions of indexing, a similar analysis of a demand-elasticity "shock", the neo-classical cost curve, and the statistical correlation between real wages and employment when noise is applied to the nominal wage. Of course, in real life, given that the elasticity of demand represents the structural competitiveness of the economy, it is most unlikely that it would change suddenly: the experiments in Figures 7.2.3 and 7.2.4 below are more to be seen as demonstrations, albeit in a dynamic context, of the distributional theory of the Imp-Mac model. Alternatively, they could possibly be seen as the result of shocks to the conjectural character of expectations under the force of some exogenous/cyclical disturbance, but this could be regarded as a somewhat treacherous interpretation as it is liable to lead to inconsistent expectations. Alternatively, one might imagine some one-time event of a character that the appearance of inconsistent expectations was a plausible, perhaps inevitable, consequence.

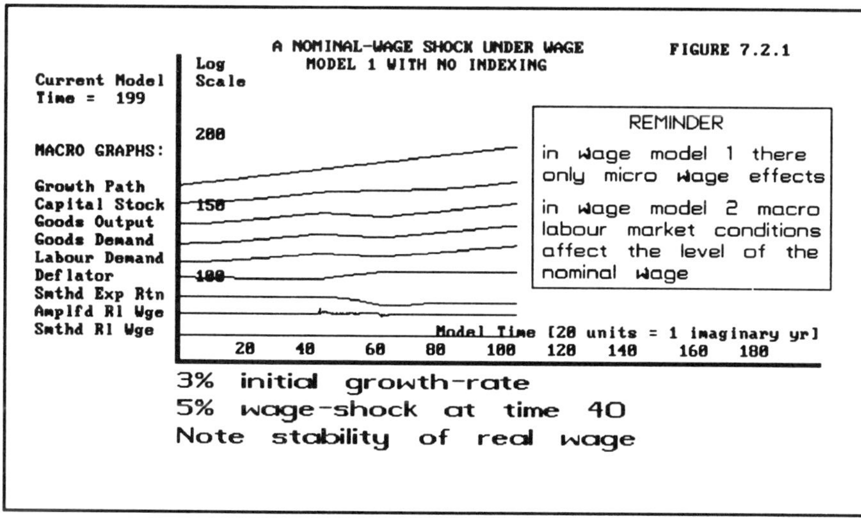

7.2.1 Nominal wage shocks without and
7.2.2 with indexing

In *Figure 7.2.1* we have the results of a wage shock under conditions which are in one respect benign, in another damaging. Neither wages nor government expenditure are indexed, so that after the first nominal boost to wages, the effect is gradually subject to inflationary attrition and in consequence eventually fades. The period of inflation is short and moderate, and full price stability is fairly soon regained. The price level, however, is permanently raised. The government does not index its expenditure and there is consequently a permanent depression of real expenditure and real aggregate demand, hence of output and the demand for labour. In the absence of wage model 2, the negative pressure in the labour market leaves nominal wages unaffected. (More precisely, there is no secondary reduction after the initial boost.) Throughout it all, profit-maximizing prices move exactly in proportion to nominal wages, and the real wage is constant. The expected return on capital falls, on account of permanently lower real profits in relation to the capital stock.

Economic growth is eventually resumed at the initial rate, but the old path is not regained. It is the scenario for an economy where the government has a strong aversion to inflation, and less concern with the permanent output loss: the government would perhaps say that provided growth resumes, the one-time trade of inflation for output

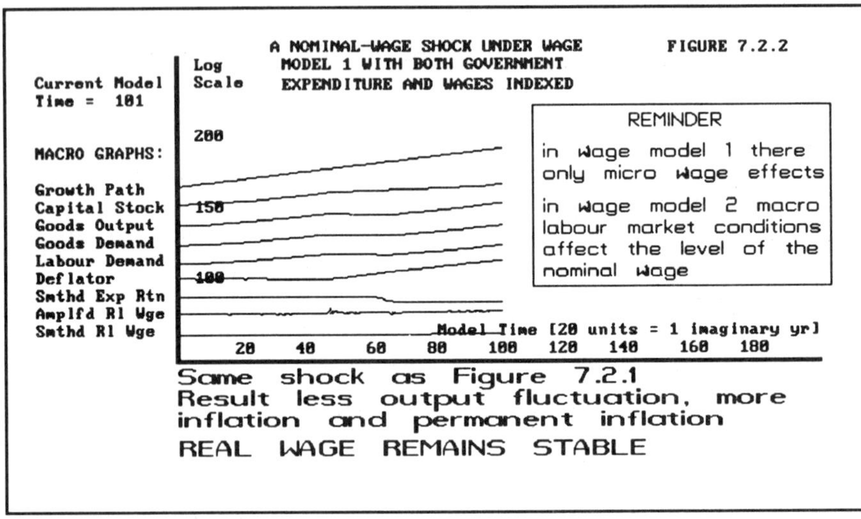

was satisfactory. The government might well argue that the permanent loss of labour demand was due to excessive wages, but, if by this would be meant excessive real wages, the proposition would be fallacious. The initial cause of the problem is the rise in **nominal** wages, leading to inflation, leading to depression of real demand in line with government policy.

Moving from Figure 7.2.1 to *Figure 7.2.2*, we obtain the "classic", or more precisely "classic neo-Keynesian", 1970s-type, stagflation scenario, but on a moderate scale. Because government expenditure is indexed, the "stagnation" phase is shorter and less severe. The reader will notice, however, that the difference between the two cases is less than might be supposed: although the long-term result cannot be seen on the display printed in the book, the user who experiments with this example will find that in neither case is the original growth path ever recovered. Why is this? The answer is to be found in the indexing dynamics. Both wage and government expenditure are in fact indexed with quite unrealistically short lags, five model time units only (i.e. a quarter of an imaginary year) in each case. Experiment shows that in order to have full real recovery it is necessary that the indexing of wages be substantially longer than the indexing of government expenditure. The reason is the fact that when the government applies its indexing it is, each period, employing the Kahn multiplier process operating through real time, as emphasized above, so, in effect, given that wages are re-indexed at the same rate, real demand never catches up with the situation. Assuming it is impracticable in reality to force a different relationship between the two indexing lags, to escape this dilemma the government in fact must add a positive fiscal shock. In so doing however, it will create more inflation.

More significant perhaps is that in this present case the inflation becomes permanent. Unless it is possible to break out of the dilemma, the time never becomes right for full reflation.

This leads towards perhaps the most fundamental policy message of the analysis of the Imp-Mac model. A mixed economy, with free wage bargaining and free price setting, which has suffered a shock and subsequently evolved with the type of lag pattern we see in this example, is inherently unmanageable, in the sense that, given the assumptions, anti-inflation objectives and real-growth objectives cannot be reconciled. The solution has to be not so much "incomes policy" in the traditional sense, but rather a progressive evolution, publicly mediated in any expedient ways, to a less malignant lag pattern. A long period when inflation is by one means or another kept down, and confidence in its restraint may be confirmed, will tend to encourage a less-tense indexing of nominal incomes, because, given the inertia that inevitably exists in practical reality, when inflation is relatively slow, the real cost of slackness being smaller, labour suppliers (or their representatives) will be less tense. Alternatively a similar result may be obtained in a highly unionized system where a small number of unions, each representing a large proportion of the GDP, may, as in the so-called "Nordic model",[1] internalize the public interest.

7.2.3 Demand elasticity "shocks" without and
7.2.4 with wage indexing

In Figures 7.2.3 and 7.2.4 address a question which was first illustrated on the cover of the book and briefly discussed at the end of Chapter 1. We apply a "shock" which is more to be seen as an analytic instrument than as a simulation of a very plausible real-life scenario. The results represent one of the most important theoretical implications of a Keynesian system with imperfectly competitive

---

1 See Matti et al (1991).

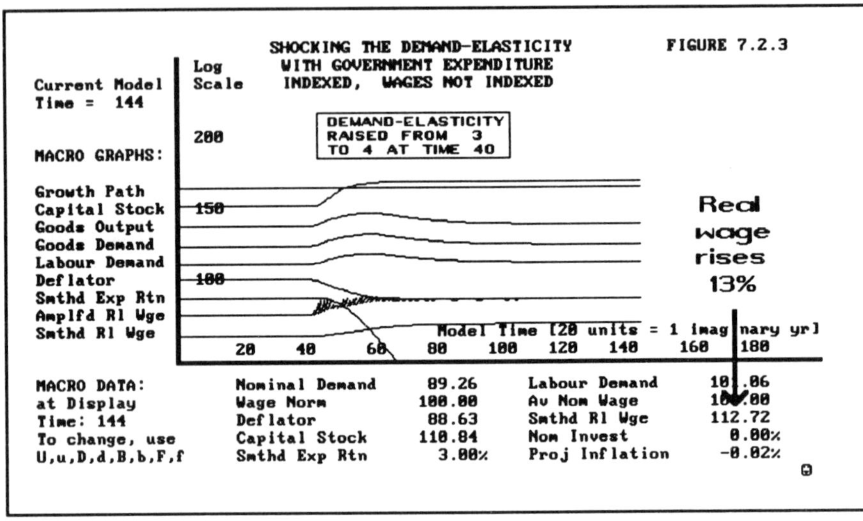

microfoundations. They tell us that in the absence of explicit macro forces such as real-fiscal or real-balance effects, the key parameters of the micro model affect the steady-state distribution but not the steady-state level of income.

In Figure 7.2.3, we impose an increase in the elasticity of demand, which firms immediately know, and which leads them to revise downwards their profit-maximizing prices. With wages not indexed, the real wage must rise, and the profit margin will fall, in fact, in accordance, after some oscillation, with the Lerner formula. Government expenditure is indexed, so the government reduces nominal expenditure - evidently the neutral response - thus holding real aggregate demand constant. But although the index-lag is short, the government's response takes time to work through the multiplier process, so firms, as they reduce their prices, at first find that the expected increase in quantity demanded is validated. But at the end of the day, this is not the case, the boom fades, and aggregate output relapses to its initial level. In this aggregate, as already mentioned, the share of wages is higher, of profits is lower. The story is intended to emphasize the original message of the original Kalecki theory-that-might-have-been (see Chapter 5), that the essential effect of the micro parameters is an effect on distribution.

In Figure 7.2.4 we impose a negative change in demand elasticity, which causes firms to raise prices. They do so, but now wages, as well

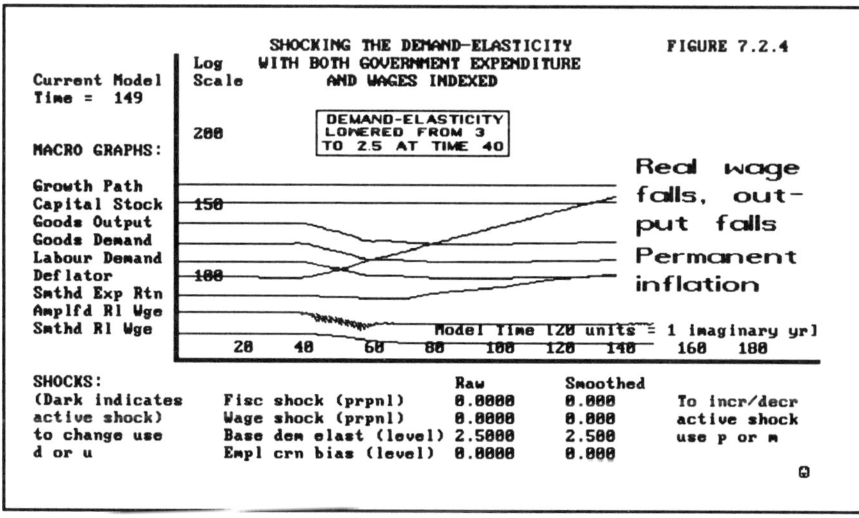

as government expenditure, are indexed. The result, as the reader can see, is that until some parameter of the situation changes, we have an economy in which in a very real sense, equilibrium does not exist. Rather than oscillations, the result is the worst form of stagflation: output is permanently depressed and inflation is fast and permanent. The Lerner formula now commands a lower real wage than the real wage at which the model set out in steady state. As fast as firms attempt to "impose" the new real wage by raising prices, however, labour suppliers "fight back" by their indexing of their nominal demands. In the ensuing permanent spiral, owing to the time-discrete operation of the multiplier process, the government, despite indexing expenditure, never catches up on real demand.

7.2.5 Effects of the neo-classical cost curve

In Figure 7.2.5 we investigate the effects of changing the assumptions to the neo-classical cost/opph curve (see Chapter 1, sub-section 1.4.5). According to the usual expectation, the effect, as much under imperfect competition as under perfect competition, should be to cause the real wage to move counter-cyclically: the share of wages in real output is constant, but output per head is itself counter cyclical. Given that we are using wage model 1, the effect should be seen through movements of prices, rather than of wages.

As will be seen, although the predicted changes in short run labour productivity (inevitably) occur, the predicted change in real wage

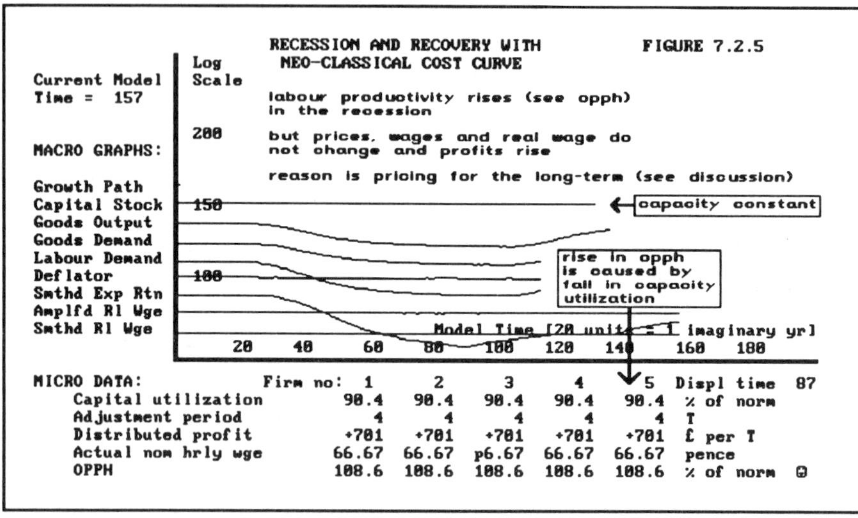

does not. This result does not negate the traditional theory, but does cast a new light upon it. The reason why the Imp-Mac model behaves in this way under these circumstances is connected with the nature of the economic-growth model and the associated pricing process. As the reader knows, the criterion for optimum price is discounted cash flow over an infinite time horizon, divided into two parts, the first of which, finite (during adjustment period) may be comparatively short. This feature, combined with the feature that, essentially for simplicity of calculation, firms are presumed to select the optimum price path from the subset of all possible paths where the "real" price, in fact, is constant through time, has the effect of making it difficult for short-term productivity changes to influence the price decision. The problem does not occur in the case of wages, where, as the reader knows, we assume that current nominal wages continue into the future. The reason for the difference of approach, of course, is that firms are treated as perceiving that they have little influence over wages but a major influence over capacity. They plan to restore capacity utilization to normal; therefore they expect productivity to become normal

It must be the case that it would be possible to earn more profit by means of a non-constant price path. Price could be raised during the period of shortage of capacity and subsequently lowered. By this standard Imp-Mac firms are simplistically long sighted. It could be

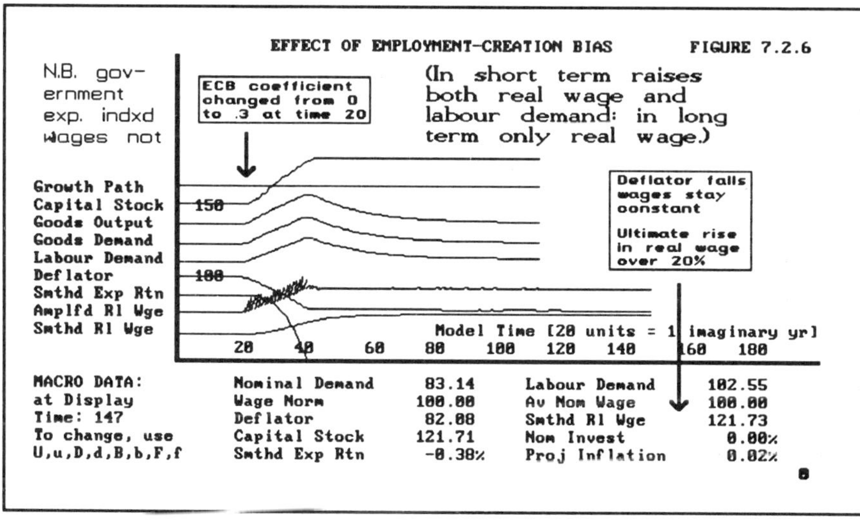

said on the other side, however, that the traditional approach leans the other way: firms are assumed rather short-sighted. More specifically, the "long period" is indeed long, so long, in fact, as Keynes himself is said to have believed, as to be elusive. In other words, the traditional approach often seems to take capacity as forever fixed, and to ignore the possibility that firms' minds could be influenced by the knowledge that they themselves plan that it shall not be fixed.

7.2.6 Effects of employment-creation bias

Figure 7.2.6 follows up in further detail the major question first raised at the end of Chapter 1 (Figure 1.2B): will employment-creation bias actually create employment? There the change in the ECB coefficient was quite mild, from 0 to 0.1. Here it goes up to 0.3. The effect is to change the criterion of optimization to a weighted average of discounted cash flow and discounted future employment (more precisely, the firm's discounted future demand for labour), the weight of the latter being 30% and of the former, 70% (0.3 and 0.7; for reminder, see Chapter 6, footnote to expected benefit function, section 6.6).

This motivation could be seen as paternalistic, or alternatively, the firms' managements may see total employment as a goal that enhances their own future salaries and general satisfaction. The device cannot, however be seen as a representation of the model

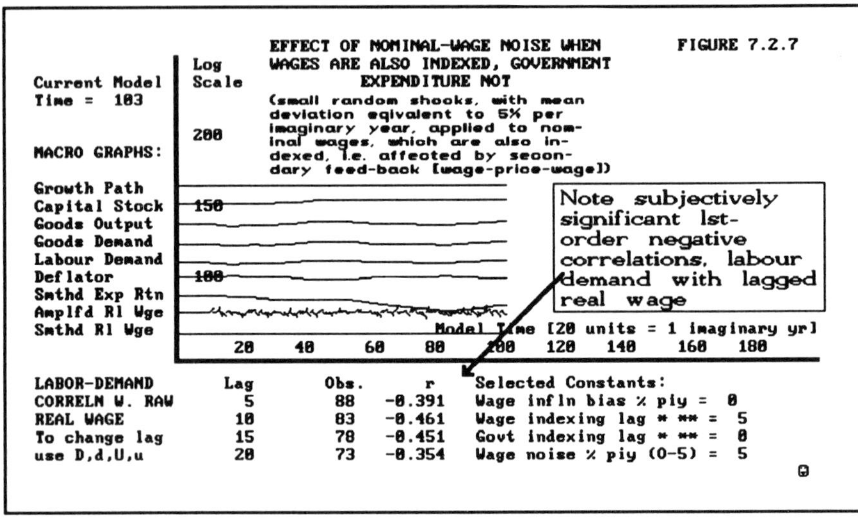

proposed by the present author in previous publications[1], because in that model, managers quite explicitly were not permitted to seek growth by moving along demand curves, as must be the case here. In effect, we are exercising the Imp-Mac model on one of its weakest points, namely the absence of a cash-flow or profitability constraint on growth or output. The result remains interesting neverthless.

Desiring to create more employment, firms desire to sell more output. Therefore their first response is to lower prices, and, in consequence, a significant rise in macro output and employment occurs. The increase in employment has no effect on nominal wages, because we are using wage model 1. Therefore real wages substantially increase. However, for the usual reasons, in Figure 7.2.6, we have also indexed government expenditure. In due course, therefore, nominal expenditure falls and real output relapses. As in the case of elasticity of demand, the whole effect falls on distribution. Unless government policy is less neutral, if firms try to "create" employment, they will succeed in creating higher real wages, lower profits, but no more jobs! Of course, the government could pursue another policy. But, as we saw in Chapter 1, if the government believed that an

1 See e.g. Marris, R. (1964b).

increase in the demand for labour was desirable, it could achieve this by a simple fiscal boost, without waiting on any change of heart from firms, and, also, without "interfering" in the distribution of income.

7.2.7 Perturbing the nominal wage with and
7.2.8 without real fiscal effect

Figures 7.2.7 and 7.2.8 demonstrate a rather crucial experiment. A small amount of random noise is applied to the random wage norm and, as can be seen, there is a consequent perturbation, but no trend, of the real wage. (It was mainly for the purpose of making this visible that the "amplified" curve was created.) Does this or does this not produce "correlations" between the real wage and the demand for labour? The answer is that in one case it does and in the other it does not. What is the difference? The answer is that in the case, namely the first run, where quite significant-looking lagged negative correlations appear, wages are indexed but government expenditure is not; in the second figure, the opposite situation holds.

It is important to be clear about the process that produce the "significant" correlations in the first Figure. Since we know the full specification of the Imp-Mac model, we know there cannot be an economically significant causal effect. The run starts with the nominal wage norm at steady-state level. The norm immediately receives a small shock, which in due course leads to some small price changes. Eventually these price changes cause a small index-movement of the wage norm. In the meantime the wage norm has received another random shock, and a further overlapping process begins, and so on, all combining together to produce the actual statistics at a given moment of model time.

The results make clear, however, that real output and employment is also being perturbed. Why is this? The answer is that because government expenditure is not indexed, any perturbation of the deflator produces perturbations of real government expenditure, producing in turn sequential effects on aggregate real demand through the Kahn multiplier process. The causality is not direct, but indirect. The first cause of the perturbation in aggregate demand is the perturbation of the nominal wage.

If econometric tests are applied to the above data, false inferences may be drawn if the model is not correctly specified. In a test for pure causality, the two series are integrated, and causality from real wage to employment is found in the sense that the real wage

A REPORT FROM ECONOMETRICS

Given that we know the actual structure of our model and what is happening to it, we thought it would be interesting to submit the data of some runs to a colleague trained in the "start of the art" econometric techniques, often referred to as "Granger" techniques (after the pathbreaking paper, Granger, 1969), where the nature and existence of causality can be tested without prior specification of an underlying model structure. This colleague, Dr. A. Sembenelli, of the CERIS research institute, Turin, knew enough about the Imp-Mac Model to know what the numbers were, but was not informed of the detailed simulation programme. He produced a thorough report, the conclusions of which, probably wrongly, we here only summarise. The summary assumes that the reader is reasonably familiar with the techniques and terminology.

It was first reported that the labour demand series was apparently non stationary, while the real wage series was. Therefore they cannot be integrated of the same order. Therefore they cannot be co-integrated and there cannot be long run causality, in either direction, between them. By contrast, both the labour demand and the nominal wage series are not stationary and it is possible to test for co-integretion between them. Two tests were run, both leading to acceptance of the null hypothesis. The same applied when the regression equation was reversed.

So it was concluded that in the short run changes in nominal wages Granger-cause changes in labour demand. No reverse relation was detected. Changes in real wages Granger cause changes in labour demand, but the reason for that seems to be some kind of impact of changes of nominal wages on the level of the real wage.

Even the reader who is not familiar with the methodology will see that these are the correct conclusions. Full marks to my colleague, and to Granger!

significantly improves on a pure autoregressive model of labour demand. This conclusion is amplified in the box. Alternatively, in a more traditional simultaneous-equations model, there is a major possibility of mis-specification unless the actual variables of the actual mechanism are explicitly defined. This is a specific advantage of simulation. For once we actually and completely know our model, and may observe how it performs as a data-generating process imitating the more typical econometrician's situation where we can only hypothesize the model. It is conceivable that some previous

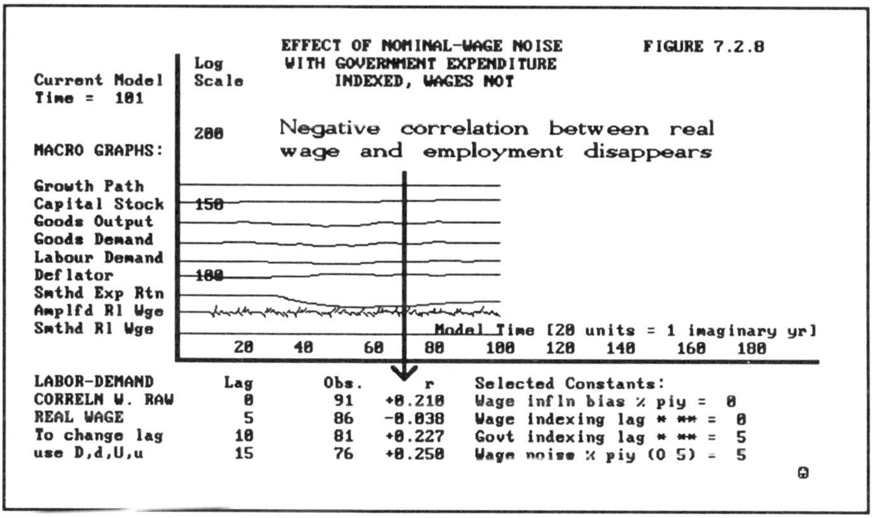

results suggesting significant causal relationships can be explained, not, of course, by exactly the story above but by richer similar stories.[1]

7.2.9 Conclusions on the real wage

This is therefore a good point to summarize the author's propositions, as now confirmed or illustrated by the Imp-Mac model concerning the relation between real wages and employment in Keynesian economics. The basic proposition is that as a matter of pure theory, for genuinely Keynesian labour-demand models, no fundamental relationship exists. Both statistically and theoretically, the movement of the real wage during a Keynesian cycle may be in either direction. The neo-classical cost curve could produce an endogenous counter-cyclical effect, but the neo-classical cost curve is not generally empirically supported. Furthermore, as seen above, if present, it will not necessarily produce the neo-classical result. From this basic proposition follows the conclusion that apparent correlations, if

1 Godley et al (1989) describe another extremely interesting data-generating process which could also explain otherwise mysterious correlations.

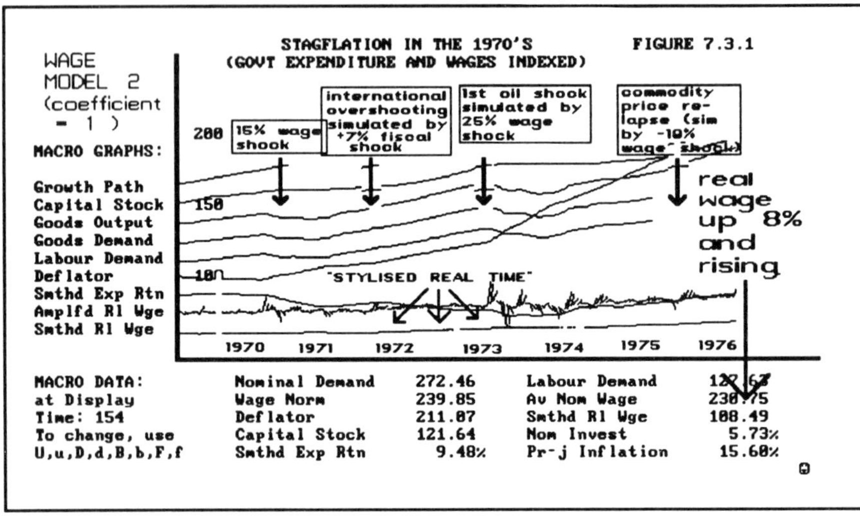

observed, are due to the interaction of nominal wages disturbances with aggregate real demand.

But, as we shall now see, that is not the end of the matter.

7.3 Stagflation

The general ideas and themes behind *Figures 7.3.1 and 7.3.2* have already been introduced in the Introduction (passage headed "personal testament") to this book and in the introduction to the present chapter. As already mentioned, we are compelled to simulate the oil and commodity shocks as if they were wage shocks. In both Figures we are using wage model 2, with the coefficient = 1. The reader should know that if wage model 2 is not used, or if it is used with a rather smaller coefficient, the simulation does not track actual events well, the disturbances to real output, and the rates of inflation, coming out too high. The implication seems to be that the relationship between nominal wage and demand pressure in the labour market, so clearly established in the previous era, had not disappeared, but, rather, under the welter of shocks, could not be so simply observed.

7.3.1 Stagflation in the 1970s

The figures are intended to be fairly self-explanatory. The essential theme, already mentioned above, is that in the 1970s inflation was worse and output fluctuation less severe, because, on the whole, governments, fiscally and monetarily, were more lenient. This is more true in Europe than in the US, where the money was kept tight in 1974/5. Consequently, in the US, there was a shorter, sharper, recession at that time, followed by a much lower inflation rate. The US was also considerably insulated from the impact effect of the oil first oil shock by virtue of her severe control of domestic energy prices.

Nevertheless, Figure 7.3.1 contains an important surprise. At the end of the period, the real wage has risen by a substantial amount. It will be found, furthermore, that this result is not obtainable unless all the main ingredients of the previous history are included, most especially the "fiscal overshoot" of 1972, which prevented a fall in real demand which would have in turn dampened nominal wages and also, as it turns out, real wages. Why do we here, in, without any contrivance, successfully simulate a moderate real-wage overrun, obtaining results so different from those obtained in the preceding section? The answer has already been hinted at. The first essential ingredient was the sheer size of the shocks. With large, in place of huge, shocks, the results are not obtained. Also essential is what may be called "super-indexing" of government expenditure, as just mentioned, in 1972. In short, the real-wage overrun that did occur in the middle and late 1970s was ultimately caused by economic shocks which, we have argued, were in turn military and political in origin.

In a more peaceful world, such as one hopes to see in the future ("more peaceful" in the sense of less military expenditure and or actual fighting by nations with major industrialized economies), there is no good reason to believe that a gradual progression to low inflation and steady economic growth (or whatever economic growth is appropriate to the human race's environmental aspirations), without new or special measures such as incomes policies. What is basically required is a well-coordinated, neo-Keynesian, politically-neutral international macroeconomic-management policy. Some elements of such a policy have been put in place towards the end of the 1980s, but in Europe, at least, unemployment is still unacceptably high and growth unnecessarily low. In the author's own country, the UK, the coefficient of the wage equation, despite a great weakening of trade union power, is higher than in most other countries and is still causing great problems in economic management. On the whole, the conclusion seems to be that whatever their other disadvantages may be, large nations, or rather large economies, can more easily be endowed with benign economic macro-dynamics than small ones. Where, however, a nation is very small and its people very public spirited, a rather different, "Nordic" conclusion may be reached. But the fundamental point is that a mixed economy is essentially prone to the Keynesian weakness of having no automatic mechanism, monetary, fiscal or otherwise, to control either the dangers of inflation or the dangers of recession. But by conventional neo-Keynesian demand management, using as many fiscal and monetary instruments as possible, the task is indeed, as has been proved, feasible. Faced with extraordinary shocks, however, while total breakdown may be avoided (if one thinks about it the remarkable thing about the period 1973-86 is that results were not worse) only under "Nordic" circumstances is there likely to be much hope of maintaining all objectives within reasonable limits. In particular, a traditional sacrifice of output and employment in order to purchase disinflation may be inevitable.

7.3.2 Stagflation in the 1980s

Figure 7.3.2 illustrates this for the 1980s. We cannot show the entry into the decade with an "overrun" real wage which, as a matter of history, gradually came down, because the initiation process of the model does not have the power to do that. But we see the effect of the second oil shock under conditions, most especially in Europe, of stricter government fiscal and monetary policy, resulting in the so-called "great recession" of 1981-1985. By the end of the decade, with the exception of the author's own country, the general picture was beginning to seem to converge toward the situation that might have been in 1990 had the Viet-Nam war, the Middle-East wars, the Afghanistan war, and the economic shocks resulting therefrom, never occurred. Of course, the old growth path can never be fully regained, especially if by that path we mean an exponential trend fitted from 1950 to 1970. Outside the US, which was already slow growing, and Japan, who was having her miracle, fast growth among already rich countries was already inevitably slowing down, however, as technical diffusion filled in technological gaps. We cannot know exactly where we should have been if these things had not happened. In the future there is no reason why we cannot have good growth without significant inflation, but we shall of course be measuring growth differently, i.e. net of negative environmental costs.

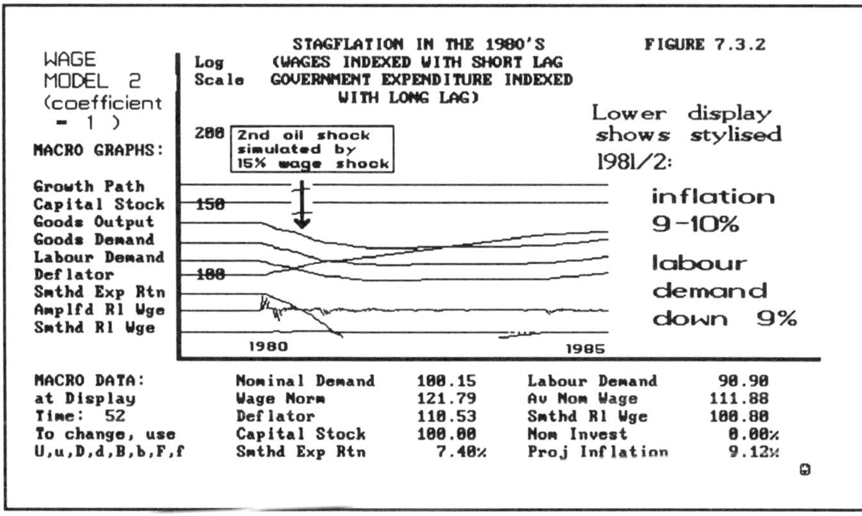

7.4 A Final Conclusion

Of the various things we hope the Imp-Mac Model has demonstrated, there is an implied conclusion which has profound political importance for the future. A modern economy is a Keynesian economy with awkward stagflationary dynamics. If it is shocked, it is not easy to stabilize and stabilization cannot be achieved by turning one wheel. Furthermore, even with the best governmental will in the world, the effect of exogenous global macro shocks, such as wars, may be very long lasting, with all the attendant problems of learning and others going under fashionable names such as hysteresis. This is not something that capitalism must be ashamed of: it is a consequence of success. Two closely related final conclusions follow.

The basic conclusion is that the delicate pragmatic task of macroeconomic management presents a difficult challenge to democratic systems where governments must place themselves before the electorate with a periodicity that is uncomfortably short in relation to the practical dynamics of the macroeconomy. Apart from the fact that many necessary macro measures are net vote losers, there is a more subtle problem of accountability. A substantial part of the typical situation faced by the typical government in the OECD world at any one time is the result of events and policies over which it had no control. But here again we face a fact of life. We want democracy and we want good macroeconomic performance; the two are not inevitably consistent. Importating ideology into this difficult situation makes self-inflicted wounds. Democracy, government by consent, differences of opinion about distribution and ethics, these are the valid concerns of politics and politicians. The question of the techniques of macroeconomic management, except where they have distributional spill-overs (and in most countries there is evidence of strong cross-party consensus on the crucial issue of inflation versus output), deserve to be defended from the pollution of ideology.

The related conclusion echoes the end of our Introduction. Irrelevant ideology is a common reason why otherwise apparently sane governments tie their hands by renouncing the use of some policy instruments.[1] The ideological act of self-incapacitation is of course usually rationalized by reference to some kind of economic theory. How has the Imp-Mac model contributed to such debates? In effect the model has only one policy instrument, or more precisely, two alternative modes in each of which there is only one instrument. In one mode government expenditure is not indexed, in which case the instrument is the nominal government expenditure. In the other mode government expenditure is indexed in which case the instrument is real. If we think of the Imp-Mac programme as a computer game with economic stabilization as the objective, and only this one knob to press, we can quickly see that it is a very difficult, if not impossible game! The moral, of course, is more knobs.

---

1 See the footnote discussion of the "Tinbergen theorem" in the section on the Keynesian Theory in the Introduction, above.

Appendix
Software Instructions

Hardware requirements

The programme was written on an **IBM AT** with **"EGA"** graphics capability. It has also been successfully tested on a range of makes of the subsequent generation of IBM Personal-System-2 compatibles with "VGA" graphics running in DOS. The displays are for a screen of **640 x 350 pixels** set for **16 colours.**

The software

The disc in the flap at the back of the book contains, inter alia, a file **IMP-MAC.EXE,** which is a stand-alone "executable" programme, meaning that if it is placed in a directory, and that directory is the current directory, on typing **IMP-MAC** (including the hyphen) from the DOS command line, or alternatively calling the it from a batch file, the programme will run.

The **source code,** in **Microsoft Quickbasic 4.0,** is available on the disk as a set of **ASCII text files,** with extensions **.BAS.** These are further discussed below.

Most of the **technical help** required to run the programme is provided internally. Its **economic meaning** is explained in **Chapter 1,** especially **section 1.3,** of this book. The detail, including explanations and definitions of the **user-editable constants** are in **Chapter 6,** especially **section 6.3.**

Running the programme

(1) Call the programme in one of the ways described above. The **main menu**, will appear;
1. to **run** the programme, select and enter **"Do/display new run"**
2. to **return to DOS**, select and enter **"Quit"**
3. for **other main-menu facilities**, see below

(2) If **"Do/display new run"** is selected, the **constants-editing** screen, which has its own help in footnotes, will appear. The screen will display the current values of constants, either default values or values employed in last run. To change values, select and enter **"edit"** from the screen sub-menu and follow instructions, using **"ENTER"** where necessary.

(3) When constant editing is complete, select and enter **"run"** from the screen sub-menu and the programme will initialize itself consistently with the selected constants (see Chapter 1 subsection 1.3.1 and Chapter 6 section 6.7), and then run.

(4) Alternatively it is possible, from the constants-editing sub-menu, to return to the **main menu** or to **quit** the Imp-Mac programme directly and return to DOS.

(5) When the programme runs, the **upper screen** displays **macro graphics** and initially the **lower screen** displays instructions; by successively pressing **"ENTER"** the lower screen can be made to display various kinds of numeric data, namely **micro data** relating to each individual firm, **macro data**, **order books**, **initial constants**, lagged **correlations** between real wage and demand for labour and finally a window enabling the user to **shock** the programme and also to review the current state of shocks.

(6) The programme can be **paused** at any time by pressing the space bar, re-started by pressing it again.

(7) To **manipulate lower-screen displays,** follow screen instructions.

(8) To **shock** the programme, call shock display as described above. Four shocks are available (see 1.3.7)
1. *fiscal shock*
2. *wage norm*
3. *base demand elasticity*
4. *employment-creation bias*
Instructions for operating the shocks are built into the displays.

(9) To **quit the run** at any time, press **"q" or "Q"**. The run ends and the display reverts to constant editing, holding, as indicated, the existing values of the constants. The data of the run, up to the point where it was quit, is also held in memory (for saving or down-loading into text files) until a new run actually starts. The only way to lose the data of the current run is to start another run, to return to DOS or otherwise clear the memory. To re-display the data of a run before it has been replaced select and enter **"Display run in memory"** from main menu.

Saving and re-calling runs

There is a facility for saving all the data of a run and subsequently recalling the macro and micro data and manipulating both the macro displays. To use this facility proceed as follows,

(1) *Preparations*

(i) make a direct sub-directory of the root directory of Drive C, named **"IMP-MAC"**
(ii) put **IMP-MAC.EXE** into the **IMP-MAC** directory
(iii) make the following IMP-MAC sub-directories
MIC-DAT, MAC-DAT, CON-DAT, SHK-DAT, DES-DAT
—these sub-directories will be used to store **micro-data, macro-data, constants-data, shocks data** and brief **descriptions** of stored runs entered by the user at the time of saving, respectively.

(2) *General points*

(i) always run the programme with the **IMP-MAC directory** current
(ii) when the save-load facility is used the programme employs an **index file** for identifying saved runs; this resides in the IMP-MAC directory, has an extension of .IMI and can be created with a user-selected name; to avoid error-messages, however, a default index file is also provided on the disc; at first use, this file, named "DEFAULT.IMI", should be placed in the IMP-MAC directory
(iii) the facility uses a procedure in Quickbasic known as **block**-save or -load, which permits fast data transfer and is necessary for handling the large quantity of data; this procedure works perfectly on the hardware specified above, e.g. IBM AT or the OS/2 based Compacq computer; there have been reports of difficulties with some other machines which otherwise run the main programme perfectly.

(3) *Activation*

(i) to **save** a run, first quit it; the main menu will be displayed; select **"save run"** and follow displayed instructions
(ii) to **load** a run, select **"load old run"** from main menu and follow instructions; data of run currently in memory will be replaced
(iii) to **view** a recalled run, select **"Display run in memory"** from main menu.

Other main-menu facilities

(1) **"Display curves"**

this facility enables the user to **view the curves of the main economic relationships** in the Imp-Mac Model, including the effects of changing their coefficients; when a display is entered the value of the coefficient is the value current in memory as displayed in the constants-editing screen; if the coefficient is changed by the user during display, the new value becomes the current value; the curves displayed are,

1. *Investment Cost*
   curve of the "**Penrose Effect**", see 1.2.3, 1.4.9, and 6.6
2. *OPPH*
   short-run **OPPH curve** (effect of varying capacity utilization on opph), both "empirical" and "neo-classical" forms are selectable, see 1.2.3, 1.4.5., 6.6 and 7.2.5
3. *Wage*
   curves displaying the effects of the **nominal-wage models,** (wage model 1 and wage model 2; see 1.2.1. 6.1 and 6.6)

(2) **"Edit old-runs index"**

this facility permits **renaming** or **deleting** old runs

(3) **"Create macro data text file"**

this facility permits the user to select macro data from the run in memory to download into **ASCII files** which can be printed or transported into other software, e.g. for statistical analysis; the facility was used to obtain the test of Granger causality in runs of the Imp-Mac Model discussed in sub-section 7.2.7.

Running speed

Given the large number of calculations to be made by each firm in each cycle, the programme was written to run as fast as possible, with most data stored as integer numbers. On the IBM AT on which the programme was written, when the economy is in steady state, the speed was 1.3 cycles per second. On an a fast 386 machine this should be doubled.

Source-code

As already indicated, the source code is provided on the disk in **ASCII** text files, all with extension **.BAS**, one of which **IMP-MAC.BAS** is the master programme, also known as the "main module", one, **IM-SETUP.INC**, is a so-called "Include" file, and the other four are subsidiary modules; finally **IMP-MAC.MAK** is the special Quickbasic file which calls the other files to assemble the whole programme for editing or for running in the editing environment, as discussed below. Apart from being readable in DOS or software that can import ASCII files, these files can in principle be modified by the user, but for that purpose **Microsoft Quickbasic 4.0** or a later version is required or alternatively a capacity for translating from this language into another language and the editor for that language.

Apart from the .EXE and .MAK files, the disk files are:

IMP-MAC.BAS	—main module, includes model programme cycle (see Chapter 1, section 1.3)
IM-CURVE.BAS	—activates "Display Curves" from main menu (see above)
IM-EFUNC.BAS	—does misc calculations e.g. DCF
IM-GRAPH.BAS	—operates run graphics display
IM-MISC.BAS	--does miscellaneous operations, especially user interfaces and other main-menu facilities (see above)
IM-SETUP.INC	—("INCLUDE" file), does technical preparations for programme.

Readers who possess Quickbasic, desiring to edit the programme, proceed as follows:

(1) Put all the above files into a directory and make that directory current

(2) Activate Quickbasic as **QB/ah IMP-MAC.BAS**
(3) Quickbasic will then seek then seek and obey IMP-MAC.MAK resulting in the loading of the editor, the display of IMP-MAC.BAS (main module) and the loading of the sub-modules listed with .BAS extensions listed above. The .INC file is named at the beginning of IMP-MAC.BAS and will be called from the current directory if the programme is run in the editing environment. It can also, by following Quickbasic instructions, be edited.
(4) The programme can then be edited and also run in the editing environment. The edited programme can be re-compiled into a new .EXE file. Such work requires knowledge of Quickbasic.

References

ADELMAN I. (1982) Simulation of Economic Processes, *International Encyclopaedia of Statistics*. (1987) Simulation Models, in Eatwell et al (1987) op cit.

AKERLOF, G. with Yellen, J. (1985) A Near-Rational Model of the Business Cycle with Wage and Price Inertia, *Quarterly Journal of Economics*.

ALOGOSKOUFIS, G. with Smith, R. (1989) The Phillips Curve and the Lucas Critique, *Discussion Paper in Economics 89/4*, Birkbeck College, London University.

ANNAN, N. (1989) The Upper Class and the Underworld, *New York Review*, 13 April 13. (1990) *Our Age*, London, Weidenfeld. ARROW, K. with Hahn, F. (1971) *General Competitive Analysis*, San Francisco, CA, Holden-Day. (1986) Rationality in an Economic System, in Hogarth and Reder (1986) op cit.

ASPRAY, W. (1990) John Von Neumann and the Origins of Modern Computing, MIT Press.

AUMANN, R. (1961) The Core of a Cooperative Game, *Transactions of the American Mathematical Society*. With Drêze, J. (1974) Cooperative Games with Coalition Structures, *International Journal of Game Theory*.

BAIN, J. (1956) *Barriers to New Competition*, Harvard University Press. (1972) *Essays on Price Theory and Industrial Organization*, Boston, Mass, Little Brown.

BALDASSARRI, M. (ed) (1989) Keynes and the Economic Policies in the Eighties, *Rivista di Politica Economica*, Rome.

BARRO, R. with Grossman, H. (1971) *A General Disequilibrium Model of Income and Employment, American Economic Review*. (1976) *Money, Employment and Inflation*, Cambridge University Press.

BAUMOL, W. (1959) *Business Behaviour, Value and Growth*, New York. (1971) On the Behavioural Theory of the Firm, in Marris and Wood (1971) op cit. With Panzar and Willig (1982) *Contestable Markets and the Theory of Industry Structure*, New York, Harcourt Brace.

BENASSY, J-P. (1975) Neo-Keynesian Disequilibrium Theory in a Monetary Economy, *Review of Economic Studies*. (1977) A Neo-Keynesian Model of Price and Quantity Determination in Disequilibrium, in Schwödiauer, G. (ed) *Equilibrium and Disequilibrium in Economic Theory*, Dordrecht, Netherlands, Reidel Publishing. (1982) Developments in Non-Walrasian Economics and in the Microfoundations of Macroeconomics, in Hildenbrand, W. (ed) *Advances in Economic Theory*, Cambridge University Press. (1986) *Macroeconomics: an Introduction to the non-Walrasian Approach*, Academic Press, New York, NY.

BENNET, R. see Bergmann, B. (1986).

BERGMANN, B. (1974) A Microsimulation of a Macroeconomy with Explicitly Represented Cash Flows, *Annals of Economic and Social Measurement*. With Bennet, R. (1986) *A Microsimulated Transactions Model of the United States Economy*, Johns Hopkins University Press. (1989) A Simulation Model of the Labour Market, *Journal of Economic Perspectives*.

BERTRAND, J. (1883) Les Faux Mathématiciens, *Journal des Savants*.

BIANCHI, P. (1989) Survey of Oligopoly Theory, *Rivista di Politica Economica*, Rome.

BILS, M. (1987) The Cyclical Behaviour of Marginal Cost and Price, *American Economic Review*.

BLANCHARD, O. (1987a) Aggregate and Individual Price Adjustment, *Brookings Papers on Economic Activity*, Vol 1. With Kiyotaki, N. (1987b) Monopolistic Competition and Aggregate Demand, *American Economic Review*. The Dynamic Effects of Aggregate Supply and Demand Disturbances, *American Economic Review, Proceedings*.

CANTILLON, R. (1755) *Essai sur la Nature du Commerce en General*, London. Fletcher Gyles; Eng trans, 1931, London, Macmillan.

CARLSSON B. (1991) Productivity Analysis: a Micro to Macro Perspective, in Deiaco, E. (ed) *Technology and Investment*, London, Pinter Publishers. See also Eliasson, G. (1991).

CASAROSA, C. (1981) The Microfoundations of Keynes's Aggregate Supply and Expected Demand Analysis, *Economic Journal.*
CHAMBERLIN, E. (1933) *The Theory of Monopolistic Competition*, Harvard University Press.
CHICK, V. (1983) *Macroeconomics After Keynes*, London, Phillip Allan. (1991) The Small Firm under Uncertainty: a puzzle of the General Theory, in Gerrard and Hillard op cit.
CLOWER, R. (1960) Keynes and the Classics: a Dynamical Perspective, *Quarterly Journal of Economics.* (1965) The Keynesian Counter-Revolution: a Theoretical Appraisal, in Hahn and Brechling (eds) (1965) op cit. (1967) A Reconsideration of the Microfoundations of Monetary Theory, *Western Economic Journal.*
COSTELLO, J. (1988) *The Mask of Treachery*, London, Collins.
COURNOT, A. (1838) *Researches sur les Principes Mathématique de la Théorie de la Richesse*, Paris, France, repub English, 1929, N. Bacon (trans), London, Macmillan.
CYERT, R. with March J. (1963) *A Behavioural Theory of the Firm*, Englewood Cliffs, NJ, Prentice Hall.
CRICK, F. (1989) The Recent Excitement about Neural Nets, *Nature* (12 Jan), London. With Koch, C. (1990) Towards a Neurobiological Theory of Consciousness, *Seminars in the Neurosciences.*
DAVIDSON, P. (1981) Post-Keynesian Economics, in Bell, D. and Kristol, I. (eds) *The Crisis in Economic Theory*, New York, Basic Books.
DEBREU, J. with Scarf, H. (1963) A Limit Theorem on the Core of an Economy, *International Economic Review.*
DIXIT, A. (1980) The Role of Investment in Entry Deterrence, *Economic Journal.*
DIXON, H. (1987) A Simple Model of Imperfect Competition with Walrasian Features, *Oxford Economic Papers.*
DORNBUSCH R. with Blanchard, O. Drêze, J. Giersche, and Layard, R. (1986) *Employment and Growth in Europe*, Brussels, Belgium, Centre for European Economic Policy Research. DOW, C. (1990) How can Real Wages ever get Excessive?, Keynes Lecture, British Academy, available as *Discussion Paper No. 196*, National Institute of Economic Research, London.

DREZE, J. (1975) Existence of an Exchange Equilibrium under Price Rigidities, *International Economic Review*. With Snessens H. (1986) A discussion of Belgian Unemployment, *Economica*. See also with Aumann, R. (1974) op cit.

DUNLOP, J. (1938) The Movement of Real and Money Wages, *Economic Journal*.

EATON, B. with Lipsey, R. (1980) The Theory of Market Preemption, *Economica*.

EATWELL, J. with Milgate, M. (1983) *Keynes' Theory of Value and Distribution*, London, Duckworth.

EATWELL, J. with Milgate, M. and Newman, P. (eds) (1987) *The New Palgrave Dictionary of Economics*, London, Macmillan.

EDGEWORTH, F. (1881) *Mathematical Psychics*, London, Kegan Paul.

ELIASSON, G. (1977) Competition and Market Processes in a Simulation Model of the Swedish Economy, *American Economic Review*. (1978-) (ed, with others) *The Micro to Macro Model of the Swedish Economy, IUI Conference Reports*. (1989) *Modelling the Experimentally Organized Economy in MOSES Code*. (1991) with Carlsson B. and Taymaz, E. *The Productivity Puzzle*, IUI Working Paper No 289. All foregoing after (1978-) pub by Industrial Institute for Economic Research (IUI) Stockholm.

ELTIS, W. with Sinclair, P. (1988) *Keynes and Economic Policy*, London, UK National Economic Development Office, with Macmillan. (1989) Contribution to the general debate, in Baldassarri (1989) op cit.

FRIEDMAN, J. (1983) *Oligopoly Theory*, Cambridge University Press.

GALBRAITH, J. (1967) *The New Industrial Estate*, Boston, Houghton Miflin.

GASKINS, D. (1971) Dynamic Limit Pricing, *Journal of Economic Theory*.

GERRARD, B. with Hillard, J. (eds) (1991) *New Perspectives on Keynes*, Aldershot, England, Edward Elgar.

GIERSCHE, H. (1986) Economics as a Public Good, *Banco Nationale del Lavoro Quarterly Review No. 158*, Rome, Italy.

GODLEY, W. with Neild, R. (1962) *Prices and Employment in the Trade Cycle*, Cambridge University Press. With Coutts, K. and Moreno-Brind, J. (1989) Pricing in U.K. Manufacturing Industry under Conditions of 'Stagflation', *Manchester School*.

GOLDBERG, E. (1989) *Genetic Algorithms*, Reading, Mass, USA, Addison-Wesley.

GORDON, R., (1990) What is the new Keynesian Economics?, *Journal of Economic Literature*.

GRANGER, C. (1969) Investigating Causal Relations by Econometric Models and Cross-Spectral Models, *Econometrica*.

GROSSMAN, H. see Barro, R. (1971), (1976).

HAHN, F. with Brechling, F. (eds) (1965) *The Theory of Interest Rates*, London, Macmillan. (1977) Exercises in Conjectural Equilibria, *Scandanavian Journal of Economics*. (1978) On non-Walrasian equilibria, *Review of Economic Studies*. (1980) Unemployment from a Theoretical Viewpoint, *Economica*. (1987) Conjectural Equilibrium, in Eatwell et al (1987) op cit. (1990) The Next 100 Years, *Economic Journal*. See also with Arrow, K. (1971) op cit.

HALL, R. and HITCH, C. (1939) Price Theory and Business Behaviour, *Oxford Economic Papers*.

HARCOURT, G. (1988) *Post-Keynesianism*, Bulletin of Economic Research, reprinted in Pheby (1989) op cit.

HARSANYI, J. (1966) A General Theory of Rational Behaviour in Game Situations, *Econometrica*.

HART, O. (1979) Monopolistic Competition in a Large Economy with Heterogeneous Products, *Review of Economic Studies*. (1982) A Model of Imperfect Competition with Keynesian Features, *Quarterly Journal of Economics*. (1984) Imperfect Competition in General Equilibrium, in Arrow, K. and Honkaphohja, (eds) *Frontiers of Economics*, Oxford, Basil Blackwell. (1985) Monopolistic Competition in the Spirit of Chamberlin, *Review of Economic Studies*. HEBB, D. (1949) *The Organization of Behaviour*, New York, NY, John Wiley.

HEIMLER, A. and Milano, C. (1989) Capacity Utilization and Profit Margins in Italian Industries, *Rivista di Politica Economica*, Rome.

HEFLEBOWER, R. (1960) Observations on Decentralization in Large Businesses, *Journal of Industrial Economics*.

HICKS, J. (1937) Mr. Keynes and the Classics, *Econometrica*. (1974) *The Crisis in Keynesian Economics*, Oxford, Basil Blackwell.

HILLARD, J. see Gerrard, W. (1991).

HINES, A. (1962) The Effect of Union Bargaining Strength on the Phillips Curve, *Review of Economic Studies*.

HODGES, A. (1983) *The Enigma of Intelligence and the Life of Alan Turing*, London, Hutchinson.

HOGARTH, M. with Reder M. (eds) (1986) *Rational Choice*, Chicago University Press.
HOLLAND, J. et al (1986) *Induction: Processes of Inference, Learning and Discovery*, MIT Press.
ICHIISHI, T. with Neyman, A. and Tauman, Y.(1991) *Game Theory and Applications*, London, Academic Press.
JACKMAN, R. with Layard, R. and Nickell, S. (1991) *Unemployment*, Oxford University Press.
KAHN, R. (1929) *The Economics of the Short Period*, Fellowship Dissertation, King's College, Cambridge, 1st pub Italian, 1983, Turin, Editore Boringhieri, 1st pub English, 1989, London, Macmillan. (1931) The Relation of Home Investment to Unemployment, *Economic Journal*. (1972) *Selected Essays on Employment and Growth*, Cambridge University Press. (1984) *The Making of Keynes' General Theory*, Cambridge University Press.
KALDOR, N. (1934) Mrs. Robinson's Economics of Imperfect Competition, *Economica*. (1935) Market Imperfection and Excess Capacity, *Economica*. (1940) A Model of the Trade Cycle, *Economic Journal*. (1957) A Model of Economic Growth, *Economic Journal*. With Mirrlees, J. (1962) A New Model of Economic Growth, *Review of Economic Studies*. (1966) Contribution to debate on theories of distribution, and "Neo-Pasinetti Theorem", *Review of Economic Studies*. (1983) Keynesian Economics after 50 Years, in Worswick, D. and Trevithick, J. op cit, Cambridge University Press.
KALECKI, M. (1936) Pare uwag o teorii Keynesa, *Ekonomista*, Poland, first pub English, Targetti and Kinda-Haas (1982) op cit. (1938) The Determinants of the Distribution of the National Income, *Econometrica*. (1970-72) *Selected Essays*, 3 vols, Cambridge University Press. See also Osiatynsky, J. (ed) (1990) *The Collected Works of Michal Kalecki*, Oxford, Clarendon Press.
KAMIEN, M. with Schwartz, N. (1975) Cournot Oligopoly with Uncertain Entry, *Review of Economic Studies*.
KEYNES, J. M. (1921) *A Treatise on Probability*. (1930) *A Treatise on Money*. (1936) *The General Theory of Employment, Interest and Money*, (1940) *How to Pay for the War*. See also Moggeridge, D. (ed) op cit (1973-) *The Collected Writings of John Maynard Keynes*. All these works London, Macmillan.

KIYOTAKI N. (1985) Macroeconomics of Imperfect Competition, Doctoral Dissertation, Harvard University. (1988) Multiple Expectational Equilibrium under Monopolistic Competition, *Quarterly Journal of Economics*. (1989) with Wright, R. On Money as a Medium of Exchange, *Journal of Political Economy*. See also with Blanchard, O. (1987) op cit.

KUHN, T. (1962) *The Structure of Scientific Revolutions*, Chicago University Press.

LABINI, P. S. (1956) *Oligopoly and Technical Progress*, Eng trans 1969, Harvard University Press.

LANZILLOTTI, R. (1958) *Pricing in Big Business*, Menasha, Ill.

LAWSON, N. (1988) Keynes and Economic Policy: Introduction, in Eltis and Sinclair (1988) op cit.

LAYARD R. with Nickell, S. (1985) The Causes of British Unemployment, *National Institute Economic Review*, London. (1986) The Rise in Unemployment, *Economica*. See also with Jackman, R. (1991).

LEIJONHUFVUD, A. (1968) *On Keynesian Economics and the Economics of Keynes*, Oxford University Press.

LERNER, A. (1944) *The Economics of Control*, New York, NY, Macmillan Corporation.

LINDBECK, A. (1983) The Slow Down in Productivity Growth, *Economic Journal*, papers of Royal Economic Society Conference, London, 1982.

LIPSEY, R. (1960) The Relationship between Unemployment and the Rate of Change of Money Wages, *Economica*. See also with Eaton, B. (1979) op cit.

LUCAS, R. (1970) Capacity, Overtime and Empirical Production Functions, *American Economic Review*. (1972) Expectations and the Neutrality of Money, *Journal of Economic Theory*. (1981) *Studies in Business-Cycle Theory*, Oxford, Basil Blackwell.

LUCE, R. with Raiffa, H. (1957) *Games and Decisions*, New York, John Willey.

MALINVAUD, E. (1977) *The Theory of Unemployment Reconsidered* Oxford, Basil Blackwell. (1988) *Real Wages and Employment*, Stamp Memorial Lecture, London University.

MANKIW, N. G. (1985) Small Menu Costs and Large Business Cycles: a Macroeconomic Model of Monopoly, *Quarterly Journal of Economics*. (1988) Imperfect Competition and the Keynesian Cross, *Economics Letters*, North Holland Press. (1991) with Romer, D. (eds), *New Keynesian Economics*, MIT Press.

MARCH, J. (1978) Bounded Rationality, *Bell Journal of Economics*. See also with Cyert, R. (1963) op cit.

MARCUZZO, C. (1988) *Richard F. Kahn: Un Discepolo di Keynes*, Milan, Italy, Garganzzanti; English version, *Richard F. Kahn: A Disciple of Keynes*, Modena, Department of Economics Discussion Paper No. 29.

MARIMON, R. with McGrattan, E. and Sargent, T. (1989) *Money as a Medium of Exchange in an Economy with Artificially Intelligent Agents*, Economics Working Paper E-89-29, Hoover Institution, Stanford University.

MARRIS, R. (1963) A Model of the Managerial Enterprise, Quarterly Journal of Economics. (1964a) *The Economics of Capital Utilization*, Cambridge University Press. (1964b) *The Economic Theory of Managerial Capitalism*, Macmillan, London. With Wood, A. (eds) (1970) *The Corporate Economy*, Harvard University Press. (1972) Why Economics Needs a Theory of the Firm, *Economic Journal* (suppl). (1979) *The Theory and Future of the Corporate Economy and Society*, North-Holland Press. With Mueller, D. (1980) The Corporation, Competition and the Invisible Hand, *Journal of Economic Literature*. (1990) Imperfect Competition and the Debate on Keynesian Economics, *Rivista di Politica Economica*, Rome, Italy.

MARRIS, S. (1984) Managing the World Economy, *Essays in International Finance*, Department of Economics, Princeton University. (1985) *Deficits and the Dollar*, Institute for International Economics, Washington, DC.

MATHEWS, R. with Bowen, A. (1988) Keynesian and other Explanations of post-War Economic Trends, in Eltis and Sinclair (1988) op cit.

MATTI, P. with Pekkarrinen, J. and Rowthorne, R. (1991) *Social Corporatism: A Superior Economic System?*, Oxford, Clarendon Press, in association with UNU WIDER, Helsinki.

McCALLUM, B. (1983) The Liquidity Trap and the Pigou Effect, *Economica*. (1986) On "Real" and "Sticky-price" Theories of the Business Cycle, *Journal of Money, Credit and Banking*. (1988) The Role of Demand Management in the Maintenance of Full Employment, in Eltis and Sinclair (1988) op cit. (1989) The Development of Keynesian Macroeconomics in Baldassarri (1989) op cit.

McCLELLAND, J. see Rumelhart, D. 1988.

MODIGLIANI, F. (1958) New Developments on the Oligopoly Front, *Journal of Political Economy*.

MOGGRIDGE, D. (ed) (1973-) *The Collected Writings of John Maynard Keynes*, 30 vols. (1976) *Keynes*. Both works London, Macmillan.

MUELLBAUER, J. with Portes, R. (1978) Macroeconomic Models with Quantity Rationing, *Economic Journal*.

MUELLER, D. (1972) A Life Cycle Theory of the Firm, *Journal of Industrial Economics*. With Marris, R. (1980) The Corporation and Competition, *Journal of Economic Literature*.

MUSU, I. (1979) Sul Capitolo Terzo Della *Teoria Generale*, *Rivista Internazionale di Scienze Economiche*, Padua, Italy.

MUTH, J. (1961) Rational Expectations and the Theory of Price Movements, *Econometrica*.

NASH, J. (1950) The Bargaining Probem, *Econometrica*. (1951) Non-Cooperative Games, *Annals of Mathematics*.

NEGISHI, T. (1961) Monoplistic Competition and General Equilibrium, *Review of Economic Studies*. (1979) *Microeconomic Foundations of Keynesian Macroeconomics*, North-Holland Press.

NEYMAN, A. see Ichiishi, T.

NG, Y-K. (1980) Macroeconomics with Non-Perfect Competition, *Economic Journal*. (1982) "—a reply", *Economic Journal*. (1986) *Mesoeconomics*, Wheatsheaf Books, Brighton, England.

NIKAIDO, H. (1975) *Monopolistic Competition and Effective Demand*, Princeton University Press.

NICKELL, S. see with Layard, R. (1985) and with Jackman, R. (1991).

NORDHAUS, W. (1972) The Worldwide Wage Explosion, *Brookings Papers on Economic Activity*, Washington DC, Brookings Institution.

ODAGIRI, H. (1981) *The Theory of Growth in a Corporate Economy*, Cambridge University Press. (1991) *An 'Economic' Theory of Japanese Management*, Oxford University Press.

OSIATYNSKI, J. (1990) *Collected Works of Michal Kalecki*, Vol 1, Oxford, Clarendon Press, (Vol 2 due 1991).

PARETO, V. (1897). *Cours d'Economie Politique*, Lausanne, Swizerland, Biblioteque Universitaire. (1905) *Manuale d'Economia Politica*, 1st French lang, 1927, 1st English, 1971, London, Macmillan.

PASINETTI, L. (1962) Rate of Profit and Income Distribution in Relation to the Rate of Economic Growth, *Review of Economic Studies*. (1974) *Growth and Income Distribution*. (1981) *Structural Change and Economic Growth*, both books, Cambridge University Press.

PATINKIN, D. (1956) *Money, Interest and Prices*, Evanston, Ill, Row, Peterson. (1982) *Essays on Keynes*. Chicago University Press. (1984) Keynes and Economics Today, *American Economic Review, Proceedings*. (1987) article on Keynes in Eatwell et al (1987) op cit.

PEKKARINEN, J. see Matti, P. (1991).

PENROSE, E. (1959) *The Theory of the Growth of the Firm*, Oxford, Blackwells, and New York, John Wiley.

PHEBY, J. (1989) *New Directions in Post-Keynesian Economics*, Aldershot, England, Edward Elgar.

PHELPS, E. (1968) Money-wage Dynamics and Labour Market Equilibrium, *Journal of Political Economy*.

PHILLIPS, A. (1958). The Relation between Unemployment and the rate of Change of Money Wage Rates in Great Britain, 1861-1957, *Economica*.

PIGOU, A. C. (1910) A Method of Determining the Numerical Values of Elasticities of Demand, *Economic Journal*. (1920) *The Economics of Welfare*, (1941). *Employment and Equilibrium*. (1945) *Lapses from Full Employment*; all books London, Macmillan.

ROBINSON, J. (1933) *The Economics of Imperfect Competition*, London, Macmillan.

ROMER, L. (1988) The New Keynesian Economics and Output Employment Trade Offs, *Quarterly Journal of Economics*.

ROTEMBERG, J. (1987) The New Keynesian Microeconomic Foundations, *Macroeconomics Annual*, New York, National Bureau of Economic Research.

ROWTHORNE, R. see Matti, P. (1991)

RUMELHART, D. with McClelland, J. et al (1988) *Explorations in Parallel Distributed Processing*, 3 vols, MIT Press.

SARGENT, T. (1979) *Macroeconomic Theory*, Orlando, Florida, Academic Press. See also with Marimon, R. (1989) op cit.

SAWYER, M. (1985) *The Economics of Michal Kalecki*, London, Macmillan. (1988) *Post-Keynesian Economics*. (1991) The Relationship between Keynes' Macroeconomic Analysis and Imperfect Competition, in Gerrard and Hillard op cit.

SAY, J.-B. (1803) Traité d'Economie Politique, Paris, Rapilly.

SCARF, H. (1967) The Core of an N-Person Game, *Econometrica*.

SELTEN, R. (1975) Re-examination of the Perfectness Concept for Equilibrium Points in Extensive Game, *International Journal of Game Theory*. With Marshak, T. (1977) Supergames and Oligopolistic Equilibria, *Quarterly Journal of Economics*.

SHAPLEY, L. (1969) On Market Games, *Journal of Economic Theory*.

SHEPHARD, R. (1970) *Theory of Cost and Production Functions*, Princeton University Press.

SHUBIK, M. (1959) *Strategy and Market Structure*, New York, John Wiley. (1967) (ed) *Essays in Honor of Oscar Morgenstern*, Princeton University Press. With Nti, K. (1981) Entry in Oligopoly Theory, *Eastern Economic Journal*. (1984) *A Game Theoretic Approach to Political Economy*, MIT Press. (1987) Cournot, in Eatwell et al (eds) op cit.

SIMON, H. (1957) *Models of Man*, New York, NY. (1959) Decision Taking in Economics, *American Economic Review*. With Newall, A. (1972) Human Problem Solving, Englewood Cliffs, NJ, Prentice Hall. (1982) *Models of Bounded Rationality*, MIT Press.

SKIDELSKY, R. (1983) *John Maynard Keynes: hopes betrayed*, London, Macmillan.

SMITH, R. (1989) see ALOGOSKOUFIS, G. (1989).

SNOWER, D. (1984) Imperfect Competition, Underemployment and Crowding Out, *Oxford Economic Papers*.

SOLOW, R. (1956) A Contribution to the Theory of Economic Growth, *Quarterly Journal of Economics*. (1970) *Growth Theory*, Oxford University Press. Some Implications of Alternative Criteria for the Firm, in Marris and Wood, (eds) (1970) op cit. (1981) Wage Bargaining and Employment, *American Economic Review*. (1986a) Unemployment: Getting the Questions Right, *Economica*. (1986b) Monopolistic Competition and the Multiplier, in Heller, W. (ed) *Essays in Honor of Kenneth J. Arrow Vol 2*, Cambridge, Cambridge University Press.

SONNENSCHEIN, H. with Roberts, D. (1977) On the foundations of the theory of monopolistic competition, *Econometrica*. Oligopoly and Game Theory, in Eatwell et al, (eds) (1987) op cit.

SOWELL, T. (1972) *Say's Law: an Historical Analysis*, Princeton University Press.

SPEAR, S. (1989) Learning rational expectations under computability restraints, *Econometrica*.

STARTZ, R. (1989) Monopolistic Competition as a Foundation for Keynesian Macroeconomic Models, *Quarterly Journal of Economics*. (1990) Notes on Imperfect Competition and the New Keynesian Economics, *Working Paper 90-32*, University of Washington, Seattle.

STEUER, M. (1988) Culture and Optimality, *Theoretical Economics Working Paper No. 206*, Suntory Toyota Centre for Economics, London School of Economics, London.

STIGLITZ, J. (1984) Price Rigidities and Market Structure, *American Economic Review, Proceedings*.

SWEEZY, P. (1939) Demand under Conditions of Oligopoly, *Journal of Political Economy*.

SYLOS-LABINI, see LABINI, P. S.

TARGETTI, F. with Kinda-Hass, B. (1982) Kalecki's Review of Keynes' *General Theory*, *Australian Economic Papers*. (1988) *Nicholas Kaldor - Teoria e Politica Economica di un Capitalismo in Mutando*, Bologna, Italy, Il Mulino.

TARSHIS, L. (1939) Real and Money Wages: a Comment, *Economic Journal*.

TAYMAZ, E. (1991) see Eliasson, G. (1991).

THIRLWALL, A. (1986) A General Model of Growth and Development on Kaldorian Lines, *Oxford Economic Papers*. (1987) *Nicholas Kaldor*, Brighton, England, Wheatsheaf Books.

TINBERGEN, J. (1939) *Statistical Testing of Buiness Cycles*, Geneva, League of Nations. (1952) *On the Theory of Economic Policy*, North Holland.

TOBIN, J. (1972) Inflation and Unemployment, *American Economic Review.* (1982) *Essays on Economics: Theory and Policy*, Cambridge, Mass, MIT Press. (1989) Is Keynesian Theory still a Useful Tool in the Economic Conditions of Today?, in Baldassarri (1989) op cit.

TREVITHICK, J. with Worswick, D. (eds) (1983) *Keynes and the Modern World*, Cambridge University Press.

TSIANG, S. (1989) *Finance Constraints and the Theory of Money*, Academic Press, London.

TURING, S. (1959) *Alan R. Turing*, Cambridge, England, Heffer.

TUSTIN, A. (1953) *The Mechanism of Economic Systems* London Heineman.

UZAWA, H. (1969) Time Preference and the Penrose Effect in a Two Class Model of Economic Growth, *Journal of Political Economy.*

VON NEUMANN, J. (1928) The Theory of Party Games, *Mathematische Annalen.* With Morgenstern, O. (1944) *The Theory of Games and Economic Behaviour*, Princeton University Press. (1958) *The Computer and the Brain*, Yale University Press.

WALRAS, L. (1874) *Elḗments d'Economie Politique Pure*, Lausanne, Switzerland, L. Corbaz.

WEINTRAUB, R. (1979) *Microfoundations*, Cambridge University Press.

WEITZMAN, M. (1981) Increasing Returns and the Foundations of Unemployment Theory, *Economic Journal.* (1984) *The Share Economy*, Harvard University Press.

WILLIAMSON, O. (1964) *The Economics of Discretionary Behavior*, Englewood Cliffs, NJ, Prentice Hall. (1970) *Corporate Control and Business Behaviour*, Englewood Cliffs. (1985) *The Economic Institutions of Capitalism*, New York, NY, The Free Press.

WINSTON G. (1982) *The Timing of Economic Activities*, Cambridge University Press.

WOOD, A,. (1975) *The Theory of Profits*, Cambridge University Press.

WORSWICK, D. see Trevithick, J. (1983).

YARROW, G. (1976) On the Predictions of Managerial Theories of the Firm, Journal of Industrial Economics.

ZAMAGNI, S. (1984) *Economia Politica*, Rome, La Nuova Italia Scientifica, Eng lang edn, *Microeconomic Theory*, 1987, Oxford, Basil Blackwell.

Index